Victorian Paper Art and Craft

Victorian Paper Art and Craft

Writers and Their Materials

DEBORAH LUTZ

Great Clarendon Street, Oxford, OX2 6DP,
United Kingdom

Oxford University Press is a department of the University of Oxford.
It furthers the University's objective of excellence in research, scholarship,
and education by publishing worldwide. Oxford is a registered trade mark of
Oxford University Press in the UK and in certain other countries

© Deborah Lutz 2022

The moral rights of the author have been asserted

Impression: 1

All rights reserved. No part of this publication may be reproduced, stored in
a retrieval system, or transmitted, in any form or by any means, without the
prior permission in writing of Oxford University Press, or as expressly permitted
by law, by licence or under terms agreed with the appropriate reprographics
rights organization. Enquiries concerning reproduction outside the scope of the
above should be sent to the Rights Department, Oxford University Press, at the
address above

You must not circulate this work in any other form
and you must impose this same condition on any acquirer

Published in the United States of America by Oxford University Press
198 Madison Avenue, New York, NY 10016, United States of America

British Library Cataloguing in Publication Data

Data available

Library of Congress Control Number: 2022939962

ISBN 978–0–19–885879–9

DOI: 10.1093/oso/9780198858799.001.0001

Printed and bound by
CPI Group (UK) Ltd, Croydon, CR0 4YY

Links to third party websites are provided by Oxford in good faith and
for information only. Oxford disclaims any responsibility for the materials
contained in any third party website referenced in this work.

Acknowledgments

Many years of research and writing went into this book, and it was finished at long last during a worldwide pandemic. I have benefited deeply from the generosity and expertise of many, especially Talia Schaffer, Susan Griffin, and Sharon Marcus. I was lucky to have two brilliant writing groups that contributed hugely to this book by reading drafts. Early parts were workshopped with the convivial New York set: Carolyn Berman, Tanya Agathocleous, Caroline Reitz, Tim Alborn, and, once again and always, Talia Schaffer. The heavy lifting was done by the delightful Kentucky/Ohio/Tennessee collective: Ellen Rosenman, Susan Ryan, Marion Rust, Nancy Henry, Mary Jean Corbett, Maura O'Conner, Jill Rappaport, and, again, Susan Griffin. And I have yet others to thank for reading drafts and providing ideas, objects, citations, and more, especially Deidre Lynch, Natalie Dykstra, John Kucich, and, again, Sharon Marcus. Still other conversations and the sharing of findings were key in the development of this project, especially with Andrew Stauffer, Karen Sánchez-Eppler, Ellen Gruber Garvey, Rachel Buurma, Christine Nelson, and Elizabeth Denlinger. I am grateful to Jacqueline Norton at Oxford University Press for her support and deft editorship.

In 2016, Cat Aboudara invited me to speak at the Smithsonian, where I presented a preliminary view of this research, and I remain grateful for discussions of the project then and at many other venues as my work continued: the keynote for the Victorian Studies Association of Ontario, Toronto; Birkbeck College, the University of London; the Victorian Research Seminar, English Faculty, Oxford University; the New York Romanticists' Friendly Society and the Henry W. and Albert A. Berg Collection of English and American Literature of the New York Public Library; the Rosenbach, the Philadelphia Free Library, the Schick Lecture, Indiana State University; the Morgan Library and Museum, New York City; the North American Victorian Studies Association Conference; the University of Calgary; the Massachusetts Historical Society; the Conrad-Caldwell House Museum, Louisville; the University of Victoria; the Grolier Club, New York City; the

Victorian Seminar at the Graduate Center of the City University of New York; and numerous talks at the University of Louisville.

Many friends and colleagues inspired and encouraged me, especially Polly Shulman, David McAllister, Andrea Olinger, Karl Swinehart, Benjamin Friedman, Nikki Cosentino, Maggie Nelson, Pam Beatty (for help with Latin translations and the history of the *Book of Common Prayer*), Tony Sebok, Cara Murray, Jean Mills, Rachel Szekely, Melissa Dunn, Kristi Maxwell, Glynis Ridley, and my sister Pamela Lutz. I benefited from a number of crack research assistants through the years, and I want to thank in particular Hayley Salo, Reid Elsea, Kelly Carty, Michelle Peña, Taylor Gathof, and Benjamin Poe.

This book exists as a testament to the assistance I have received from librarians, archivists, and curators at libraries, archives, and museums in the United States, Great Britain, and Western Europe, many of whom went out of their way to be helpful. I made so many visits to the British Library I have lost count, but I want to thank in particular Sandra Tuppen (for her patience and kindness); Alexandra Ault; and Alexander Lock, for sitting with me while I looked at Virginia Woolf notebooks, and for being so kind, interested, and interesting. I have also lost count of the visits I have made to the Berg Collection at the New York Public Library, but I remember in particular the assistance of Mary Catherine Kinniburgh, Carolyn Vega, and Lyndsi Barnes. At the Morgan Library, John Vincler, Maria Isabel Molestina, and others pulled many mounds of papery things for me out of storage, often the same things two or three times. Lisa Darms and Charlotte Priddle at the Fales Collection, New York University, shared piles of albums with me, as did Jim Holmberg and others at the Filson Historical Society, Louisville, KY; Jeremy Parrett at the Manchester Metropolitan University, All Saints Library, who gave me the history of Harry S. Page; and John Pollack at the University of Pennsylvania Special Collections, for many kindnesses and for being as enthusiastic as I was. I owe a debt of gratitude to Sarah Laycock, Amy Roebottom, and Ann Dinsdale at the Brontë Parsonage Museum, Haworth, West Yorkshire, and Elizabeth Denlinger (once again) at the Pforzheimer Collection, New York Public Library, for sharing her deep knowledge and friendship. At the London Library, Mandy Southern, Samantha Gibson, and Dafydd Sinden let me page through many of Charles Reade's albums; thanks also to Daniel Sudron at the Calderdale archive, Halifax; Dave Goulding at the John Rylands Library, University of Manchester; and Chris Hyland, Archives & Local History, Manchester Central Library. I thank Karla Nielsen for those enchanting conversations in the Southern

California sun about Brontë manuscripts, marginalia, and so much more at the Huntington Library.

Other collections I haunted: the Bodleian Library, Oxford University; the Houghton Library, Harvard University; Princeton University Special Collections; the Beinecke Library, Yale University; the Burke Library, Columbia University; the Wellcome Collection, London; Carlyle House, London; Shibden Hall, Halifax; the Victoria and Albert Museum, London; the British Museum, London; the Elizabeth Gaskell House Museum, Manchester; the Keats House Museum, London; the Charles Dickens Museum, London; the Sir John Soane Museum, London; the Florence Nightingale Museum, London; the Thomas J. Watson Library, the Metropolitan Museum of Art, New York City; the Keats-Shelley House, Rome; and the Sigmund Freud Museum, Vienna.

A short essay in *Victorian Review*—"The Paper Museum" (vol. 43, no. 1 [2017], pp. 25–30)—became part of Chapter 2. Another essay in the same publication—"Emily Brontë's Paper Work" (vol. 42, no. 2 [2016], pp. 291–305)—was reworked and became parts of Chapters 3 and 4. I thank the journal for permission to publish those pages here.

This project would not have been possible without support from the Thruston B. Morton Endowment, which generously paid for the travel to these many archives, libraries, and museums and for various permissions. A sabbatical from the University of Louisville helped me complete this book.

A National Endowment for the Humanities Fellowship also provided much-needed time and funds for this project, and I am very grateful and honored to have received it. An Andrew W. Mellon Foundation Fellowship at the Huntington Library allowed me to spend a month researching in their rich collections, and I'm grateful for that honor as well.

Finally, I want to dedicate this book to my dear mother (1942-2022), whose passion for greeting cards, notebooks, books, reading, and crafts of all sorts gave me an early love for the subjects of the following chapters.

Contents

List of Illustrations   x

   Introduction   1
1. Marginal Scribbling and Defacing   9
2. Collecting and Recollecting   34
3. Researching and Performing   63
4. Reusing, Tearing, and Folding   93
5. Crafting   119
   Afterword   143

Notes   146
Bibliography   201
Index   220

List of Illustrations

1. Emily Brontë's one-page manuscript with numerous poems and notes. Brontë Parsonage Museum, Bonnell 127 — 5
2. Charlotte Brontë's diary page in the family's *Russell's General Atlas of Modern Geography*. The Morgan Library & Museum. PML 129886. Bequest of Helen Safford Bonnell, 1969 — 17
3. Doodle probably drawn by Charlotte Brontë in the *Russell's General Atlas of Modern Geography*. The Morgan Library & Museum. PML 129886. Bequest of Helen Safford Bonnell, 1969 — 19
4. George Eliot's inscription in her copy of *The Linnet's Life* (1822). George Eliot and George Henry Lewes Collection, General Collection, Beinecke Rare Books and Manuscript Library, Yale University, GEN MSS 963, Box 56. By kind permission of the Estate of George Eliot — 29
5. An illustration by one of Charlotte Brontë's Roe Head school fellows in an album. Roe Head Album (1831–40), Brontë Parsonage Museum, C109 — 40
6. A contribution by a friend to Maggie Strickland's 1890s friendship album that includes micrography and cut-paper designs. Margaret Strickland Papers; MSS 77; box 8, folder 5; Fales Library and Special Collections, New York University Libraries — 42
7. Souvenir album probably created by Georgina Lucy Byron (ca. 1829–31). Private collection. Used by permission — 57
8. Anonymous souvenir album (ca. 1859). Brontë Parsonage Museum, E 2013.2 — 58
9. Album of British mosses, 1854–73. MS Coll. 1151, Kislak Center for Special Collections, Rare Books and Manuscripts, University of Pennsylvania — 60
10. George Eliot's handwritten paper label on her notebook that says "Quarry for Middlemarch." Houghton Library, Harvard University, Lowell 13. By kind permission of the Estate of George Eliot — 72

LIST OF ILLUSTRATIONS   xi

11. One of George Eliot's travel diaries, labeled in her hand: "Journeys to Normandy in 1865 and Italy in 1864." George Eliot and George Henry Lewes Collection, General Collection, Beinecke Rare Books and Manuscript Library, Yale University, Journal 1864–5, GEN MSS 963, Box 18. By kind permission of the Estate of George Eliot   75

12. First page of Emily Brontë's "Gondal Poems" notebook. © The British Library Board, Add. MS. 43483   86

13. Charlotte Brontë's tiny booklet with a wallpaper cover, called "There was once a little girl and her name was Anne," ca. 1826–8. Brontë Parsonage Museum, B78   97

14. Calendar card with George Eliot's notes for a novel on the verso. George Eliot and George Henry Lewes Collection, General Collection, Beinecke Rare Books and Manuscript Library, Yale University, notes 1876, GEN MSS 963, Box 23. By kind permission of the Estate of George Eliot   99

15. George Eliot's notes for a novel, on verso of Fig. 14. George Eliot and George Henry Lewes Collection, General Collection, Beinecke Rare Books and Manuscript Library, Yale University. By kind permission of the Estate of George Eliot   100

16. Virginia Woolf's repurposed notebook, made from a copy of Isaac Watts's *Logic*. Henry W. and Albert A. Berg Collection of English and American Literature, The New York Public Library, Woolf notebook, No. 1, "Warboys, Aug. 4–Sept. 23, 1899"   104

17. Emily Brontë's manuscript of "I'm happiest when most away," with a few lines still visible from "To a Wreath of Snow / by A.G. Almeda." Henry W. and Albert A. Berg Collection of English and American Literature, The New York Public Library, E13   112

18. Verso of Brontë's manuscript pictured in Fig. 17, with "Weaned from life and torn away." Henry W. and Albert A. Berg Collection of English and American Literature, The New York Public Library   113

19. Hand-crafted paper dolls sewn to a page of Miss Jane Edwards's friendship album, dated 1830–70. The Jane Edwards album, © The British Library Board, Add 57724   122

20. Volume handbound in an old dress by Edith and Kate Southey. John Constance Davie, *Letters from Paraguay* (G. Robinson, 1805). Rare Books, Special Collections and Preservation, River Campus Libraries, University of Rochester, Rochester, NY   130

21. Sampler made by Mary Frances Heaton, ca. 1852. Mental Health Museum, Wakefield, SR2015.323   135

22. Anna Atkins's photogram, part of *British Algae: Cyanotype Impressions*. Spencer Collection, The New York Public Library, Eng. 1843 93-440   140

Introduction

> The next morning, very early, I received a note from Miss Pole, so mysteriously wrapped up, and with so many seals on it to secure secrecy, that I had to tear the paper before I could unfold it.
>
> Elizabeth Gaskell, *Cranford*[1]

Small slips of paper—cut, folded, or sealed—take on a cryptic radiance in *Cranford* as they did in Gaskell's own busy writing activities and routines. In the quotation above, the opening of the packet reveals generous, if officious, friendship between women, as will the "opening" of many such real-life packets in the following chapters. The shining possibility contained in a leftover scrap of paper will be of central significance to this study; it will comprise, if you will, the main meal. As an author—of letters, essays, a biography, stories, novels—Gaskell worked with paper and understood its romance. Taking to heart Gaskell's enchanting of her medium, *Victorian Paper Art and Craft* cares about folds, tears, and snipped-out holes. How sheets are fastened together with such tools as gummed wafers, seals, needle and thread, ribbons, brads, and more matters.[2] Doodles, scribbles, inscriptions, marginalia, and witty drawings will be considered in turn, as will anything written or drawn on versos. We will pay attention to bindings, especially when handmade or repaired, alongside bookmarks, notebooks, albums, and commonplace books. Proximity and association will be germane, but so will, crucially, "haptic" texts and artifacts—volumes, pages, and papery objects that are not just for reading or writing (or in some cases not at all for reading and writing), but that have an added element that makes us aware of their status as objects in the world, rather than windows to look through.[3] I find meaning in the contingent, the incidental, the crammed in, and the supplemental. What Walter Benjamin calls "booklike creations from fringe areas" will be paramount.[4] Texture comes before texts in some cases, as does the tactile before the visual. Sensory encounters with paper, books, and other writing materials will form part of this study of the Victorian writing life. In other words, minor things that have been mostly overlooked—notes scribbled in the margins, anonymous albums gathering dust, tiny shreds of manuscript—will be noticed. Often such small-bore artifacts and inscriptions have been disregarded or even discarded because they were made by women or became female-coded and tied to the domestic sphere, like friendship albums and paper crafts.

This book is deliberately granular. Looking after such small details has been aligned, historically and philosophically, with the feminine, Naomi Schor argues. She writes that

> to focus on the detail ... is to become aware ... of its participation in a larger semantic network, bounded on the one side by the ornamental, with its traditional connotations of effeminacy and decadence, and on the other, by the everyday, whose "prosiness" is rooted in the domestic sphere of social life presided over by women ... the detail is gendered and doubly gendered as feminine.[5]

In this sense, my methodology is marked by the domestic, the everyday, and the feminine, even though not all of the artifacts and practices explored here lend themselves to gendered readings, as with, for example, marginalia and notebook-keeping.[6] Elevating understudied minutiae—what's found on the edge of vision, in the footnotes of biographies—reshapes the sensory history of working with and on paper during the Victorian era. *Victorian Paper Art and Craft* locates the pleasures taken by these authors when crafting compositions. Drawing this out further: what satisfactions might we find in reanimating these mostly forgotten side notes, detours, and material glyphs?

The intensely local concentration of *Victorian Paper Art and Craft* elucidates how composition grew out of creativity with the materials of writing (and reading, drawing, note-taking, and handicraft), leading to inspiration and experimentation. I apply these terms broadly: Charlotte Brontë composing poems and diaries in the margins of printed books, Eliot jotting ideas on her blotter, Elizabeth Barrett Browning sewing paper to paper as a means to edit her poems, or Jane Austen using straight pins for her "cut and paste." Album culture plays a role, as a space where writers such as Gaskell and Anna Atkins created text-and-collage gifts for friends, or stored material memories. Notebooks, journals, and commonplace books were essential tools for the work of Eliot, Michael Field, and Emily Brontë. Paper crafts and needlework served as text composition outside the bounds of paper, ink, and pen, especially in the case of samplers. The platforms on which writing and drawing happened—the desk, slate, paper, book, album, pattern, wall, and so on—carried weight, as related to and generative of the themes of the writing. This expansive view of what creativity with textual (and material) things meant was common to the Victorians, but the authors discussed here were extravagant even among their self-reflexive contemporaries in their undoing, remaking, miniaturizing, encrypting, reusing, and transforming. The edge of the page, the width of the margin, and the covers of the book were limiting factors but also provocations to push on further.

Writing could be collaborative, playful, theatrical, or worked out in fiction through characters who also perform writing. Eliot, for instance, represented her male writing persona and almost-obsessive research and note-taking in her fiction with such characters as Casaubon and his pigeonholes, pamphlets, and synoptic tabulation. Katherine Bradley and Edith Cooper wrote together as Michael Field, a man who impersonated Sappho in his writings and who curated a journal of many volumes. Emily Brontë drew herself composing on the sheet of paper she was composing, and she created Catherine Earnshaw as a self-conscious writer-in-the-margins. Some of these performances celebrated the traditionally feminine, while others borrowed the greater authority and agency of the masculine or imitated (or made fun of) male Romantic poets who could easily roam the world, like Byron. Craft-like elements in assembling manuscripts (and narratives) appear in these authors' activities and works, tethering their productions to a domesticity that is radical. Charlotte Brontë practiced various paper crafts, and her Lucy Snowe in *Villette* is hyper-aware of the page, ink, seal, envelope, and quasi-magical power of letters, which require burying in drawers, boxes, bottles, and the earth.

The extant manuscripts by these writers and their methods of piecing them together—the paper they used, the spaces they wrote in, and surfaces they wrote on—contribute to our understanding of their craft in its most material form. Heeding their creative acts broadens our idea of the "book" and the "page." Drawing, tearing, folding, and burning manuscripts released meaning in unusual ways. Sewing together one's own codex using household waste, reusing paper patterns for needle-cases to compose poems, and creating text using chemicals and sunlight were ways to open up what writing and publishing could be. These incipient book forms—or what Alexandra Gillespie and Deirdre Lynch call "unfinished" books—currently fall outside of conventional book history.[7] But placing such forms on the fringe of that history not only heavily underscores the material nature of book parts and book uses but also opens a line of communication between that history and less-excavated ones, such as domestic crafts aligned with women's and servants' work. Furthermore, paper had a strong relationship to the body and the household, with its high rag content and its reuse to wrap food before wood pulp became its main ingredient in the 1880s. Reduced to its material components, composition was a sort of paper art, not only a piecing together of notes from notebooks and other sources but also cutting and attaching parts using glue, cloth, pins, and needle and thread. The writers considered here practiced these arts, often as a means to reach both outside and deeper inside. Embedding was part of their process—writing about writing, sheet represented on sheet, paper inside a book (or box or album), book in a hand, and the body in a reading space. Collecting mementos in an album and weaving together a novel from disparate parts both involved curating what can be thought of as a box or museum of the self.

* * * * * *

The following chapters developed out of a curiosity in artifacts I stumbled upon in archives over decades while researching my two previous books. They weren't central—or in some cases even relevant—to those projects, but they stuck in my mind as worthy of contemplation. Peripheral to my studies, these accidental artifacts have also been peripheral to other histories and accounts. I set them aside as so many others did, as orphans with no place. But here I take them up in order to keep in focus their marginality, insignificance. Some of these objects have been explored by other scholars, but their material nature has only been slightly touched upon or not at all, as with Eliot's notebooks and Emily Brontë's poetry manuscripts. Others have received no scrutiny or recognition, such as hundreds of friendship albums, handmade bookmarks, and a variety of paper crafts. When their textual natures are put aside, they stand forth as mute things. Given their silence, I often had to speculate about them, so the readers of this book will, I hope, open themselves to the suppositious, to fugitive meaning, and in general to the mystery of these strays. Such gaps and stillness can overtake most scholars in the archive. Carolyn Steedman calls this research a "type of activity that has given rise to a particular form of writing, whose practitioners believe to be about what *is not* as much as what has been found; a form of writing which celebrates the constraints on it, constraints which—so it is said—are made by the documents themselves: what they forbid you to write, the permissions they offer."[8] I felt permitted to write about the grimy folds in one of Emily Brontë's poetry manuscripts (see Fig. 1), for instance, which possibly had no significance to anyone at all. Well, except for me. (And maybe,

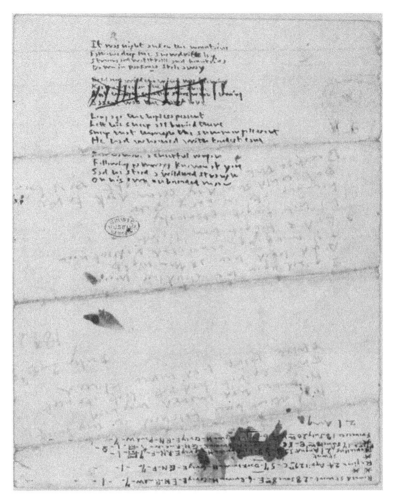

Fig. 1 Emily Brontë's one-page manuscript with numerous poems and notes. Brontë Parsonage Museum, Bonnell 127[9]

eventually, you?) A driving force of this project has been what Helena Michie and Robyn Warhol call "archival desire and archival romance."[10] Or, as they say in the title of their marvelous book: *Love Among the Archives*. Others talk about the "cult of the archive," its fetishization, and a sort of fever or sickness for (in) it.[11] I have felt, done, and fallen ill of all of these and more. Embodiment was an aspect of the love I felt; a sense that I might come closer to those writers' bodies that had done that folding, cutting, stitching, scribbling, and binding. And that somehow that said something significant about my own writerly process and body, although it was never entirely clear what. What does it mean to be one who does creative labor with paper? Then these papery leaves and artifacts have their own kind of physical heft: inky fingerprints, bodily smells, or dirty edges. Unfolding slips of paper has an eroticism to it, Terry Eagleton muses in relation to found letters, an intimacy, even a violent intrusion into a secret "crevice or fissured place where the stirrings of desire can be felt."[12] The absorbency of paper during much of the nineteenth century is attested to by the fact that women used linen and paper together as menstruation pads. The diarist Anne Lister called her period "cousin," and she writes of one night: "had slept in cousin-linen with paper as usual."[13] While I don't think I've encountered blood on any of the archival matter I've handled, I've certainly come upon bodily leavings.[14]

The body appears as a kind of refrain in these chapters, but they are organized around objects and the activities done with and in them. They move from a more conventional understanding of texts to increasingly loose and radical versions of reading and writing material. Chapter 1 considers books from writers' libraries that they have marked, autographed, and supplemented with matter such as pressed plants, feathers, and fingernail scorings. These haptic texts, thickened with time and adaptation, gained singularity, with meaning developing when samples of the real were left behind. Eliot used some of her books to memorialize—to observe a passing moment, to remember a personal exchange—while in others she wrote comments, indexes on their endpapers, and other glosses of a scholarly nature. Charlotte and Emily Brontë, contrarily, penned diaries in their books, doodled in them, and generally defaced them. This thinking of the published, printed volume as paper with blank spaces inciting script, as a bearer of relationships and memory, as a magical object set in place and time, and as a space that could be inhabited shaped these writers' own creative acts.

Chapter 2 examines another sort of volume. Attempts to preserve the embodied moment, to capture and keep experience, Victorian albums (especially friendship, autograph, and botanical) were gatherings of pressed objects that could seem to spring off of the page—moss, locks of hair, ribbons, feathers, valentines, lace, and other material memories. Attached with paste, wafers, thread, or straight pins, theater programs, printed menus for special meals, lecture flyers, letters, and the like needed to be folded out to be read—three dimensional layers that required the hand as well as the eye. Such assemblages influenced writers like Gaskell, a collector of personal ephemera who used her fiction to think about the pulling together of fragments (bodies, scraps, reused household items, and memories).

Chapter 3 takes up a related activity, that of researching. Writers such as Eliot, Michael Field, Charles Reade, and Emily Brontë kept commonplace books, notebooks, journals, diaries, almanacs, and other sorts of memoranda as fodder for their writing lives. Eliot, along with many of her contemporaries (like Anne Lister), inhabited the initially blank books that she bought at shops, usually stationers, and she recognized the ways they inhabited her. They often had pockets (where she stored things), attached pencils, and clasps, and she pasted paper labels on the front or just inside, where she also affixed newspaper articles or extra sheets. She sometimes sewed another cover on top when the original one wore out, re-stitched the binding when it began to fall apart, and cut out tabs from fore-edges to alphabetize. Eliot's novels in particular evolved out of this magpie collection of quotes, poems, and sayings of others, a network of associations seen most obviously in the epigraphs in *Middlemarch*.

Chapter 4 explores a different sort of collecting method. Tracing the reuse of domestic items as part of the writing, creating, and reading process for many authors in the nineteenth century, this chapter considers rebinding books with repurposed clothing, stitching wallpaper onto a manuscript booklet, ripping off a corner of a letter and using its blank side to compose a poem, taking an old ledger and turning it into a souvenir album, and other types of thrifty activities. In many cases of reuse, restricted choice (and space) enriched aesthetic decisions rather than limiting them, especially when it came to Emily's poetry manuscripts. Thinking of paper (and books) as more than a carrier of text (or as a carrier of just one text) brought fragments of everyday life into the creative process.

Finally, Chapter 5 moves even further away from more traditional ideas about "authorship" to focus on the notion of "writing" as a more experimental act. Here I consider the uses of paper and text-related materials for talismanic, decorative, and artistic purposes. Needlework skills helped authors revise manuscripts or craft blank books to be filled with composition. Writing needn't include ink, as Victorian women were adept at exploiting. Embroidery on paper, pinpricks through paper, cut-out silhouettes, pincushions with text in pinheads, and needle-books inscribed or shaped like books locate the work of women's hands in a continuum of craft. Samplers provided a mode of composition so labor-intensive that the makers sometimes invested them with magical significance. The Victorian novelist and botanist Anna Atkins made albums of seaweed, ferns, flowers, feathers, and lace using Sir John Herschel's cyanotype technology, an early form of camera-less photography that marked the shadow of the object directly on the page. Atkins also made these "photograms" of her handwriting, turning text and autograph into ghostly absence.

Micro-histories and case studies comprise this book, giving it the feel of a book-box. This is a method of analysis honed by the Victorian "object lesson": material culture readings of Victorian novels that focus closely on one micro-history to elucidate the whole, such as mahogany furniture in *Jane Eyre*.[15] Open this book-container like the lid of a chest and find inside vivid objects, pieces of flotsam, and miscellaneous articles and cloth to turn over in the hands (although this might prove difficult if you are reading this on a computer).[16] Use all of the senses, even taste and smell, but also, critically, touch. Perhaps the reader will feel invited to write in its margins, tear off the flyleaf for a piece of scrap paper, dwell in its spaces, and explore all of its nooks and crannies. Press a flower here, leave a theater ticket as a bookmark, give it away to a friend with an inscription expressing admiration and love for the recipient.

1
Marginal Scribbling and Defacing

> For books are not absolutely dead things, but doe contain a potencie of life in them to be as active as that soul whose progeny they are.
> Milton, *Areopagitica* (copied by George Eliot into a notebook)[1]

> Language has a body and the body has a language; graphology is concerned with the bodily aspect of the language of handwriting and with the expressive aspect of the body of handwriting.
> Walter Benjamin, "Review of the Mendelssohns' *Der Mensch in der Handschrift*"[2]

In *Wuthering Heights* (1847), Catherine Earnshaw's small library—really just a moldering pile—still occupies her oak bed-cabinet decades after her death and is linked closely to her selfhood and body, through her handwritten diary in the margins of the books. This is a fictional space, of course, inside other fictional places (with the books also containers of a sort) created by Emily Brontë, whose library (as much as it ever existed) was dispersed a handful of years after her death. Brontë opened up many imaginary boxes and rooms that had writing in them, as we shall see, almost as if the text itself created the opening, like in her poems scratched on caves or dungeon walls by imprisoned speakers. George Eliot, Charlotte Brontë, and other authors that will be taken up here also felt that books encompassed place and moments in time, turning them into haptic holders for memories. These authors not only made books (by writing them and having them published); they also put themselves into books, and drew themselves out of them. Running through much of their writing is an attention to the tactile, sensuous qualities of volumes, an appreciation of the published, printed book as presenting gaps for script, as a holder of friendships and memories, and as an expanse that could be indwelled. These attitudes also shaped their own artistic acts, whether this meant composing in significant spots, as we see with

Charlotte Brontë scribbling poems and snippets of fiction in the margins of schoolbooks and bibles; caring for the surface on which writing happens, as with Emily Brontë's graffiti; or recognizing how identity is fundamentally shaped by found text, as with George Eliot's near obsession with epigraphs and commonplacing. The paratextual for these authors stretched radically outside the more traditional definition of the term, in some cases jumping the boundary of the book and the page altogether.[3] Moreover, in an uncanny way, Catherine's marked-up books in *Wuthering Heights* work as apt fictional stand-ins for Victorian books—and especially women's books—more generally.

Lost Libraries

Recovering a general notion about what nineteenth-century readers wrote in the margins of their books (and why) or what sorts of objects they slipped between the leaves is difficult, especially when those readers were women. Only a small sample of their marginalia survive (or can be identified as such), so conclusions are necessarily based on small samples. Consequently, in this chapter I focus on details, case studies, micro-histories, and fictional moments. Karen Sánchez-Eppler calls approaches to studying marks in books "methods for an impossible subject."[4] The absence of these books and libraries is itself significant, of course. William H. Sherman points to the fact that "catalogues and indexes tend to be organized by surname," which "makes the textual traces of women more obscure or diffuse ... Books purchased by or given to women tended to disappear behind the surname they adopted when they married and to be subsumed into their husband's estate."[5] More generally, women's personal libraries were less likely to be kept together (or even exist in the first place) than men's, their books mostly vanishing into larger collections (or altogether), thus losing their association with them. Furthermore, before the Married Women's Property Acts of 1870 and 1882, wives had no independent legal rights, including that of making a will. Wealthy women who collected books sometimes tried to retain them as a group posthumously, as in the case of Hester Piozzi (1741–1821), a writer and celebrity (who is read by Mary Garth in *Middlemarch*); Lady Anne Clifford (1590–1676), who filled her books with notes; and Frances Mary Richardson Currer (1785–1861), a "bibliomaniac" in Yorkshire.[6] In Samuel Richardson's *Clarissa* (1747–8), the unmarried Clarissa Harlowe writes of her library in her will: "I bequeath all my books in general, with the cases they are in, to my said cousin Dolly Hervey. As they are not ill-chosen for a woman's library, I know that she will take the greater pleasure in them ... because they were mine; and because there are observations in many of them of my own writing; and some very judicious ones written by the truly reverend Dr. Lewen," reflecting a means for women of the time and later to keep their libraries whole, as a physical manifestation of their constructed selves.[7]

While we do not know the thoughts George Eliot (to take another example) had about her own library's fate—she had around 10,000 volumes when she died—she did create a character whose heart's desire lies in his collection remaining intact, with his name inscribed over the door.[8] In *Romola* (1862-3), Bardo de' Bardi spends his days copying manuscripts, making scholarly emendations in his books, and having his daughter Romola write marginal notes and copy down extracts in commonplace books for him at his direction (activities with which Eliot herself filled her time). His obsession develops, in part, because he leaves his great piece of scholarship unfinished, lamenting that "there will be nothing else to preserve my memory and carry down my name as a member of the great republic of letters—nothing but my library and collection of antiquities."[9] (Eliot later created Casaubon, who dies before his book appears in the world and leaves only a shining row of notebooks.) Bardi's superstition about inanimate objects—he wears "massive prophylactic rings" (53)—means his library represents not only his labors and his only possibility of being remembered, but something more. Tito's dispersal of Bardi's collection enacts Bardi's second death, as if the books all together make up his body. While Eliot completed her great works—her brilliance contained in the books she produced rather than ones she amassed—her fate was, nevertheless, something like Bardi's. Most of her books are now missing, and those that still exist were kept through a series of lucky chances, despite her status as one of the most beloved authors of her time, a sort of secular saint. The majority of Eliot's and George Henry Lewes's possessions were inherited by Lewes's son Charles, who eventually donated some of their books—around 2,500 volumes—to the Dr. Williams's Library in London.[10] In 1882 Charles wrote to the library's trust about giving them his "Father's valuable library" and requesting that it be "kept as a separate little library—called the George Henry Lewes Library—on distinct shelves."[11] In 1977, William Baker published the first serious catalogue of this collection, naming it "The George Eliot–George Henry Lewes Library," finally calling attention to the approximately 150 volumes with Eliot's marginalia and hundreds of additional titles she actively used, many for research for her novels.[12]

Other female writers, now canonical, fared even worse. The books that belonged to the Brontë sisters (and the family as a whole) were mostly auctioned off by Charlotte's husband, Arthur Nichols, after Patrick, the father, died in 1861 (the rest of the family predeceased him), along with kitchenware, furniture, beds, and most of the contents of the parsonage. Listed in the auction catalogue in lots, mostly without their titles or authors, the books were not sold, or bought, as association items, but rather just as dusty tomes.[13] No one thought to collect them or keep them together, even relic hunters of Charlotte Brontëana, who were already active at the time of the auction. Before he died, Patrick had given away some of Charlotte's books, mostly to the family's servants; Nichols carried a few away; and locals who came upon others eventually sold them to collectors, but only a fraction of the library can now be located. Jane Austen, to add another example, had little money to spend on books, and approximately twenty books known to have belonged to her survive.[14] By all accounts, the family had a good library in the rectory in Steventon, Hampshire, but it was almost completely sold off when her brother James and his family took over the house, in anticipation of being given their father's living. Austen wrote in a letter that "my father has got above 500 volumes to dispose of" and some of her own books were also sold.[15] Most of Austen's reading came from circulating libraries or establishments like the Chawton Reading Society, where presumably she wrote no comments. (If she did, they were not saved as Austen marginalia.) Other eighteenth- and nineteenth-century writers who have left behind books with studious or creative marginalia include Lucy Aikin (1781–1864), a poet and critic; Florence Nightingale (1820–1910), whose glosses mostly related to her profession as a nurse; Elizabeth Barrett Browning (1806–61), who left extensive notes in her Greek and Hebrew bibles and her volumes of the Greek dramatists; and Lady Bradshaigh (1708–85), who rewrote parts of Richardson's *Clarissa*, especially the ending, in her copy, given to her by Richardson himself.[16] The poet Felicia Hemans (1793–1835) often illustrated "her favourite books with the thoughts excited by their perusal, and with such parallel passages from other writers as bore upon their subject."[17] Books belonging to Harriet Martineau (1802–76), a founding member of the London Library and a leading intellectual and novelist of her day, do not survive (as far as I have been able to trace).

Not only lost is the possibility of a more systematic study of these authors' habits of marginal notation and bookmarking, but also the volumes they possessed as kinds of physical evidence—even relics of a sort. Marking the book one is reading can be a way to lay claim to it, to impress oneself on it.[18] The marks that last (if any do) are mostly verbal, but glosses might also be inkless, and pressing literal.[19] The fictional character Lydia Languish comments, in Richard Brinsley Sheridan's *The Rivals* (1775), that she always knows when Lady Slattern Lounger has taken out a book from the circulating library before her because she leaves it soiled and dog-eared: "She has a most observing thumb; and, I believe, cherishes her nails for the convenience of making marginal notes."[20] A nineteenth-century reader complained about others leaving "scratches of pins, scorings of thumbnails, and divers marginal illustrations, executed by means of a crow-quill, or a black-lead pencil."[21] Pinpricks and thread sewn into the page also indicated spots to return to.[22] Lucy Snowe, another fictional character, knows that her beloved professor has been in her desk because he has left her books perfumed by his cigar smoke in Charlotte Brontë's *Villette* (1853). While Dorothy and William Wordsworth carried a copy of William Withering's *Arrangement of British Plants* (1796) when out rambling, recording in the margins the place and date when they found a specimen discussed in the book, others went a step further, adding a sample of the plant itself, pressing it between the leaves next to its representation.[23] When one Sydney Biddell, for example, went on a pilgrimage in 1879 to Haworth to visit "Brontë Country," he brought along a copy of Gaskell's biography of Charlotte, making notes and adding pieces of the place itself—a daisy, a leaf from a blackcurrant bush, and a spray of heather.[24] Charles Lamb celebrated "sullied" volumes like these and the "worn out appearance, nay, the very odour (beyond Russia) ... of an old 'Circulating Library' Tom Jones, or Vicar of Wakefield! How they speak of the thousand thumbs, that have turned over their pages with delight!—of the lone sempstress, whom they may have cheered ... Who would have them a whit less soiled?"[25] Holding one's place, like E. B. Browning did in her bible with a feather and Eliot in her Hebrew grammar with a leaf, shows reading paused, ended, emphasized, or not done at all, the book being used merely as a container, its cover like a lid (as with the Dodson sisters in Eliot's *The Mill on the Floss* [1860], whose "Bibles opened more easily at some parts than others ... because of dried tulip petals, which had been distributed quite impartially").[26] Leigh Hunt praised the habit of adding a lock of one's hair when giving books to friends, to be used as a bookmark, and Peter Stallybrass sees the bookmark more generally as the prosthetic of the index finger—this finger a simple form of an index.[27] The manicule, a hand with a pointing finger drawn onto the page, fixes the "index" directly onto the margin.[28]

Handwriting or other supplements to books lend them added haptic qualities, combining as they do printed words on a page with residues of embodied interaction. Haptic books call on all the senses—touch, smell, sight, and even taste (when Francis Bacon wrote that "Some *Bookes* are to be Tasted, Others to be Swallowed, and Some Few to be Chewed and Digested," he didn't mean it literally, but, nevertheless, eating bibles "for their curative or prophylactic powers" continued into the nineteenth century).[29] Lamb calls this the book's "topography of blots and dog's-ears ... the dirt [from] having read it at tea with buttered muffins, or over a pipe."[30] They share characteristics with what Geoffrey Batchen calls "hybrid objects," which he uses to describe nineteenth-century photography that contains a material addition, like a lock of hair or scrap of paper with writing tucked into a daguerreotype case.[31] Something like photographs, then, these haptic texts work as souvenirs—remembrances of reading or spending time with a book open before one. With the Gaskell biography carried on a pilgrimage mentioned above, the book itself, and even the handwriting in the margin, wasn't enough to preserve the experience. The pressed plants add a spatial localism to the book-as-container, tethering it to a spot in nature, with its distinct flora. A volume has a biography—it can bear "traces of its many social interactions," Andrew Stauffer argues—and books function as "platforms upon which readers elaborated their own identities."[32] Acts of reading, gift-giving, and preserving carved into the paper, glued onto the pages, or closed up in its leaves turn the book into a little museum of material memory.[33]

Engagement versus Resistance

Eliot usually marked her books in the manner approved by teachers and conduct manuals.[34] A serious scholar and intellectual, Eliot set herself learned tasks, and the jottings in her library show her talking back to authors, sometimes arguing or agreeing with them. She read the authorities on pulling knowledge out of reading, in particular Erasmus, Locke, and Isaac Watts. They encouraged "the exercise of your own reason and judgment upon all you read" by adding remarks, indexes, corrections, and other sorts of comments wherever they would fit.[35] Heather Jackson explores the push for reading with a pen in hand in the eighteenth and nineteenth centuries and how marginalia became such a habit that printers routinely left space between the lines of books, interleaved blank pages, and maintained wide margins, to encourage readers' annotations.[36] Young women especially were exhorted, Kate Flint explains, to "keep a written record of their reading, with résumés of its contents; to note discrepancies between different authors ... they were advised to underline or to mark in the margin important passages."[37] Eliot made indexes on the front or back endpapers of her books, with lists of topics and page numbers she might return to, and she underlined or marked passages as she went along, often setting down remarks.[38] Like Eliot, Austen sometimes followed the approved models for active reading, such as in her copy of Charles Dilley's *Elegant Extracts* where she inserted Austenian phrases like "a lie" or "that was impossible" (in other books she favored "fiddlededia"). On the inside of the back cover she has made a sort of index, titled "To be read." (She gave this book to her niece, inscribing it with her niece's name—"Jane Anna Eliz:th Austen / 1801.")[39] In the four volumes of Oliver Goldsmith's *The History of England* (1771), which seemed to have survived the sale, her brother wrote "James Austen Steventon," and other members of the family, mostly male, scratched various notes, such as "8 August 1845" next to a passage in the first volume. Austen herself made a chronology of significant events Goldsmith explores in the front of volume 1.[40]

Eliot's marginalia (and Austen's) were not like the sort she complains of in her 1856 essay "Silly Novels by Lady Novelists." She faults frivolous women who mark up "frothy," "prosy" literature; those

> class of readers to whom these remarks appear peculiarly pointed and pungent; for we often find them doubly and trebly scored with the pencil, and delicate hands giving in their determined adhesion to these hardy novelties by a distinct *très vrai*, emphasized by many notes of exclamation.[41]

In her male persona (anonymous in this case), Eliot shows "his" disdain for—and distance from—these women reading female-coded novels, with their fatuous "delicacy" and enthusiasm. Eliot bands with other men censorious of female marginal notes, which are to be distinguished from serious (or sarcastic) male ones, like Thackeray, who wrote in *Fraser's Magazine* in 1843,

> It is a wonder how fond ladies are of writing in books and signing their charming initials! Mrs. Berry's before-mentioned little gilt books are scored with pencil-marks, or occasionally at the margin with a ! –note of interjection, or the words, "Too true, A. B." and so on. Much may be learned with regard to a lovely woman by a look at the book she read in.[42]

"Little gilt books" exist more for show than reading, for being charming rather than intelligent. Yet this sort of performance for an audience with marginal observations was common across genders. In some of the books owned by Eliot and Lewes, for instance, we find Leigh Hunt's annotations alongside Eliot's and Lewes's. For instance, in the four volumes of Henry Hallam's *Introduction to the Literature of Europe* (1837–9), Lewes recorded on a flyleaf: "the marks and remarks signed L.H. in these volumes are those of Leigh Hunt." Jackson explains that books with inscriptions by friends, family, and the famous were treasured, circulated, or even sold as "enhanced," and "borrowers sometimes asked permission to copy the notes" of others into their own books, recording the fact on the flyleaf.[43] A sort of communal conversation develops, something that Dickens wrote about in relation to a library in Broadstairs. In his 1851 *Household Words*, he finds the "leaves of the romances, reduced to a condition very like curl-papers, are thickly studded with notes in pencil: Sometimes complimentary, sometime jocose." One "young gentleman" writes "O!" with sarcasm "after every sentimental passage." But a "Miss Julia Mills has read the whole collection of these books. She has left marginal notes on the pages, as 'Is not this truly touching? J.M.' She has also italicized her favourite traits in the description of the hero ... She adds, 'How like B.L. Can this be mere coincidence? J.M.'"[44] While Eliot frowns upon certain types of "feminine" reading, she managed to read with her mind and her body, and she created female characters who occupy both roles.

While Eliot's notes in her books usually show a respect for them, much of the Brontës' marginalia function like small-scale graffiti. For example, Charlotte added a bit of diary on the back pastedown of *Russell's General Atlas of Modern Geography*, penned upside down, impressing her own identity on the printed book (see Fig. 2):

> Brussels—Saturday morning Oct. 12th 1843—First Class—I am very cold—there is no fire—I wish I were at home With Papa—Branwell Emily—Anne and Tabby—I am tired of being amongst foreigners it is a dreary life—especially as there is only one person [her professor] in this house worthy of being liked—also another [the professor's wife] who seems a rosy sugar-plum but I know her to be Coloured chalk.

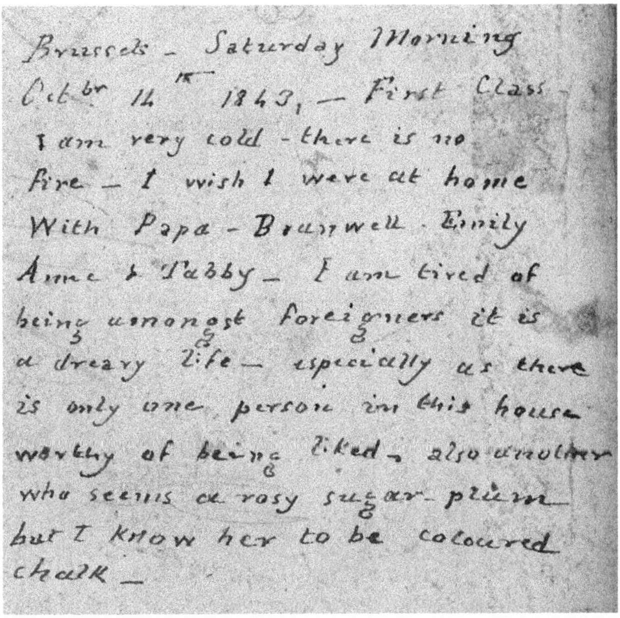

Fig. 2 Charlotte Brontë's diary page in the family's *Russell's General Atlas of Modern Geography*. The Morgan Library & Museum. PML 129886. Bequest of Helen Safford Bonnell, 1969

She affirms not that she is reading, learning, or teaching the text as her contemporaries were taught to do, but rather daydreaming about home, musing unhappily about her bodily presence in time and space (and her desires for a married man, under the nose of his wife). Charlotte's inscription does not fit into the type Eliot ridicules in her essay on silly women, since Charlotte doesn't even pretend to be taking in the book, too enthusiastically or otherwise. Much of the Brontë marginalia that still exist express reading distracted, stopped, or not done at all. Two geography textbooks that belonged to the Brontë siblings provide good examples of this, and also of the sometimes-communal nature of their defacing—the *Russell's* already mentioned and the evocatively titled *A Grammar of General Geography*.[45] They filled most of the white spaces with rows of numbers, doodles, lists of characters to be incorporated into fiction (Charlotte, into *Shirley*), self-portraits, and what seem to be snippets of notes to each other, such as, written sideways on a pastedown in *Russell's*, probably by Emily to Charlotte about a French term for an essay she was composing for school: "what is is [sic] the word used to express the enlitenment [sic] of a room" (see Fig. 3). In the *Grammar*, Emily shoehorned into the index of real places fantasy locations from Gondal.[46] Under the "g's" she has added "Gaaldine A large Island newly discovered in the South Pacific" and "Gondal a large island in the north pacific." In the "u's" are found "Uls a kingdom in Gaaldine governed by 4 Sorceresses," and Zelona and Zedora are added to the "z's." Charlotte composed poems or bits of fiction in two bibles; in *Grammatical Exercises, French and English*; in *A New and Easy Guide to Pronunciation and Spelling*; in an exercise book entitled *Cahier d'Translations from English to German*; and elsewhere, and she has her Angrian characters pen personal marginalia as well.[47] Anne wrote a poem in *Thoughts in Younger Life on Interesting Subjects* (1778), and on *The Remains of Henry Kirke White* one of the Brontës drew an open book in the margin of the open book.[48] The Brontës' treatment of books fits well into Leah Price's account in *How to Do Things with Books in Victorian Britain*: volumes were put to work as notebooks (especially when paper was scarce), but also as boxes to store or flatten things.[49] More lasting than this treatment, however, is the *writing* part of the Brontës' non-reading (and especially the depiction of this in their novels)—in the margins of the book from which they are distracted, in many cases working out ideas and themes that would later appear in their fiction and poetry.[50] Others did this: in her *Mentoria; or, The young ladies instructor* by Ann Murry, Austen composed an elegiac poem in pencil, upside down on the inside front cover and title page, and signed it "Jane Austen / June 29th / 1785." (When she later gave the book to her niece, she added: "Jane Anne Eliz:th Austen / 1801.")[51] Joseph Conrad began some of his own novels in the margins of novels he read, and Thomas Hardy often composed poems in margins, like in a pocket Milton, where he also wrote "1866 Westbourne Park Villas."[52] John Keats wrote original poems in a number of his books, including Chaucer, Shakespeare, Milton, and Dante.[53] A Miss Welch composed a poem in 1818 in *Isabella, Countess of Carlisle's Thoughts, in the form of maxims to young ladies*, thereby not following those maxims.[54] These writers appropriate others' texts and subordinate public (because published and reproduced) works, making them personal and repurposing them with (and by) their own desires. Like graffiti, these marks left behind say, "I was here."[55]

This feeling for writing *on* something, important for authors attentive to the act, calls to mind desks and tables—the ground on which the paper or

MARGINAL SCRIBBLING AND DEFACING 19

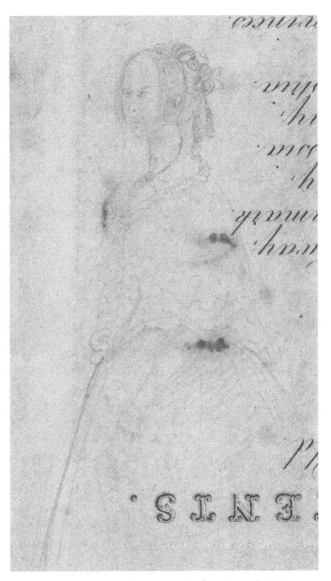

Fig. 3 Doodle probably drawn by Charlotte Brontë in the *Russell's General Atlas of Modern Geography*. The Morgan Library & Museum. PML 129886. Bequest of Helen Safford Bonnell, 1969

book rests while receiving text. George Eliot had a leather blotter which she laid out on her desk and used as a surface on which to put the paper or notebook she wrote on or in.[56] At some point, Eliot began writing on the blotter itself, a sort of doodling, although more thoughtful and organized—ideas for poems she might write and some of her favorite quotes from her reading. She filled the surface of the blotter with tiny script, in her characteristic purple ink. When she wrote on a page on top of this blotter, she was using writing (on leather) as a foundation for more writing, with text under the text she was creating, as if the words underneath might influence or help along the words being produced on top. Or, she might have wanted to have text that inspired her next to or underneath the text she produced, a way of thinking of (hand)writing as emanating or haunting. Her blotter, and marginalia more generally, have qualities of quasi-palimpsests, in that writing partially (or temporarily) obscures other writing, or is layered on top of it, and paper (or leather) is used for a second or third text, creating the possibility that the supplemental, tangential, or marginal text might become the most important text (depending on the reader), as is now true for the marginalia of Eliot, Austen, and the Brontës, but also, as we will see, for the fictional Catherine Earnshaw's.

Reimagining marginalia and, especially, doodling as kinds of graffiti brings into focus how "language entered into relations with the material world," as Juliet Fleming remarks, and poems carved into windows, written on walls, and inscribed or painted on jewelry, fruit trenchers, pots, and other surfaces not the book or the page announce that a "choice of appropriate material support" matters, that these texts "understand themselves to be written on something."[57] "Inscription poems" cut into glass or stone appear often in eighteenth-century gothic fiction, as Deidre Lynch remarks, blazoning "their status as writing, their constitutive scriptiveness."[58] Scratching one's autograph or lines of verse into a window, wall, or piece of furniture was a practice that continued into the nineteenth century, a means of claiming one's place in time and space, another way of impressing oneself *onto*.[59] In *Adam Bede* (1859), Wiry Ben makes fun of Seth Bede's absent-minded sloppiness by planning to write on a door he made, "Seth Bede, the Methody, his work," which is something like signing a piece of artwork, or writing "his book" with one's name on a flyleaf.[60] Eliot wrote in her journal that when she visited Goethe's house with George Henry Lewes, "We wrote our names near one of the windows."[61] Emily Brontë carved an "E" into the gate-legged parlor table where she did much of her writing, scratched her signature into a piece of jet jewelry (with Charlotte scratching hers onto another, attached piece), and doodled on a wall in her bedroom, potentially acts of resistance or defiance.[62] Another way of saying "I was here," this defacing leaves a bit of the self behind—a graphic trace of one's presence passing through as one might do with an autograph in a book, or marginalia with initials. Emily created characters who left behind handwritten text for others to read, in situ. Poems are "found in (or on)" or "written on (or in)" various spaces in Gondal and Angria, so a surrogate reader (the one who found the text) is written into the work, as is the surrogate writer.[63] Many characters in Gondal end up in dungeons or prison caves and they write while there, usually as a means to speak of the heart's yearning for what is on the other side of the walls, where nature holds sway. Poems such as "Written in the Gaaldine Prison Caves to A.G.A."; "From a Dungeon Wall in the Southern College," signed "J.B. Sept. 1825" (a Gondal date); and "From a D.W. in the N.C." (D.W. is dungeon wall and N.C. Northern College—colleges have dungeons in Gondal), signed by "A.G.A. Sept. 1826" (another Gondal date) picture a writer at work in specific locations (and times) and doing their work on walls (or in caves).[64] The poem "Written on the Dungeon Wall—N[orthern] C[ollege]" by "M.A." tells of the speaker's "vain repining" in "constant darkness" and thoughts of her friends whose "careless young eyes are closed in sleeping" and "brows are unshadowed, undimmed by woe."[65] The speaker ends with the feeling that it is better that she should "pine alone" than have her friends near, because then she would be even more haunted by the thought of them. M.A. addresses those who will later find these verses, imagining that they might even be the "friends" she refers to (or, more likely, other prisoners). The writing surface and the space where the text was composed become part of the poem's imaginary structure—the prison walls are what the poem is about.[66] The speaker composes the text to be found by someone who will inhabit the same space, declaring, once again, "I was here" and "here, I felt this," but also the rebellious idea of art as escape, from imprisonment and the powers that be.[67]

Like Emily, Eliot believed in the significance of found texts, as can be seen in her love of epigraphs (what she called mottoes), used so heavily in her later novels and copied on her blotter (and in her notebooks). In *Middlemarch*, she imagines the long life of a scrap of writing and how circumstances might bring it to the eyes of the only person who can understand its true import.

> Who shall tell what may be the effect of writing? If it happens to have been cut in stone, though it lie face downmost for ages on a forsaken bench, or "rest quietly under the drums and tramplings of many conquests"; it may

end by letting us into the secret of usurpations and other scandals gossiped about long empires ago … Such conditions are often minutely represented in our petty lifetime. As the stone which had been kicked by generation of clowns may come by curious little links of effect under the eyes of a scholar, through whose labours it may at last fix the date of invasions and unlock religions, so a bit of ink and paper which has long been an innocent wrapping or stop-gap may at last be laid under the one pair of eyes which have knowledge enough to turn it into the opening of a catastrophe.[68]

An inscription in stone or jottings on a piece of wrapping might "unlock religions" or open a catastrophe, as happens when Raffles picks up a bit of paper from a fireplace at Riggs's house to steady his flask against its leather casing. By a chain of morally fraught chance occurrences, Bulstrode's address on this slip leads to the return of his secret past, which unravels his life and those connected to him.

The effect of found writing on Maggie Tulliver in *The Mill on the Floss* works differently, but it "unlocks religions" for her in a personal way, emanating a strange energy that Eliot found herself in her reading, but also in the physicality of books, in their ability to capture time and memory.[69] As we have seen, books represent the possessor's identity and work as additions to (or fond friends of) the body; they are part of the world of objects that form what Eliot calls "first ideas":

> There is no sense of ease like the ease we felt in those scenes where we were born, where objects become dear to us before we had known the labour of choice, and where the outer world seemed only an extension of our own personality: we accepted and loved it as we accepted our own sense of existence and our own limbs. (*The Mill on the Floss* 187)

When the Tullivers in *The Mill on the Floss* must sell these dear things, their home resonates with the "shadows of departed objects—the daily companions" of their lives (214). Maggie sees books, especially, as these daily companions, like "our dear old Pilgrim's Progress that you [her brother Tom] coloured with your little paints." They are the family relics that tell most feelingly of the past, akin to her father's "quarto Bible" with the family records on the flyleaf (197). Maggie recognizes Philip Wakem's "hand" on a letter delivered to her during the crisis of her life because she has seen her own name written in it, "long ago, in a pocket Shakespeare which she possessed" (406). She stands in for the reader, especially for Mary Ann(e) Evans (as reader), who adored the same books, and showed it in similar ways. But Maggie also represents us, perhaps writing our name in our copy of *The Mill on the Floss*.[70] Marks in used volumes have an almost magical ability to spring to life. When Bob gives Maggie a pile of tattered books, she encounters an anonymous reader in *Imitation of Christ*, by Thomas à Kempis, bringing a "strange thrill of awe." "She took up the little, old, clumsy book with some curiosity: it had the corners turned down in many places, and some hand, now forever quiet, had made at certain passages strong pen-and-ink marks, long since browned by time. Maggie turned from leaf to leaf, and read where the quiet hand pointed" (236). The dead hand of the active reader, along with the dead author à Kempis, whose ideas but not touch are represented, shift Maggie's emotional life.[71] She thinks to herself, "Here, then, was a secret of life that would enable her to renounce all others secrets,—here was a sublime height" (237). Maggie, not so different from the "female" readers who enthuse too much in margins, loves reading, perhaps too much according to some lights. She personalizes and internalizes her books, practices discussed by Lynch in her history of literature loving. Lynch describes book "kissing"—which we can imagine Maggie doing—by writers like Charles Lamb and Leigh Hunt when they couldn't contain their enthusiasm.[72]

Reverence versus Irreverence

This notion that books might be relics or that previous readers can possess us, as with Maggie, are forms of bibliomancy—the feeling that books were haunted by some force. This belief clings most commonly to the bible, seen in swearing with one's hand on it, a faith believed in by Magwitch in *Great Expectations*, who pulls "a greasy little clasped black Testament out of his pocket" for this purpose.[73] The Tulliver family bible in *The Mill on the Floss*, with its handwritten record of marriages, births, and deaths on the flyleaf, has fetishistic powers. Mr. Tulliver believes in its special status—for attesting and promising—and he asks Tom to:

> "Write as your father, Edward Tulliver, took service under John Wakem, the man as had helped to ruin him, because I'd promised my wife to make her what amends I could for her trouble, and because I wanted to die in th' old place, where I was born and my father was born ... and then write, as I don't forgive Wakem ... I wish evil may befall him ... write as you'll

remember what Wakem's done to your father, and you'll make him and his feel it, if ever the day comes. And sign your name Tom Tulliver." (291)

Tom in his turn makes Maggie "vow solemnly to me, with your hand on my father's bible, that you will never have another meeting or speak another word in private with Philip Wakem" (278). He has her swear on the flyleaf with manuscript, however, as if the handwriting rather than the "word of God" strengthens the promise. In her earlier work *Adam Bede*, Eliot has Dinah open her bible randomly "for direction," because she "always lighted on some clear word to tell me where my work lay."[74] Wondering if Hetty Sorrel might need her guidance, Dinah sits in an almost dark room:

> She knew the physiognomy of every page, and could tell on what book she opened, sometimes on what chapter, without seeing title or number. It was a small thick Bible, worn quite round at the edges. Dinah laid it sideways on the window ledge, where the light was strongest, and then opened it with her forefinger.[75]

The tactile text, with a face to be "read" with fingertips, seems almost embossed on the page, as books for the blind were at this time, or words carved into wood or jet. Treating volumes as totems or fetishes dates to the beginnings of the codex. The anathema or book curse, for instance, grew out of scribal traditions, with owners believing that their books wouldn't go missing or be stolen with phrases like "he who steals this book shall be damned in eternal fire" written in them.[76] Fleming points to an "esoteric literalism, an almost magical way of thinking about the physical properties of language ... the fact that it is born of and bound in matter" during the Renaissance, but many of these ideas persisted.[77] With Eliot, as her belief in a God waned, she poured ever more feeling into her faith that books—and other humanist endeavors and productions—had messianic qualities and abilities.

Many treasured books more for their associative properties than for the text to be read in them. Charlotte and Emily Brontë—and other members of their family—also found an expanding richness between the boards of books, and they brought this notion often into their fiction.[78] To open a book and gently pass "over the characters the tips of her fingers," as Paulina in *Villette* (1853) does, is to be in the owner's presence once again, their time together lodged in the ink, paper, and leather.[79] Matter between the leaves marks moments and experiences, as in Anne's *Agnes Grey* (1847) when the title character preserves the primroses given to her by Mr. Weston in her bible, planning to "keep them always."[80] Volumes in the Brontë library have plants pressed in them, such as an 1827 book of botany and a brown leather copy of *Songs in the Night*, and various sorts of bookmarks, like Charlotte's watercolor sketch of a stone cross and two attached pages of Mme de Staël's *Corinne* (a book Maggie reads in *The Mill on the Floss*) tipped into the aforementioned *Russell's*.[81] In an 1829 diary, Charlotte ponders a primer that belonged to her now-dead sister Maria: "Once papa lent my Sister Maria a Book it was an old geography one and she wrote on a Blank leaf papa lent me this Book. The Book is an hundred and eleven years old it is at this moment lying Before me while I write this I am in the kitchen of the parsonage house Haworth."[82] Maria's presence (and absence) is felt in the family home by this tome she left behind. Another book-relic belonging to their mother Maria, Southey's *Poetical Works and Remains of Henry Kirk White* was salvaged when a ship carrying her possessions beached on the Coast of Devonshire, and the box that held them was "dashed to pieces."[83] Their father Patrick inscribed it, in Latin, after her death, "This was the book of my dearest wife; and it was preserved from the waves. So then always will it be preserved," thus pointing to the numerous layers of "remains"—of Henry Kirk White, Maria Brontë, and, eventually, the Brontë family.[84] He implies that the inscription might make the book immortal, as an inscribed curse might strike down its thief.

The volumes that saints, royals, historical figures, and other "celebrities" handled and used found their way into museums, such as one that St. Boniface (680–755), an Anglo-Saxon missionary, was holding when the "pagans" martyred him, still showing "gashes from the murderer's sword."[85] Volumes cherished as personal relics, associated with a beloved, hold an added sense of embodiment when containing manuscript.[86] Stephen Nichols sees annotation as "like the saint's relic, an artifact imbued with the power of an absent presence: in short, metalepsis, in the sense of substituting an indirect expression for a direct one."[87] For example, the inscription "Richard Brereton, Pembroke College, Oxford, 1741" in a 1730 copy of Milton's *Paradise Lost* was added to when it was passed or sold on, and it eventually became a memorial of a William Holder, as is detailed under the first autograph in a different hand: "The Gift of / Sarah Holder / to / Mary L. Holder. / in memory of / Willm Holder Gent, / who died June 15, 1810 …. 'He's gone, and left corruption here, / Where no corruption doth appear: / Where Seraphs bright their praise sing, / To God our father, and Our King.'"[88] This volume holds, but does not show, corruption—that is, it represents the body now fully corrupted.[89] Giving a book as a present, with one's own graphological trace, in some cases was an intimate gesture, like a touch or caress. Jackson explains that writing marginal notes in a volume as a gift to a friend was especially common among middle-class women.[90] Hester Piozzi "cultivated friendships by sharing books" she annotated, especially for "particular friends."[91] Edith Simcox, a writer in love with George Eliot, gave her books with various sorts of handwritten blessings. In her *Some Questions of the Day* (1875) she wrote, "From one who admires and appreciates George Eliot's great intellectual gifts. 'And this is the Promise that He hath promised us, even Eternal Life.'" In *Natural Law: An Essay on Ethics* (1877), Simcox added various manuscript incantations, including "To Whom with idolatrous love this book is dedicated" and addressing Eliot as "heaven ... with a tender smile upon her gracious lips, and yearning prophecy in the melting depths of her unfathomable eyes" (when she received it, Eliot wrote on the flyleaf " Marian Evans Lewes / June 21 1877").[92] Simcox worked in the long-established tradition of giving a marked book to woo—the handwriting (or "voice") seducing the reader while she read silently, alone.[93] Gillian Silverman sees books "as a technology of intimacy."[94] Coleridge, probably the most active writer of marginalia in the nineteenth century (and the one who first used the term in this way), wrote intimate comments in volumes he gave or lent to women; Byron annotated books for his lovers, and Keats, in a letter to Fanny Brawne, noted that he was "marking the most beautiful passages in Spenser, intending it for you."[95]

In gifts from George Eliot's friend Sara Sophia Hennell (whom Eliot addressed as "Beloved Spouse" or "Leiber Gemahl"—"dear husband") of her own books, she includes not only the current date but also a span of years that the book represents, inscribing them as material memories of their time together.[96] In Hennell's *Thoughts in aid of Faith* (1860), she wrote on the flyleaf: "Marian Evans Lewes—To the dearly beloved Translator / of Feuerbach's 'Essence of Cht' – in grateful / remembrance of how much I owed to her / during the season of happy intercourse / the 'German' period of our lives— / S.S.H/May 22n 1860."[97] Hennell's attention to temporality follows the habit, common at the time, of recording where and when the reading of a book happened, what Stauffer calls "date-marking," which reminds us that books are "objects in time."[98] Anne Brontë, for instance, kept an account of her progress in her red leather bible, writing on the second page, "began about December 1831 What when and how shall I be when I have got through?"[99] The movement of the self through time is calculated through reading time and through an imaginative leap to a future state that corresponds with pages of the book. Akin to the practice of subtracting the date of publication from the year when the reader buys or reads the book, date marking brings those years into the book, as it "lived" through them.[100] Anne may have imagined the bible either "knowing" or going to "witness" what would happen to her, in another kind of bibliomancy. Perhaps she even thought that writing in the bible might be a form of blessing or prayer for the future, a good luck charm. E. B. Browning included, along with her copious annotations of her Greek and Hebrew bibles, some marginal dates, including, "I finished reading the last line of this bible, at Sidmouth, Sept. 25th 1833."[101] Noting when and where in her life this ending occurred, she marked it down as it marked her, on that day in Sidmouth. Eliot date marked as well: in her copy of Carl Eduard Geppert's *Die altgriechische Buhne* (1843) she penciled on the final page: "read Feby-March 1844."[102] In John Kitto's *The Lost Senses, Deafness* (1845), she wrote at the end, "read April 1845 with intense interest," and in Torquato Tasso's *Le Gerusalemme Liberata* (1835), "Mary Anne Evans / Finito Luglio, 1841."[103] An especially rich example of this gesture can be found in her copy of Wordsworth's *The Prelude* (1850), a poem immensely important to her writing and identity.[104] She owned the volume for at least thirteen years, according to the dates handwritten in it, and read it aloud, or had it read aloud to her, with two different husbands. The earliest manuscript comes at the end and was written by George Henry Lewes: "Read second time (aloud to Polly [a nickname for George Eliot]) at Niton, reclining on the cliff or in the long grass, July 1867." They went to this village on the Isle of Wight, England, to try to restore their failing health, Eliot particularly struggling to write *The Spanish Gypsy*, which has many echoes of Wordsworth. The specificity of the grass and cliff locates the poem *there* for them, as if the reading surrounds and holds onto that spot in time and geography, lets them possess it, as a performative experience.[105] This rereading was heard by Eliot in her beloved Lewes's voice, making the volume a kind of aural relic: did she hear his voice when she opened it later, especially after his death? She experienced the poem again with her new husband John Cross, during their honeymoon. She recorded this scene of reading on the first page of the poem: "Begun with J. at Wildbad [Germany] in our walk on a Sunday morning, July 1880. Finished Aug. 23." Eliot chose not to write this on the same page as the earlier inscription, although there was room, as if she felt the two records of experience, during two Julys, should be many pages apart. They bracket the text, embedding this poem she adored into her living hours, marking it as it touched and changed her.[106] While *The Prelude* is far from being a "silly" novel written by a "silly" woman, it gathers around it notes with a similar type of enthusiasm, eagerness, and embodiment.

Eliot's sense that reading picks out and preserves a moment and its setting was shared by many in the nineteenth century, such as Mary Russell Mitford, who associates books she reads with the places (and set of hours) in which she reads them in her *Recollections of a Literary Life* (1852). Marcel Proust, when reflecting on reading Victorian authors in the 1880s (including Eliot's novels, which influenced his own work), also found that the physical volume evoked a scene of reading, and that many of one's memories—one's past itself—could be recovered only through opening a book, as if experience could be caught between the two covers. Proust writes about reading Ruskin:

> There are perhaps no days of our childhood we lived so fully as those we believe we left without having lived them, those we spent with a favorite book. Everything that filled them for others, and that we dismissed as a vulgar obstacle to a divine pleasure: the game for which a friend would come to fetch us at the most interesting passage ... the dinner we had to return home for, and during which we thought only of going up immediately afterward to finish the .interrupted chapter, all those things with which reading should have kept us from feeling anything but annoyance, on the contrary they have engraved in us so sweet a memory, that if we still happen today to leaf through those books of another time, it is for no other reason than that they are the only calendars we have kept of days that have vanished.[107]

The physical book itself seems to enclose those vanished days—the game, the sunrays, and the dinner—activities remembered only because he was reading while they occurred and because they came to inhabit the volume. Of Eliot's cherished volumes, the one most bound up with her identity was a childhood copy of *The Linnet's Life* (1822), given to her by her dear father, whose hair she preserved after his death (see Fig. 4).[108] She wrote on the flyleaf,

> This little book is the first present I ever remember having received from my Father. Let anyone who thinks of me with some tenderness after I am dead take care of this book for my sake. It made me very happy when I held it in my little hands and read it over and over again, and thought the pictures beautiful, especially the one where the linnet is feeding her young. / Marian Evans Lewes.

Fig. 4 George Eliot's inscription in her copy of *The Linnet's Life* (1822). George Eliot and George Henry Lewes Collection, General Collection, Beinecke Rare Books and Manuscript Library, Yale University, GEN MSS 963, Box 56. By kind permission of the Estate of George Eliot

The book stands, to some extent, as a replacement for Eliot herself, since after she is dead, this is the object that should be treated with tenderness, as if it were an adjunct to her body, now in the grave.[109] In such everyday objects as this book about birds, she locates a secular divine, part of her project of atheistic realism. The nostalgic tone of so much of Eliot's writing appears here, too – the sense that all could be redone or once again revisited, with innocent eyes, like a child in Wordsworth whose days are bound each to each with natural piety. Or, as she writes in *The Mill on the Floss*, "but heaven knows where that striving might lead us, if our affections had not a trick of twining round those old inferior things—if the loves and sanctities of our life had no deep immoveable roots in memory" (188).

Turning from *The Mill on the Floss* to the earlier *Wuthering Heights* is to move from Maggie's reverence for books, and Eliot's marking of time in and with them, to Catherine Earnshaw's resistance to them, especially religious texts, and Brontë's wasting of time (in and with them). While in the former novel books can seem to have magical qualities, ones that might lead to escape, in the latter books feel more like containers or even prisons. More than most novels, *Wuthering Heights* feels as if it has an interior, or many interiors, made more potent by the fact that the book takes the name of a building with rooms. Can readers dwell in or penetrate *Wuthering Heights* in the way that Heathcliff inhabits or Lockwood enters Wuthering Heights? Inside the rooms of Wuthering Heights are more books (mirroring the book in which we find them). Some of these imaginary books have writing in their margins or even running over their margins to cover, or take the place of, the printed text. The texts inside of texts (inside of Wuthering-Heights-as-text) elaborate, Carol Jacobs remarks, the novel's "own textuality."[110] One way this works is through representing a surrogate author in Catherine Earnshaw, who writes in the margins of her books a diary that Maggie Berg sees as a "microcosm of the novel," mirroring Emily Brontë writing *Wuthering Heights*.[111] Furthermore, the urban stranger Lockwood works as a surrogate reader of found text, arriving at this remote place with a desire to understand the narrative of these closed-off people, similar to readers of the novel struggling to make sense of a story almost over when they open the book.[112] Not long after his arrival in the area and his rental of Heathcliff's other house, Lockwood makes his way to Wuthering Heights, curious to know more about his taciturn landlord. He enters the house through a doorway inscribed like the flyleaf of a book—"Hareton Earnshaw 1500"—as if the house is a volume opened by going through this entrance. Because of a heavy snowstorm, Lockwood is forced to spend the night in the unfriendly place, with snarling dogs and other misanthropic inhabitants. A servant takes him to the bed of the long-dead Catherine. This "large oak case, with squares cut out near the top, resembling coach windows" entered by sliding back the "paneled sides" is reminiscent of the reading closets common during the Renaissance, when this house was first built.[113] This room within a room represents "the innermost recesses of Emily Brontë's text," James Kavanagh remarks, emphasizing the novel's many nooks and crannies.[114] Lockwood and the reader first meet the central character Catherine through her "writing scratched on the paint" of the window ledge enclosed in the paneled bed. "This writing, however, was nothing but a name repeated in all kinds of characters, large and small—*Catherine Earnshaw*, here and there varied to *Catherine Heathcliff*, and then again to *Catherine Linton*" (51). As Lockwood begins to drift off, these "white letters" become "as vivid as spectres—the air swarmed with Catherines" (51). The autograph scored into paint is linked to an autograph on the flyleaf of one of her books: "Catherine Earnshaw, her book" and an unspecified date (which must be in the 1770s). These texts

Catherine once carved and scribbled come alive with her presence, at least in Lockwood's dreamy state.[115] He continues to "decipher her faded hieroglyphics," finding that "scarcely one chapter" of these books of sermons and other religious text "had escaped a pen-and-ink commentary—at least, the appearance of one, covering every morsel of blank that the printer had left" (51). Like the Brontës themselves, Catherine doesn't write in the margins for what Lockwood calls "legitimate purposes." She doodles irreverently, such as an "excellent caricature of ... Joseph, rudely yet powerfully sketched," and jots down a "regular diary, scrawled in an unformed, childish hand" (51). Catherine is not an Eliot or even a "silly" reader, but a defacer, thus even worse than those complained about earlier, who scratch with fingernail and quill.[116] Even though she has filled all of these books, Lockwood only reads a few snippets of her diary before he nods off. The window to Catherine's writing closes with his eyes, leaving the reader (of *Wuthering Heights*) unable to discover the other stories she pens, as if it were possible for her (the reader) to enter the book the way Lockwood penetrates this "innermost recess"— and read more. A *mise en abîme* opens up, with books inside the book that is *Wuthering Heights*, and marginalia inside volumes that are themselves inside a volume that might have marginalia.

With interiors come surfaces. Like Eliot, Brontë presents the material on (and in) which the writing happens. The graffiti, scored into the paint, could be read with hands in the dark, like braille, and the books carry their years and place by being mildewed, "dreadfully musty" things piled in a corner, evoking paper damp to the touch, darkened with organic matter. One of the "antique" volumes, burned by Lockwood's candle, perfumes the bedspace "with an odour of roasted calf-skin," calling to mind the possibility of cooking and eating their animal flesh. The skin with which the books are bound brings to mind Catherine's skin, especially when Lockwood cuts and makes bleed that skin—or that of her ghost, during another dream generated by her handwriting in which Catherine as a girl knocks on the window, trying to return to her bed.[117] The sleeping cabinet works as a stand-in for her body, as do the books, impressed long ago with her hands and handwriting, which tell of the fate of her body. The text and its foundation localize, create space and time, but also emanate and move—continuing to haunt Lockwood and Wuthering Heights and, ultimately, *Wuthering Heights*.

These dogmatic volumes represent imprisoning cages or boxes, just as the house itself and its rooms imprison—the young Heathcliff and Catherine after the Earnshaw parents die and Catherine's brother Hindley takes over as the despotic ruler. Later, when Isabella Linton marries Heathcliff, she has to work hard to make her escape and Cathy, Catherine's daughter, coerced to marry Heathcliff's son Linton, flees by climbing out of the window inside the bed-cabinet and down the tree. As a child, Catherine finds these books oppressive, and she and Heathcliff attempt to escape from being force-fed them by the servant Joseph. She records this escape from them, in their very pages:

> An awful Sunday! ... H. and I are going to rebel—we took our initiatory step this evening. All day had been flooding with rain; we could not go to the church, so Joseph must needs get up a congregation in the garret; and, while Hindley and his wife basked down-stairs before a comfortable fire, doing anything but reading their bibles ... Heathcliff, myself, and the unhappy plough-boy, were commanded to take our prayer-books ... I could not bear the employment. I took my dingy volume by the scroop, and hurled it into the dog kennel, vowing I hated a good book. (51–2)

Rather than using these books for reading, Catherine asserts her selfhood in and on them, claiming her experience by overwriting, crowding out the block of printing in the middle of the page. Not only does she write on them and throw them, she rips the back off of *The Helmet of Salvation*, and Heathcliff does something that Joseph calls "pawsed his fit into" the first part of the *Broad Way to Destruction*.[118] While this treatment of books, normally expensive at the time, is meant to be shocking, these types of religious tracts were often given away for free or cheaply, being subsidized by members of religious societies, like the Bradford Auxiliary Bible Society that the Brontës' clergyman father Patrick belonged to, which distributed free bibles to the poor of the area. In *Jane Eyre*, the hypocritical headmaster of Lowood Mr. Brocklehurst gives the young Jane tracts like these to scare her into submission. Such free books were ripe for reuse, as notebooks, albums for "scraps," pressed plants, and the like.[119] Despite this, defacing these books works as a form of rebellion; Berg sees Catherine's diary as a marginal space that combines an "image of her social marginalization with an exploration of writing and reading as acts of resistance."[120] While Catherine and Heathcliff attempt various types of escape, including death, the ultimate one, these scribbles work as the most lasting type of revolt, in part because they provide a witness in the future. In fact, Catherine's glosses replace the published words, since the reader never sees them (except for the title of one sermon, which turns into a dream). The printed text becomes the paratext here, the "marginal" writing the only thing worth reading. Moreover, Catherine *writes* instead of passively reading, a key point for the Brontës, whose work became a means for young women (Charlotte especially, with her Jane) to present to the world their own thoughts and ideas, their own version of reality that included more than "making pudding and knitting stockings ... playing on the piano and embroidering bags."[121] In a self-reflexive move, Catherine even records the act of writing itself, acknowledging that she isn't reading these books but merely using them as notebooks or diaries. She tells us that she "reached this book" (the one she is writing in) "and a pot of ink from the shelf, and pushed the house-door ajar to give me light, and I have got the time on with writing for twenty minutes" (53). Catherine says, like those imprisoned poets writing on their prisons, "I was (am) here, writing."

Catherine's paratexts represent the books that once belonged to Victorian women, in part because they feel haunted, reminding us of women's lost libraries. The absence of these writers' real-life, tangible books and the identities they once embodied feels ghostly, just as Catherine's books do in the novel—found serendipitously by a stranger in that weird bed. Volumes still present can also have this quality, especially when someone long dead has scribbled in them. Reading old books, Virginia Woolf remarked, helps us "feel that the present is not all; that other hands have been before us, smoothing the leather until the corners are rounded and blunt, turning the pages until they are yellow and dog's-eared. We like to summon before us the ghosts of those old readers who have read their *Arcadia* from this very copy."[122] Eliot's books have a different quality, yet her writing of, in, and about physical volumes expresses their power to deeply mark the emotional, and even the bodily, life of individuals, in ways not always rational. All of these women explored textual and material boundaries and also sometimes exploded them, with texts migrating out of the book, in the way that Catherine's autograph appears to move from flyleaf to window ledge, and things that were not texts migrating into books, like pressed plants, feathers, smells, and impressions.[123]

2
Collecting and Recollecting

> From your book I take a leaf,
> By your leave do take:
> Art is long, though life be brief,
> Yet on this page my mark I'll make.
> Walter Crane,
> his mark.
> Walter Crane, written in Constance Wilde's album[1]

Even more than the haptic books discussed in Chapter 1 with their marginalia, locks of hair for bookmarks, and date and place stamping, nineteenth-century albums let in the object world from outside, creating a reading, writing, and touching continuum, and foregrounding their own material nature.[2] Always present with and in the album is the body that made, displayed, and looked through it, providing a meeting place for the book and skin, time and space. Many of the writers discussed in Chapter 1—including George Eliot, Elizabeth Barrett Browning, Charlotte Brontë, and Elizabeth Gaskell—created and contributed to various sorts of albums, notebooks, or commonplace books. In this chapter, I suggest ways that albums worked as nascent books, or as models for how to put together a novel (and other types of writing, especially books of poetry and biography). Said another one, they are *intermedial*, in the sense that Richard Menke and others have defined it, as encouraging "connections across media."[3] But, more than this, I explore how nineteenth-century albums lead us to think newly about writing and drawing, about the book object and book form more generally.[4] Different sorts of albums did different work: as memory storage devices, gatherings of friends, and creations of interior spaces that might imaginatively be inhabited. Many had performative elements, often with attention to script as a visual form in space and on paper. Devices we associate with twentieth-century avant-garde movements, such as *mise en abîme*, asemia, *trompe l'oeil*, micrography, collage, and the *objet trouvé*, were part of the performative act of crafting and displaying them. The experimental art of

Victorian Paper Art and Craft. Deborah Lutz, Oxford University Press.
© Deborah Lutz (2022). DOI: 10.1093/oso/9780198858799.003.0003

these book-like assemblages, along with their heterogeneity, hybridity, and fragility, lead to philosophical questions about mortality and death, such as: can collections of artifacts preserve the moment, the place, history?[5]

Gaskell's album and writing work will be the central focus of this chapter, although other writers could have taken her place here (and will make guest appearances, especially Charlotte Brontë). But more than most creative people of her time, she was steeped in album culture, and much of her writing (*Cranford* [1863] especially) shares qualities with albums and suggests kinship with and growth out of the same communities, crafts, and sets of ideas. She compiled multiple "music books" where she recorded in pencil (and later traced over in ink) songs with musical notation passed on from friends and to be played on the piano and sung.[6] She carefully credited the giver, with notes such as, "copied from L.A.D.H. / February 1826 / copied Tuesday."[7] When she was twenty-one, she wrote out favorite quotations from Shakespeare, Burns, and others in a commonplace book (what we would today call a notebook or journal, for collecting and treasuring lines gleaned from one's reading, the "flowers" or "commonplaces" of literature—a form discussed at length in Chapter 3).[8] For her autograph collection, she hunted widely for letters and signatures from people she admired, mostly writers like Charlotte Brontë, Eliot, and E. B. Browning.[9] Many of these "autographs" (which could mean a bit of handwriting, not necessarily a signature) were eventually gathered into five leather-bound volumes.[10] She called these her "book"; for example, when a friend asked for a Charlotte Brontë autograph and Gaskell didn't have one, Gaskell invited her to visit and view all of her autographs: "Or come and see my book—that would be best of all."[11] Gaskell collected these sorts of souvenirs, a way of holding onto an experience, a feeling, a friendship and its gifts, by making or keeping a tangible trace. She treasured vestiges, describing letters written by her long-dead mother as "the only relics of her that I have, and of more value to me than I can express, for I have so often longed for some little thing that had once been hers or touched by her."[12]

As Gaskell's varied array of volumes suggest, categorizing albums of the time can be a complicated task. Clare Pettitt, following James Secord, uses the umbrella term "scrapbook" or "scrap" album.[13] She includes under this rubric albums with no "scraps" as we would understand them today—like cut-out strips of newspapers—but just handwritten entries and drawings. In this broad sense, all of the albums discussed in this chapter contain "scraps"—leavings of friends and associates, keepsakes of one's travels, and bric-a-brac picked up in the daily rhythms of life. My focus will be narrower, however, taking in album making alongside creative acts that become literature (and published books more generally). The two forms that are of interest here I call "friendship albums" (with "autograph albums" as a subset) and "souvenir albums" (recalling the French word, meaning "memory" or "remembrance," although also in the sense of mementos picked up while traveling).[14] I define the former as volumes contributed to by more than one person, while the latter were compiled by one person alone (although sometimes as gifts or for others to look at). Gaskell's creative work aligns most closely with the friendship album, so it will take center stage. The category of "souvenir album" could potentially be as overarching as "scrapbook," in that anything put in an album might be said to represent a memory. But I use the word to signal a personal museum making—a shaping of an identity and a narrative—through objects displayed in volume form. Photograph albums are the breed of souvenir collections most familiar to us today, yet I turn to the more haptic forms of holding onto selfhood, during the decades just before photographs swept in to replace most other types of memento gathering.

Friends in Books

Despite being popular in the nineteenth century, albums—domestic and ornamental—have been mostly forgotten in histories of the book, paper, and binding.[15] This is especially true of friendship albums, sometimes called an *album amicorum* or *souvenir d'amitié*, largely because these volumes were, by the early nineteenth century, associated with women (although men also kept them).[16] The owner requested friends to add a poem, drawing, painting, collage, lock of hair, and other art or keepsakes to her "book." Commemorating relationships and shared experience, creating witnesses to the social group, its occasion, and haunts, friendship albums were often displayed in the parlor and paged through with visitors, thus holding a semi-public quality. Collections of friends, in a sense, the volumes provided a means to show and preserve one's connections, fondnesses, communities. Gaskell kept one, writing to request from one Harriet Carter a drawing for what she calls "my scrapbook," explaining that "it does not pretend to the dignity of an album, [but] is anxiously looking forward to seeing its pages adorned by your contributions, and I will do my best in the course of winter to draw you something."[17] Friendship albums were usually chatty, anecdotal, intimate, and whimsical, with games, acrostics, lists of likes and dislikes, pasted or sewn in paper dolls, feathers, and more.[18] Many of these albums start out with a poem by the owner, asking for creative collaboration and sometimes setting up rules. Jane Nelson opened her 1820s album with one beginning, "My album is a garden plot / Here all my friends may sow / Where thorns and thistles flourish not"—inviting her group to bring their own "flowers" of verse or drawings.[19] One created at a girls' school that Charlotte Brontë attended has a "Prologue" that starts, "Whoever with curious eye this book explores / Must add some contribution to its stores" and states some rules, such as no "profane" wit.[20] Friends composed poems for the occasion that wished the compiler well, such as a few lines written by a twelve-year-old Felicia Browne (later Felicia Hemans) to her aunt Anne Wagner,

> Anne, may every Bliss be thine,
> That fond Affection can bestow!
> And Love and Sympathy combine,
> To soothe thee, in the hour of Woe,
> And Seraph Hope, around thee play,
> And smiling Peace attend thy Way![21]

In a small album belonging to the British writer Maggie Strickland, someone has filled a leaf with an acrostic with the first letter of each line spelling "MAGGIE."[22] Other verse championed friendships, such as, on a page in Anne Wagner's album that has a braid of brown hair attached to the paper with pink ribbon: "Close as this lock of hair the ribband binds / May friendship's sacred bonds unite our minds / Yrs. Sincerely, Eliza Brooks, Liverpool, June 15th -95."[23]

Derided as sentimental and frivolous (terms also used to diminish Gaskell's novels, especially *Cranford*), friendship albums are celebrated by Samantha Matthews as "symbolic stand-in[s] for the feminine body."[24] The body comes into play with these albums in myriad ways. Occasionally, leavings of actual bodies were added, such as locks of hair, as in the before-mentioned Anne Wagner album with three locks of hair tied to pages using ribbons threaded through holes in the paper. In Edith May Southey's album, a curl from a friend (dated March 1829) is held in a paper pocket glued to a page.[25] Yet another way to think of these albums as embodied is in their sensuous tactility. Shared with others, they were held in laps, turned over by multiple hands, and given narratives. Martha Langford calls this their "vestigial oral framework," and she argues that "the showing and telling of an album is a performance."[26] With covers of stamped or tooled leather, or plush velvet, and ribbons, locks, and other embellishments, they invited the caress. Pressed artifacts seemed as if they might spring off of the page—flowers, feathers, lace, and other haptic remains. Larger items pasted or sewn in needed to be folded out to be viewed or read. These volumes tell of the intimacy and empathy to be found in touch, which might close the distance that sight can open.[27] Their texture reminds the handler of those who made and decorated them, offering information about how they came into being.[28]

Friendship albums managed to be, on the one hand, commonplace, commercially made, and, on the other, singular expressions of place, emotion, and community. Blank books with "album" (or "scraps," "souvenirs," or similar terms) embossed on the cover were produced on an extensive scale, as were individual pages with ornamented frames or other embellishments that would be bound together professionally when the compiler had curated the whole. The various fashions for different sorts of albums work against an argument for their expressions of individual uniqueness, yet even the faddish ones have personal touches. Todd S. Gernes remarks that creators of "assembled books transformed the everyday prose of the object world into poetry, infusing domestic artifacts with historicity, familiarity, and selfhood."[29] Most entries in British friendship albums include the date and place, mooring them in specificity. Charlotte Brontë, who contributed to a number of these albums, composed a short religious poem, called "Stanzas On the Death of a Christian," in one Sarah Thomas's album and signed it "C. Brontë / Haworth / July 17, 1837," hence giving it the feel of a performance in a moment and a local space, kept in amber.[30] Brontë uses an album of this kind as a representation of longstanding bonds in *Shirley* with Caroline Helstone's enamel-covered "souvenir," where she memorializes moments of affection.[31] Taking a few flowers from a bouquet as she gives it to her old friend Cyril Hall, she presses them into her album, closed with a silver clasp, and pencils in the date and "To be kept for the sake of the Rev. Cyril Hall, my friend."[32] Cyril also slips a sprig into his "pocket Testament," recording her name next to it.

Not only were these store-bought, ordinary objects turned into monuments to singular groups, collections of people; they could also be highly inventive and self-aware. Poems composed on the spot for an album reflected on writing in an album as a performative act.[33] In one of Maggie Strickland's albums, a friend wrote, "When this you see, / Your shoulders shrug / For what's within an album / Is all Humbug— / Ada Sampson / July 29th 1899."[34] In another Strickland album, a friend has done this:

COLLECTING AND RECOLLECTING 39

"Lines from the pen of a bashful poetess:—"
_____
_____
_____

Amy Thyne, Oct. 4th, 1894.[35]

Often the poet made the theme of the poem the writing of the poem, along with the reason for doing it, and they imagine the page and the volume as part of their conceit, especially the pure whiteness of the sheet—a play on the word "album," which comes from the Latin "albus," meaning white—to then be sullied or darkened by the poet's ink.[36] The 1830s album of Agnes Kitching, of Milnthorpe, holds a number of these types of poems, including one called "An Address to this album":

> O Album, now that we're alone
> And none to overhear us;
> We'll poke the fire and prate awhile,
> And take a dram to cheer us.
> Your Missie is a well fared lass, …
> When next she strokes your bonnie leaves,
> And peers them with her ee,
> Just whisper lightly till her ear,
> To cast a thought to me.[37]

The poem's speaker addresses the paper and the book as agents that might help her be remembered. Ink and paper become subjects of the poem made of ink and paper, akin to the Emily Brontë prison poems (discussed in Chapter 1) found on—or being written on—dungeon walls. Matthews comments on the eroticism of poems like these and how they "register the album's subversive potential as an object that opens up a space of fantasy and the ideal in unsettling and ambiguous proximity to the embodied feminine subject."[38] Another subversive embodiment appears through the recursive recognition of the physical act and tools of writing, what Roland Barthes calls the "hand which presses down and traces a line."[39] It is as if the writer sees herself as an artist composing then and there, a historical personage inscribing her mark. On another page of Agnes Kitching's album, a different friend begins a poem, "When this little tribute I am writing, / In this book for thee, / Shall meet your eye—in friendship I ask / One little thought for me." There are at least two temporalities here: the now of "I am writing" and the future time of reading by the album owner.[40]

Yet the meta-structural desires found in friendship albums were even more varied and creative than the "here I am writing in an album" poems. On one of the pages of Charlotte's school album, to which she contributed a pencil copy of a David Cox drawing of St. Martin's Parsonage in Birmingham, a classmate made four watercolors with a *tromp l'oeil* effect (see Fig. 5).[41] One is a closed-up letter with its seal broken, exposing on the inside edges bits of deliberately illegible writing. Made to look as if it went through the mail, it has a post office mark that appears to say "Chester" on it, stray pen and pencil smudges, and a generally crumpled appearance. Another picture shows a decorated visiting-card case with its top open and a card peeking out of it, the partial text "ooke House" visible. A third depicts another visiting card, this one sitting out as if pulled from the case, with "Miss Kitson" on it, possibly the name of the artist. The fourth and most interesting item on this page is an album with illustrations and music in it, sitting open so that numerous individual pages can be partially seen. A painting of a brightly colored bird and flower on one page closely mirrors the pictures made by girls in the album itself, as do pages of music. Some of the

Fig. 5 An illustration by one of Charlotte Brontë's Roe Head school fellows in an album. Roe Head Album (1831–40), Brontë Parsonage Museum, C109

depicted leaves are heavy with handwritten text, most of it also deliberately unreadable, although the bottom of one page appears to say, "Eliza Lukis, Millport, March, 1833." These pictures invite imaginary hands to turn their pages, pull cards out of boxes, unfold and read letters, making fully manifest the actual flatness of the page but also, paradoxically, signaling a depth or *mise en abîme*. Is there another album drawn in the depicted album and, if so, does that one also have a depicted album? Such gestures add another dimension to the originally blank book, as if they reach outside of the paper and covers, or go deeper inside. The volume is given a sort of interior, as if we, the reader/viewer/handler, might be able to enter its space, inhabit it, something like how *Wuthering Heights*, as discussed in Chapter 1, opens up a rich, peopled world readers imagine entering. As a kind of display case, the album sat in the parlor or other domestic interior, rooms often exhibiting crafted or found objects—wax flowers, needlepoint, shells—turning the album into a miniature version of the room containing it.[42]

The page in Brontë's school album is one example of hundreds of these types of drawings.[43] In Eliza Threipland's circa 1812 album, for instance, there are numerous pictures of paper, including an open album with a religious poem and writing made to be unreadable on partially seen pages.[44] On other leaves, friends drew an unfurling scroll with a poem on it and a tombstone in a cemetery, with "Album" scrawled across it (perhaps a witty hostility against album culture?). In other albums, visiting cards are depicted as if thrown onto the page, each with the name of a friend; pictures of envelopes have their flaps open, showing paper inside; and scraps of paper of all sorts with text are depicted with a corner (or more than one) peeling up, as if the fictional paper can't help but fly off of the real page.[45] Pettitt writes about this *tromp l'oeil*, remarking that "the theatricality of these optical special effects, and their playful use of imagined space, references other contemporary popular forms of travel reportage in panoramas, dioramas and dissolving magic-lantern views."[46] These drawings not only call to mind these other imagined spaces but they also insist on their own and the need these makers have to represent the physical nature of the paper and the book—to thicken it, fetishize it, celebrate it.

The creators of these volumes emphasize, in various ways, the materialization of language in written form. They explore the fact that, as Joanna Drucker puts it, "all writing has the capacity to be both looked at and read, to be present as material and to function as the sign of an absent meaning."[47] Related to these pictorial devices to deepen and layer volumes, to give them extra interiority, are asemic texts (having the appearance of writing but with no semantic content) and micrography (tiny writing). The illegible writing in albums discussed earlier increases the visual properties of language by making it drawing only—a kind of pure writing—turning it into a "precise material act."[48] Emily Brontë sometimes used asemics in her illustrations, such as her pencil sketch of the dog Grasper, who has an inscribed collar with the text deliberately illegible.[49] Eliot, in an early notebook of 1834, doodled a tombstone with an urn on it, then used asemic writing for its epitaph.[50] These marks on a page that only gesture to the idea of writing share a kinship with handwriting so small one needs magnification to read it, another common visual effect in friendship albums. On one leaf of an 1890s Maggie Strickland album (see Fig. 6), a contributor pasted in an

Fig. 6 A contribution by a friend to Maggie Strickland's 1890s friendship album that includes micrography and cut-paper designs. Margaret Strickland Papers; MSS 77; box 8, folder 5; Fales Library and Special Collections, New York University Libraries

elaborate, expert, cut-paper design that radiates out from a central circle on which the Lord's Prayer has been handwritten in a tiny script.[51] Many Brontë manuscripts utilize micrography, such as Emily's poetry leaves and the miniature booklets that Charlotte and Branwell made as children. Charlotte owned (and perhaps made herself) a tiny slip of paper with, again, the Lord's Prayer written in a circle the size of a three-pence coin, a popular trick of the time.[52] Signs so tiny they can't be read draw the reader closer—almost into—the page, as the marks retreat from attempts to give them meaning. Roland Barthes remarks that, "for writing to be manifest in its truth (and not in its instrumentality), it must be illegible."[53] Like asemia, minute script announces itself as lines on paper made by the hand of a specific historical individual. It becomes drawing in addition to writing, art or craft along with text, or what Juliet Fleming calls a "commitment to a linguistic aesthetic predicated on the recalcitrant exteriority of language to meaning."[54] Susan Stewart also touches on these themes:

> The closure of the book is an illusion largely created by its materiality, its cover. Once the book is considered on the plane of its significance, it threatens infinity. This contrast is particularly apparent in the transformations worked by means of the miniature book and minute writing, or micrographia. Minute writing experiments with the limits of bodily skill in writing; the remarkableness of minute writing depends upon the contrast between the physical and abstract features of the mark. Nearly invisible, the mark continues to signify; it is a signification which is increased rather than diminished by its minuteness.[55]

The album doesn't even need legible words—what Stewart calls here "the plane of its significance"—to play with this sort of infinity, which happens through the visual properties of language and the artistic rendering of the page and book as doubly visible.

Picking up another thread from Stewart's remarks quoted above, some friendship albums were themselves miniature, part of a fad for tiny volumes of all sorts that grew, in part, out of a Victorian fetishization of books and the book form.[56] For example, Julia P. Wrightman used her circa 1850 miniature album, a "present from Margate," to collect drawings and texts from her friends, mostly minute poems decorated with painted frames.[57] Miniature books proliferated during the nineteenth century, including tiny blank notebooks, which could be carried in pockets or worn on the body.[58] Devotional texts were the most common types made minute, like Charlotte Brontë's palm-sized prayer book that closes like a wallet, with a leather tab that slips into a band, and Emily Brontë's 2½ by 3¾-inch *Psalms of David*.[59] Miniaturization attests not only to the hand and eye of the maker but also the reader. Reading such minute tomes dramatizes the reading act itself, bringing attention to the fingertips and palm being used in ways unusual with normal reading.[60] When a book is too small to read, it becomes an object to admire. Many miniature tomes were made to be beautiful objects like jewelry, with bindings of silver, emerald, enamel, gold pierced-wire, mother-of-pearl, needlework, and tortoiseshell.[61] Even normal-sized albums have this object-like quality, as we have seen, with their luxurious trappings. Elizabeth Edwards and Janice Hart point to albums' skeuomorphic qualities, in that they refer "to other objects with precise social meanings and functions. Albums are made to look like precious books, religious books … clearly a reference to medieval devotional books, the *carte-de-visite* album becoming a form of secular bible."[62] Albums thus comment on the book shape more generally as a decorative container, as something merely to look at and touch rather than to read. Is it still a book if it can't even be opened? The book object held so much value to the Victorians—as signs of education and knowledge, as familiar and comforting household possessions—that "dummy" books, or containers that looked like books, became popular. Gerard Curtis describes doctors and lawyers plumping out their libraries with shell books (just the bindings, no interiors) and Charles Dickens taking the pages out of old books to make a false bookcase behind the door of his study.[63] Book-shaped things—boxes, bookends, daguerreotype cases, maple-sugar molds, sewing cases, puzzles, flasks, and much more—were used and loved by Victorians.[64] Not surprisingly, a large proportion of these "blooks" (things that look like books) were modeled on friendship, souvenir, and photo albums.[65] Charlotte Brontë's leather, book-shaped sewing case says "Souvenirs" on the spine.[66]

Cranfordian Collections

Gaskell's writing process at certain junctures looked like the activity of putting together an album, a book of scraps, a collection of friendly tales or tales of friendship. A prolific writer, she accumulated piles of papers of her own fiction, essays, and letters. When Mary Howitt needed a quick article for a magazine, she wrote Gaskell to send her one, "for I presume it is already written and is one of the many manuscripts which lie in a certain desk drawer, and may have lain there for years."[67] The drawer as storage space for manuscripts perhaps also functioned as an organizing device, something like the tiny boxes and portable desk Emily Brontë used to hold diaries and small leaves of poetry, or the "alphabetical boxes" Charles Reade kept for loose-leaf writing ideas, notes, and useful quotations.[68] These places share a kinship with writers' volumes like the scrapbooks Virginia Woolf compiled with notes and clippings about women's education and everyday lives, which eventually served as fodder for *Three Guineas* (1938) and *The Years* (1937).[69] George Eliot's extensive research notebooks functioned similarly, as distillations of her massive reading for use in her densely intellectual novels.[70] Gaskell was a more heterogenous collector: of anecdotes, mementos, papers, letters, and crafts, and these leftovers often became part of her stories and nonfiction. She always asked in her letters for what she called "scraps," "bits," "particulars." To her friend Elizabeth Holland, she writes, "Thank you my dear for your letter ... you need never fear being too particular; you cannot give me too many minutiae," and she wants her daughter to send "*every scrap you hear*" about the Crimean war.[71] A common refrain in notes to friends: "Oh! I have so much to say,—not of any thing particular but quantities of bits and crumbs."[72] These sorts of "little details" seemed to her to be the purview of women, to be "beneath the dignity of man," who shunned "condescending to particulars" in letters.[73] The paper, pen, and other materials of her practice are openly discussed as shaping her writing. "This piece of paper tempts me to write to you," she says to a friend, and to another, to whom she often wrote very long letters, "I am not going to write a word beyond this little sheet."[74] *Cranford* has this scrappy quality, as if it were one of (or a series of) Gaskell's letters rather than a novel, or "the little daily notes, almost without beginning and without end, that one talks out on paper," as she describes her letter writing.[75] *Cranford* started out as an account of Knutsford—the small town where she was raised by her Aunt Lumb (her mother died when she was a baby)—published as an article called "The Last Generation in England." It then developed into the lightly fictionalized Duncome, in "Mr. Harrison's Confessions." Later, Gaskell imagined it as one short story, and she published it as "Our Society at Cranford" in Dickens's *Household Words*, explaining to John Ruskin, who admired the novel, "The beginning of 'Cranford' was one paper in 'Household Words'; and I never meant to write more."[76] But then, almost when she wasn't looking, it multiplied into numerous stories, which finally formed the book *Cranford*.

Although Gaskell never made this connection herself, as far as we know, *Cranford* shares many qualities with friendship albums. In other words, if an album is a nascent book, the friendship album would grow up to be *Cranford*. Given that friendship albums are filled with poetry, they would seem comparable to poetry anthologies or miscellanies rather than novels.[77] Yet a novel like *Cranford* that retains its quality of a collection—a stitching together of the types of stories told by her aunts and their friends in Knutsford—and fits uneasily into the category of a cohesive novel also presents a close kinship with albums. Many have noted its episodic, gossipy nature, its pulling against the stereotypical idea of the Victorian realist novel, with its news, yarns, and reports from the field that don't lead to a major climax or resolution. Characters make use of "fragments and small opportunities in Cranford," reusing, collecting, and *noticing* domestic tidbits.[78] Andrew Miller calls Gaskell a "narrative bricoleause" with *Cranford*, and Tim Dolin sees the novel as "organized like a collection of anecdotes printed on cards and bundled together ... reminiscent less of a conventional Victorian novel than a woman's collection."[79] Talia Schaffer shows how not only is *Cranford* "patched together out of domestic handicrafts," foregrounding women's domestic rhythms, but it is also itself "structured like a craft, its plot compiled from carefully preserved fragments." Moreover, she argues, its paper crafts work as recursive stand-ins for the novel.[80] Originally calling it *The Cranford Papers* (reminding us of Dickens's *Pickwick Papers*), Gaskell made explicit her thinking of the book as a material thing, as leaves bound together that readers will touch and open, something like a friendship album, filled with a heterogeneous hodgepodge. As with the handicrafts in the plot that work as stand-ins for *Cranford* (papers within papers), characters work as authorial surrogates in that they produce something akin to a manuscript, a bound book, a paper craft. In *Cranford*, Matty, Deborah, and Mary spend the morning "cutting out and stitching together pieces of newspaper, so as to form little paths to every chair" (57) in order to save the carpet from the dirty shoes of partygoers.[81] Schaffer connects this episode to Gaskell's own anxiety about piecing together her *Cranford* stories to make a novel. The characters in the tale sewing together paper as a figure for Gaskell putting together her manuscript remind us of the pictures of albums in albums. They both present the interiority of a world that the reader/handler can enter when she opens the cover of the book. *Cranford* thus experiments with textuality.

Gaskell's novel also celebrates odds and ends made and handled by women that retain their mark. Like friendship albums, the story coheres around tactile keepsakes that work as memorials of friendships. In and with both, women spend time together and mark these hours materially.[82] For instance, the paper candle-lighters that Matty makes by refashioning "all the notes and letters of the week" (124) become "well-known tokens of Miss Matty's favour" (212) when she uses "coloured paper, cut so as to resemble feathers" to make them. Yet such thrifty kindness runs through the whole town and the plot. There are those

> rose leaves that were gathered ere they fell to make into a pot-pourri for someone who had no garden; the little bundles of lavender flowers, sent to strew the drawers of some town-dweller, or to burn in the chamber of some invalid. Things that many would despise, and actions which it seemed scarcely worth while to perform, were all attended to in Cranford. Miss Jenkyns stuck an apple full of cloves, to be heated and smell pleasantly in Miss Brown's room. (37)

Such generosity is leavened always by a light playfulness and affection, of relishing the absurd, that runs through both the novel and many friendship albums. When Matty loses all of her money, her friends gather to contribute funds to support her. The complicated way this is set up, including how "every lady wrote down the sum she could give annually, signed the paper, and sealing it mysteriously" (222), strikes the reader as silly and stuffy, but also sweet.

Female intimacy and the sharing of material gifts drives the plots of many of Gaskell's novels, especially *North and South* (1854) and the unfinished *Wives and Daughters* (1866). In the former, Gaskell makes some of her central points about the struggles of the working classes and the need for the middle classes to witness and take action through the friendship developed between the clergyman's daughter Margaret Hale and the mill-worker Bessy Higgins. When the latter dies from inhaling cotton dust while at work, Margaret asks Bessy's sister for "some little thing to remind me of Bessy." She goes away with "a little common drinking-cup, which she remembered as the one always standing by Bessy's side with drink for her feverish lips," a kind of souvenir of her friend's life.[83] In *Wives and Daughters*, the main character Molly Gibson must create a bond with a new stepsister, Cynthia Kirkpatrick, when her father remarries. They develop a close, romantic friendship that withstands the man Molly loves almost marrying Cynthia, along with other potential conflicts and jealousies. Cynthia shows her affection for Molly by helping her dress more beautifully, using her cleverness for style and the newest fashions to give Molly's appearance flair. In a typical passage of many, Cynthia "took the utmost pain in dressing Molly ...

desirous of setting off Molly's rather peculiar charms."[84] She pulls apart a bouquet given to her by a lover and arranges the flowers in Molly's hair. In her study of female friendship, Sharon Marcus comments that "the object that epitomized friendship was the gift, which could represent the giver's body (a lock of hair), merge with the recipient's body (a ring), or be a body (a man bestowed by one friend on another)."[85] The gifts of adornment, dress, and flowers in *Wives and Daughters* remind us of the ribbons, pressed plants, and fashionable verse of the friendship album sitting in the parlor to be shown to guests—in other words, those domestic "bits and crumbs" that Gaskell most valued and that made up the best stories (and albums).

Paper Scraps

While Gaskell's writing process suggests the activity of creating a friendship album, it can also be expressively yoked to the autograph album. Her own collecting practices show the differences between the friendship and the autograph album, although in some cases the lines blur between the two (so often the case with albums, where a particular volume might have many uses and functions, thus category hopping). Autograph albums are generally collections of fragments of handwriting of famous people, often taking the form of letters written to someone else, not necessarily the album owner. The compiler would sometimes ask the celebrity directly for a sample of handwriting, or ask an associate or family member. Autographs were bought and sold, and some rare-book dealers specialized in them.[86] In contrast, with most friendship albums the creator wanted someone she knew, rather than a famous stranger, to decorate a leaf. The two breeds often vary in their material makeup: the friendship album has entries drawn directly onto the page and the autograph album has snippets of paper with handwriting attached (by sewing, gluing, or paper taping) to the leaves, often with many snippets on one sheet. Some archives catalogue friendship albums as autograph albums, and in some cases it can be hard to keep them distinct, especially when the keeper asked a famous stranger to contribute, along with their ordinary friends. Or the compiler had famous friends, such as Constance Wilde, Oscar Wilde's wife, whose "guestbook," now in the British Library, has notes from the likes of Mary Elizabeth Braddon, Olive Schreiner, and Marie Corelli, addressed directly to her, but also from relative nobodies, also friends.[87]

Autograph albums have a long history, dating to the seventh century and perhaps earlier, but they grew particularly popular in the Romantic and early to mid-Victorian periods, when collecting became more visible with the opening of public museums and historic houses.[88] Judith Pascoe explores this "culture's new understanding of the past as an idealized lost world, partly salvageable through the recovery and preservation of old objects and documents," and she calls the period a "time when the notion that objects are imbued with a lasting sediment of their owners" gained increasing traction.[89] The treasuring of ordinary bric-a-brac (playing cards, lace, and, later, stamps and valentines—all album fodder) grew out of a strong self-identifying with one's possessions. Elizabeth Fay remarks on how "objects yoke together sign and symbol, cross-functioning as metonyms of the collector's life and metaphors of his personality and spirit," as a means to explain the rise of Romantic-era house museums.[90] Lothar Müller details the popularity of autograph collecting as part of this movement, seeing them as like "historical novels ... autographs were the object of a modern passion for evidence of the past and the vanishing present ... unique specimens whose authenticity grew more important as reproduction technologies began to penetrate the world of writing, images, and three-dimensional artworks."[91] As with friendship albums, autograph albums became so fashionable by the early nineteenth century that many writers found their patience exhausted by requests.[92] Felicia Hemans complained about being asked to contribute to albums when she became famous. She wrote to a friend from Ambleside, "Here I have left behind me all the dust of celebrity: I have been only asked to write in two Albums since I came into this country."[93] Harriet Martineau also groused about the "importunity about albums" and being "despoiled of the privacy of correspondence" with her friends "by the rage for autographs."[94]

In her study of Gaskell's autograph collecting, Pamela Corpron Parker sees Gaskell's "album as an oblique form of autobiography, displaying her professional alliances with the leading cultural figures of the day."[95] Many of these figures were women, of course, and Gaskell worked hard to create networks of female writers as fellow supporters, providing introductions, comments on their MSS, praise, and convivial gossip, Crantord-like. She was a fan, and the letters that female writers sent her became part of her autograph collection. But she also collected autographs of people she didn't know, traded them with others, donated them to be sold for charity, and eagerly looked at others' collections. A typical request went like this: "have you been able to muster me up an autograph of Carlyle's yet? Or of Mr or

Mrs Browning's?"[96] Of the Earl of Leicester, she brags to a friend, "(oh the autographs the man has.) I am to see his collection of letters some day."[97] To a fellow enthusiast, she explained,

> I don't much care for statesmen and have a handsome quantity of unknown peers at your disposal. (I have Sir Robert Peel, Lord John Russell & etc. in the statesmen line wh[ic]h I *don't* mean to give you.) Would you like a royal William Frederick? ... I should rather like Washington Irving. How would your old Puritan blood have been stirred with glorious circulation, not to say ignominious envy of their possessor, if you had seen, as I did not three weeks ago Lord Nugent's grand autograph book,—*letters* from (Q. Eliz, Burleigh, Raleigh, Bacon, &c.) Oliver Cromwell, Falkland, Hampden (just like some of Shakespeare's for the exquisite & somewhat formal grace of their style, touching upon euphuism.) ... real identical yellow ragged *letters* that they had touched with the hands, (right royal hands,) now mouldering away.[98]

These last lines about the "real" speak of something vital about this collecting impulse—its desire to have a material object that *touched* history. The slippage here between the script and the person's identity (or body even) gives the former an almost magical capability to represent the person who made it. Gerard Curtis describes this approach to the autographic: "many Victorians saw both sign and signification as carriers of their own unique values, with the act of sign making having specific significance and tangible 'presence.' The graphic value of text was appreciated as being also indexical and iconic, and was treasured as such."[99] The autograph album, so unoriginal in this historical moment, was also, seen in a different light, a box of bodily traces, or a museum displaying historical artifacts.

Gaskell's love of autographs, her affection for the casual chattiness of the letter form, was matched by her attention to them as physical presences, akin to her awareness of manuscripts, albums, and other papery things. Not only did she happily send along her autograph, writing to a Mrs. Susan Deane, "Will this not do for an autograph?," she also generously offered to obtain other people's autographs for an acquaintance: "if I can send Miss Egerton Leigh any more that she will care to have (of *living* authors I have a good store), I shall be very glad indeed to send her any."[100] *Cranford* relishes the texture, look, and smell of letters.[101] In the novel, we read about "yellow bundles of love-letters, sixty or seventy years old" that have "a faint, pleasant smell of Tonquin beans" (89), giving a suggestion of taste as another sense to be used to fully appreciate letters. When Matty burns them, they are ghostly: "And one by one she dropped them into the middle of the fire, watching each blaze up, die out, and rise away, in faint, white, ghostly semblance, up the chimney" (91). With other old correspondence, the seals and postal marks matter. They were

> very yellow, and the ink very brown; some of the sheets were ... the old original post, with the stamp in the corner representing a post-boy riding for life and twanging his horn. The letters of Mrs. Jenkyns and her mother were fastened with a great round wafer; for it was before Miss Edgworth's "Patronage" had banished wafers from polite society ... the rector sealed his epistles with an immense coat of arms ... he expected that should be cut open, not broken by any thoughtless or impatient hand. (95)

A letter posted to India is imagined to be "stained with sea-waves perhaps ... and scented with all tropical fragrance" (185), picking up narrative and meaning as its surroundings cling to it.[102]

Yellowed letters that might have been destroyed were saved by being put in autograph albums. Yet this practice could also lead to their destruction, if cut up to be divided among many albums, or so they could fit into a crammed album where only a line or two was wanted.[103] This happened to many of Gaskell's own letters. For instance, the following little snippet, addressee unknown, was found in an album: "I am very fond of collecting autographs myself, so I can enter into the feeling which makes you wish for mine."[104] A kind of autograph especially valued was a fragment of literary manuscript. Gaskell explained to a correspondent that she was delighted to receive "Thackeray's preface to Rebecca and Rowens, corrected up and down by himself, and the funniest little pen and ink vignette at the end."[105] A page of her manuscript for *Sylvia's Lovers* ended up in a circa 1860s/1890s album belonging to a Mrs. Roberts.[106] Thus do Gaskell's manuscripts move from drawer to album, with the published novel a step in between.

Given Gaskell's penchant for taking scraps of stories and threading them together (as with *Cranford*), her gathering piles of manuscript in her desk drawer, and her appetite for autographs, it's not surprising that one of her favorite fictional devices is the found fragment of paper with almost-illegible text that creates a sea change in a plot. Much like *Cranford*, the two central plot lines in her earlier novel *Mary Barton* (1848) are linked to, or hinge on, bits of paper or other scraps—objects that could make up an album, but that also have that *mise-en-abîme* quality. At the heart of the novel is "a little piece of stiff writing paper" on which converge the romantic plot and the political one.[107] The love story involves a triangle between Mary Barton, her working-class lover Jem Wilson, and her wealthy near-seducer Harry Carson. The political tale revolves around Mary's father John, the starving workers, their Chartism, and the political murder of Harry Carson. The writing paper begins as a valentine "all bordered with hearts and darts" (the kind of fancy cut-paper artifact that often ended up in albums) Mary receives from Jem Wilson. When Mary and her father hear a poem written by the weaver Samuel Bamford that asks god to bless the starving poor, he asks Mary to write it down, and she records it "on a blank half sheet" of the valentine. A strip of this hybrid object is found later by Mary's aunt Esther in a hedge near where Harry's murder takes place. Now "compressed into a round shape," it is understood instantly by Esther to be "the paper that had served as wadding for the murderer's gun" (205). It has part of Mary's name written on it—"ry Barton"—and the street where she lives, in Jem's hand. When Mary sees this "corner of stiff, shining, thick, writing paper, she recognized as a part of the sheet on which she had copied Samuel Bamford's beautiful lines so many months ago—copied ... on the blank part of a valentine sent to her by Jem Wilson" (213), she knows her father is the murderer, a knowledge strengthened when she finds the rest of the sheet in his pocket. Jonathan Grossman suggests that this piece of physical evidence becomes a surrogate for the novel *Mary Barton*.[108] He argues that "Gaskell is writing with a nineteenth-century conception of her novel as a material work in her readers' hands, not as a bodiless text."[109] Paper on which writing happens changes form and use, from a mailed love token to gun wadding, or, in the case of an album, from a letter sent through the mail, then sewn into a volume to form a collection.

Many of Gaskell's plots use this same type of clue. In "The Squire's Story" (1855), for instance, a house burglar decides to tap a barrel of ginger wine in a house he is burgling. He "wrapped the spigot round with a piece of a letter taken out of his pocket ... this piece was found afterward; there are only these letters on the outside, 'ns, Esq., —arford—egworth.' On the other side, there is some allusion to a racehorse ... though the name is singular enough—'Church-and-King-and-down-with-the-Rump'" (47). This partial text, found and then eventually placed in the hands of someone who decodes it, leads to the solving of the crime. We know from Chapter 1 how Eliot set store by such discovered scraps, as with the jotting in *Middlemarch* Raffles picks up in a fireplace with Bulstrode's address on it, which leads to the unraveling of his life and those associated with him. In all of these cases, writing matters because of its material grounding, its mobility, its pliable reusability, and its being lost and then found. Gaskell would have seen these sorts of chopped-up texts, perhaps even her own, in albums. For instance, after Charlotte Brontë died, her father was besieged by fans clamoring for an autograph (as was Gaskell herself, when she wrote the first biography of Brontë). He snipped many of her letters into strips and mailed them off, making more difficult the job of biographers. In the album of one Mary Jesup Docwra, from Kelvedon, in Essex, is an 1858 note from Charlotte's father sent in reply to her request, along with a tiny bit of one of Charlotte's letters, only holding the words, "my book—no one" and then, on the line below, "ious than I am to."[110] While not exactly asemic or micrographic, such texts have magic and meaning only because of their physical status as material remnants.

When Gaskell wrote her friend Charlotte's life story, published in 1857, she laboriously gathered shreds of Brontë's life. She tried to have a daguerreotype taken of the painting of Charlotte made by George Richmond, and she contacted Charlotte's friends, acquaintances, and relations for recollections, accounts, and manuscript material in Charlotte's hand, like the then-unpublished *The Professor* and the unfinished *Emma*.[111] To one of Charlotte's friends she says, "I am becoming very anxious to receive any materials you find you can furnish me with for my memoir," and to another, "I want *every particular* I can collect."[112] She traveled all over England and to the continent, stockpiling keepsakes, papers, and stories. On one trip to Haworth, she was able to carry away "a packet about the size of a lady's travelling writing case, full of paper books of different sizes," holding the miniature booklets made by Charlotte and Branwell, along with other manuscript.[113] She gathered up her own leavings of Charlotte, like a sample of pink and mauve wallpaper Charlotte sent her in a letter of April 3, 1854 when she was putting it up in the parsonage. Gaskell noted on the back, "Slip of the paper with which Charlotte Brontë papered her future husband's study, before they were married. –ECG," turning it into the kind of assemblage she wrote about in her stories.[114] Place mattered, as itself a sort of relic, a location for a body and its experiences: "I crave for more ... and one wants the frame-work of locality because she was so much influenced by places and surroundings," she wrote to Charlotte's friend Mary Taylor.[115] Eventually she was happy to say that "I now think I have been everywhere where she ever lived, except of course her two little pieces of private governess-ship."[116] The final version of the manuscript of *The Life of Charlotte Brontë* has itself a kind of patchy, fitful quality. Sending the first part to her publisher, she wrote: "I have 100 pages quite ready,—only with so many erasures, insertions at the back of the leaves &c (owing to the unchronological way in which I obtained information) that I should much like to correct all I can myself."[117] She enlisted her daughters Marianne and Meta to copy in the complete text of many of Charlotte's letters, so their handwriting interrupts Gaskell's in places. She later went back and redacted portions of the letters, creating a layering of different "hands." The relationship between this collection of "scraps" and an album (friendship and autograph) is palpable.

Gaskell's creation of Brontë's "life" by sifting through her "remains"—a kind of reanimation of ashes, of lifeless relics—leads us back to the relationship between the volume and the body. Can a body enter a book? Two fictional albums comment on—and satirize—this need to collect embodied castoffs and put them in a volume. Wilkie Collins dreamt up an album in his *The Law and the Lady* (1875) made by the character Major Fitz-David. Bound in blue velvet and with a silver clasp, the album has ornamented, vellum pages with "tokens" of hair "let neatly into the center of each page" and inscriptions describing the end of affairs with female lovers. The first page, for instance, "exhibited a lock of the lightest flaxen hair, with these lines beneath: 'My adored Madeline. Eternal constancy. Alas, July 22, 1839!'" The erotic leavings of her body—the lock of hair—replace the autograph but also emphasizes the "graph" as metonymic of the hand. In another fictional example, Charles Dickens, in *David Copperfield* (1850), satirizes this saving of the minutiae of memory by having fashionable girls put the finger and toenail parings of a Russian prince in their keepsake albums. Here again the celebrity signature transforms into the celebrity body and its leftovers, aligning the volume and its interior with the body and its soul—or the body and its interior parts. Moreover, increasing this yoking of book and body, the history of collecting autographs runs alongside that of locks of hair, and both entered into volumes as keepsakes, as we have seen. Prizing the hair and autographs of literary figures became especially popular in the late eighteenth century, and many collections still hold them today, such as tresses from Charlotte Brontë, Mary Shelley, and E. B. Browning in the Berg Collection of the New York Public Library; Eliot in the Yale Beinecke; and in the British Library, Letitia Elizabeth Landon, Felicia Hemans, Christina Rossetti, and more Eliot. Women marked friendships with an exchange of hair as they did by drawing or writing on a leaf in a friendship album. Charlotte asked her best friend Ellen Nussey for a sample, for instance, and Lucy Snowe, in *Villette* (1853), keeps a lock from her dead friend and employer Miss Marchmont, between the leaves of a memorandum-book.

Hair could also be bound into the covers of a book or album, further destabilizing the boundary where the volume ends and the body begins. When Charles I was beheaded in 1649, his hair was used for rings and, woven with silver and gold, was bound in a volume of *Les Heures royalles, dediées au Roy*.[118] An odd leather volume at the British Library called *Percy Bysshe Shelley: His Last Days Told by his Wife, With Locks of Hair and Some of the Poet's Ashes* has two glass cavities set into the front cover—one containing a lock of Shelley's hair and one of Mary's—and an urn-shaped one in the back with a sprinkling of Shelley's ashes and bone fragments.[119] Created by the bibliophile, forger, and relic collector Thomas Wise, the volume contains manuscript letters and official documents that describe Shelley's death.[120] Another example at the British Library is a bound collection of Eliot's autograph letters with her hair let into the cover.[121] Binding books in relics that reflect—or are a piece of—their contents brings together different removes of representation, similar to what Juliet Fleming calls "autofiguration ... a delineation that closed the gap between material signifiers and ideational signifieds in the experience of signification itself."[122] Books bound in human skin provide another instance where the covering is meant to comment on the interior, such as an 1816 copy of Holbein's *Dance of Death* rebound anthropodermically in 1893.[123] In some cases individuals requested that their flesh be tanned and integrated into a book about themselves, such as two volumes of the autobiography of George Walton, a professional thief who asked that they be bound with his own skin, after his execution in 1837.[124] These book-containers have an excessiveness about them, as if they need to provide evidence in various ways, with handwriting, with hair, bone, and skin. Standing somewhere in between an autograph album and an (auto)biography, these volumes overreach the boundaries of printing and publishing by, in part, over-materialization, as if the thing as thing can never be too material (or literal).

Another, less strange, re-imagining of the book, called extra-illustration (also grangerization), should be mentioned here in its kinship with album culture. In its simplest form, this meant rebinding a book to include one's own pages, often prints, illustrations, or title pages gleaned from taking apart other books.[125] The creator of these unique copies would then display them, album-like, to visitors. William Sherman compares extra-illustration, which in many cases involved cutting up many books to rearrange their pages into another, single volume, to scrapbooks.[126] Sometimes manuscript pages, such as letters, comprised the added material, such as a letter Gaskell wrote to one Sampson Low, which was added as an extra-illustration to a copy of John Forster's *Life of Charles Dickens* (1872–4), creating a hybrid volume, both a published biography and an autograph album.[127] In a copy of Mary Russell Mitford's *Rienzi: A Tragedy*, a letter written by Mitford has been bound into the volume, and a copy of Tennyson's *In Memoriam* has been rebound to include a slip of paper with Tennyson's signature on it.[128] Another related practice was storing—"tipping in" or binding in—autograph letters in books by the author who wrote the letter. For instance, at the Berg Collection in the New York Public Library, the card catalogue mentions numerous letters written by Eliot originally tipped into copies of her novels, a kind of storage system related to a drawer or album.[129] The owner could revere a unique copy of a novel by, in part, adding a graphic trace to it, somewhat like an association copy with inscription, but at a more distanced representational remove.

Souvenir Albums

Assembling fragments of a life for a biography was one way the collecting impulse led to a volume. Another involved putting together a more personal album, an autobiographical one, what Martha Langford calls "the cabinet of the self."[130] Unlike the friendship and autograph album as the work (or at least the display) of many "hands," the souvenir volume grows from one person gathering her own fragments of experience and arranging them in a meaningful way on the page, then in the codex, with the order of the pages creating a durational narrative. Another kind of nascent book, these creations move toward memoirs or autobiographical fiction. As with these other albums, sometimes souvenir volumes were meant to be shown. Queen Victoria started out early with her prolific album keeping, creating one of pressed seaweed as a girl and later making—or having made—various keepsake albums, such as "animal albums" with illustrations of her pets, and what she called "Souvenir Albums" with watercolors documenting ceremonies, travel, and other events.[131] It is as if the Queen needed evidence to prove these events happened, as if they didn't unless represented in an album. An especially rich example of a touristic album (see Fig. 7), probably made by a British woman named Georgina Lucy Byron (kinship to Lord Byron unclear) between 1829 and 1831, takes Gaskell's "scrap" collecting to another level of extremity. The small album that closes with a clasp contains fragments of houses and landscapes she visited, such as a piece "cut from the carpet on the left-hand side of the chimney in Madame Bainville's drawing

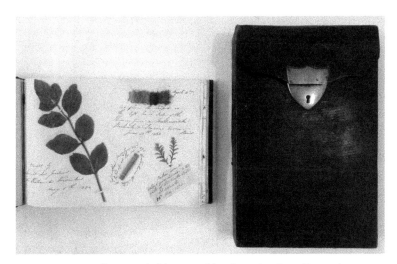

Fig. 7 Souvenir album probably created by Georgina Lucy Byron (ca. 1829–31). Private collection. Used by permission

room, Paris, June 20th, 1830"; a snippet of wallpaper, "from the bed-room where Napoleon slept on his way from Elba to Paris, L'Hotel des Cinq Mineurs, Joigny, June 29, 1830"; a square of wood, "from Queen Bertha's Saddle at Payenne, who lived in the 10th Century. Sept. 19"; numerous plants, labeled with the place and date of their gathering; and even hair plucked from a goat and a cat's whiskers.[132] Rather than needing to collect proof of friendships, or linkage to the famous, the keepers of travel books like this one bring home samples of places, to indexically represent the whole of the locality and experience, to remember but also to affirm: "I was here. Look, I have proof." Byron's album reminds us of the tourists' graffiti explored in Chapter 1, but here the materiality of the experience is gathered, rather than left behind with a physical mark. When one Lady Emilia Hornby visited Crimean war battlefields, she picked wildflowers to press into her album, carrying back with her the landscape itself, a topos of memory.[133] Charlotte's house and the moors surrounding it became sites for fan worship and collecting, evidenced by one anonymous fan (of many) who remembered a mid-nineteenth-century visit to "the home of Charlotte Brontë" (as reads the caption on an oval scrap, cut from a published source, showing the parsonage in Haworth) on a page of her album (see Fig. 8). The traveler pasted a snippet with the signature of Patrick Brontë, still living here at the time, underneath, and arranged two leaves—described in

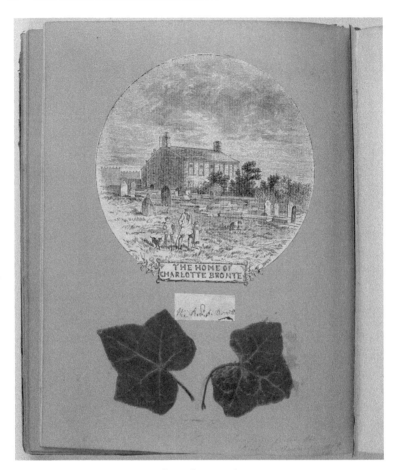

Fig. 8 Anonymous souvenir album (ca. 1859). Brontë Parsonage Museum, E 2013.2

pencil as "ivy leaves from the rectory, Haworth, 1859"—along the bottom.[134] Like other book assemblages discussed here, these volumes multiply kinds of representation, using varied means of saving moments and spaces. In the latter example, the published sketch of the parsonage didn't suffice to store or evoke engagement, to prove that the traveler had been there, seen that, met him, touched this. She needed to include the "hand" (the signature representing the body) of the local celebrity (himself a stand-in for Charlotte, now dead and out of reach). The plants that grew there meant she had stood at the site itself and was the kind of fan who made the pilgrimage. Some of these albums can seem similar to autograph albums, but with the added requirement of travel. In her study of photo albums, Langford uses Bakhtin's notion of the chronotope, "a fictional fusion of time and space."[135] With souvenir albums, this fusion emerges in an even bolder way, since with the haptic album bits of the real are subtracted from the place and brought into the space and time of the album, to be reinvigorated, re-told, when someone looks through it, in a different space and time, perhaps at home and many years later.

Botanical albums more broadly can work as souvenir albums in the sense that they carry into book form the experience of landscape, something like Eliot's placement of her reading of Wordsworth's *The Prelude* at Niton into her copy of the poem, as discussed in Chapter 1, or the practice of traveling with a guide to plants with one while out botanizing and then adding a sample of the thing itself next to the representation of it on the page. Fern, moss, flower, seaweed, and other plant collections were fashionable during the period, especially, once again, for female creators.[136] Charlotte collected ferns on her honeymoon in Ireland, and may have made an album of them, now at the Brontë Parsonage Museum. This inscription is penciled on the flyleaf: "F.E. Bell / Jan. 25th 1914 / From Mrs. Nicholls Hill House Banagher / Ferns collected and pressed by Charlotte Brontë at Killarney / On her honeymoon."[137] On each page, a band has been cut out of the heavy paper and the stem of the fern specimen has been stuck through it. A clear paste—starch, isinglass, flour paste, gum-arabic, and mucilage were mentioned in manuals on making fern albums as good ingredients—was then used to attach the fronds to the page, giving them a sense of life and motion, frozen just then. This album seems to be an account of her honeymoon, of its floral-scape and stopping points, although the memories contained here are now silent, since Charlotte didn't write anything in this album. Other botanical albums gave more details. An anonymous album of British mosses (probably a quasi-scientific study) was contributed to by a number of individuals (see Fig. 9).[138] One bunch of furry lichen, still looking fairly alive, has this handwritten underneath: "Rocks n[ea]r Saugh. Devon. May 1867. E.M. Holmes," and another gives us this precise location and day: "Powder Hill Copse, n[ea]r Cumnor, 24 April, 1861, H.B." The earth, and those who glean from it, are brought into the volume, attesting to that singular moment of gathering. Like other sorts of albums, botanical ones in some cases worked as signs of friendship between women. Margaret Stovin, an important botanist and early expert in ferns, gave two fern albums in 1833 to her friend Miss Walker that evoke her local walks searching for rare

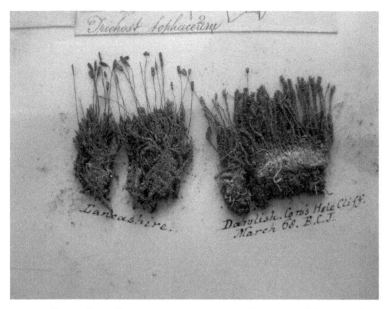

Fig. 9 Album of British mosses, 1854–73. MS Coll. 1151, Kislak Center for Special Collections, Rare Books and Manuscripts, University of Pennsylvania

breeds. On the flyleaf of one volume she wrote, "To Miss Walker, Masborough House, with Mrs. Margaret Stovin's kind regards, Newbold, 5th Feb., 1833," reminding us of Eliot and her author friends exchanging their own published books with each other, including these sorts of inscriptions.[139] Unlike one's novel in print, though, a botanical album can be an evolving process, always inchoate, lacking closure (unless one extra-illustrates one's novel, tips in letters, or continues to add manuscript notes). In a tipped-in letter dated February 4, 1833 from Stovin to Walker, she tells her friend that, "if I live and find favour in the season, I will change some of your specimens for better."[140] Stovin also created an album of pressed flowers and plants, collected in Derbyshire, for her young friend Florence Nightingale, herself heavily steeped in album culture, keeping a commonplace book, an album documenting her shell collecting, and a range of notebooks.[141] Gaskell, ever at the center of circles of successful, working women, cultivated a friendship with Nightingale and her sister Parthenope, to whom she sent ferns.[142] The naturalist, writer, and photographer Anna Atkins, the first person to make a book using photographic processes, collaborated on her plant albums in the

1850s with her best friend Anne Dixon ("dearer than a sister," Atkins called her), collecting the specimens together on walks and then compiling them into albums.[143] Atkins created the 1854 *Cyanotypes of British and Foreign Flowering Plants and Ferns* with the help of Dixon, then had it bound as a present for her, the spine stamped in gilt, "A.A. to A.D., 1854."[144]

Atkins's work signaled the sea change in album culture that came with the spread of photography. With the invention of the *carte-de-visite* photograph in the 1850s, the earlier type of album began to be mostly replaced by photographic ones, encouraging the visual over the tactile. At first it wasn't easy to put photographs in albums—they varied widely in size and most early formats were thick and heavy (printed on plate or glass)—although some determined album makers occasionally assembled them with much expense, starting in the 1840s. Yet in 1857, the French firm Marion and Company brought to Britain a new type of photographic print, called the *carte-de-visite* because of its similarity to the visiting card. Albumen prints mounted on card of a standard size, the *carte* lent itself to standardized albums that would hold them. Made with windows into which the *cartes-de-visite* could be slotted, they were only slight modifications of earlier albums, in which the windows received drawings and watercolors, or even ferns or other plants. "Cartomania," as many called it, swept Britain soon after 1860, when J. E. Mayall published the popular "Royal Album" of *carte-de-visite* photographs of the Queen and her family, and the printing of *carte* photo albums began in earnest. Queen Victoria took up the fashion immediately, glad to have yet another sort of album to make of the moment something enduring. Photos were, in a sense, moments under glass, whereas ivy leaves were the thing (and the place) itself. While some photo albums maintained haptic elements, such as handwriting under the photos, giving person, place, time, and so on, the movement was steadily away from the hand toward the eye.[145]

Friendship, autograph, and souvenir albums began to seem old-fashioned with surprising swiftness. Even as early as the 1860s, writers on fashion characterized them as fusty things made by grandmothers.[146] Those who used to assemble them were more likely now to make photo albums, yet some new forms sprang up for a time, hybrids of the friendship and the photo album.[147] Friends were asked to write verse or a note next to their photo. Many women composed albums that mingled photography with their own watercolors, often painted as backdrops or frames for the photos. Constructing whimsical photo-collages in albums became a hobby among circles of upper-class women in the 1860s and 1870s. Cutting out the heads of the *cartes* and adding them to painted tableaus such as giving them animal bodies or placing them in jewelry (the head becoming like a miniature) or on sections of fans, these women wedded the new machine-made technology with older forms of album keeping. Faces peer out of seals or stamps on painted envelopes in Georgina Berkeley's album from the late 1860s, and a boy dressed like an angel blows bubbles, which are faces from photographs. Frances Elizabeth Bree painted images of photo albums on the pages of her 1875 album, with actual photos on the painted pages: a photo album within a photo album.[148]

Both the haptic and the photo album fulfilled a need to contain, arrange, classify, and, simply, keep. Both attempted to answer the query: can moments be preserved? They partook of larger questions: how can artifacts secure the moment, the place; in other words, history? Albums, like all mortal objects, body forth the depredations of time. Representing a sort of ephemerality, they have often been discarded, in part because their tactile qualities, their need to be paged through to have any meaning at all, leads to their eventual destruction. Another reason many albums were destroyed was that their intensely personal quality made them meaningless once the compiler, and those who stored that person and her set of moments in their memory, had died. Then the album became a kind of dead letter or unmarked grave. Time's passing marks the nineteenth-century albums that lasted. Botanical albums in particular rapidly decay, but even photographic ones become faded, brittle, fall into pieces—losing their chronology. One haunting quality of most albums is the way that artifacts create shadows of themselves on their opposing pages. The rot of leaves seeps into the page pressed on top of it when it is closed; the chemicals of the photograph, or of newspaper scraps, spread as they break down over time; the ink from a print is transferred onto the facing page and then sometimes the print is removed altogether, thus leaving only a ghostly outline of what was once there. Yet this is also their glory; meant to tell of time, they are steeped in it, showing traces of the mortal hands that made and viewed them.

3
Researching and Performing

> This evening I have been reading to G. some entries in my notebook of past times in which I recorded my *malaise* and despair.
> George Eliot, in a notebook[1]

George Eliot's extensive notebook keeping, along with an ethical commitment developed in part from her reading, helped her find an outside "standing ground"—a phrase that appears in *Impressions of Theophrastus Such* (1879) and *The Mill on the Floss* to describe an ability to move out of the solipsistic concerns of the self and find an expanded understanding of the world as full of others with their competing needs, a notion key to the plot of *Middlemarch*. Eliot's fiction has many characters who can't do this, such as the failed writer Casaubon, who isn't able to move past the stage of a self-absorbed filling of notebooks. In contrast, Emily Brontë's characters (and herself, to some extent) write to express the true self in the moment, a release of deep emotion, in an amoral world where others hardly exist. For many authors of the time, notebooks offered a setting, a stage, and a collecting place for a wide array of drafts, quotations, doodles, experiments, clippings, and much more. When used as fodder for the writings of authors, notebooks are stronger forms of incipient books than albums. I begin with detailing the history of commonplace books, using Eliot and Charles Reade as case histories. Eliot's commonplace books, where she wrote down research notes and epigraphs for her novels, as well as Reade's large-format journals for story ideas, have a direct line to their published works. This takes me to a section on the wide array of Eliot notebooks, including diaries, that have an adjacency with the published book that is somewhat hazy but still suggestive. A reading of papery things in *Middlemarch* develops notions of the ethics and values assigned to different sorts of paper artifacts. While Eliot searched for a point outside the self, Emily used her notebooks to perform the self—which I take up in my last section. She approached them as final copies—as scribal publications—unlike Eliot's "quarry" notebooks. So, too, did Michael Field (the penname for the collaboration of Katharine Bradley and Edith

Cooper) create expressivist notebooks, with a mixture of personal and creative work. Another idea that runs through this chapter (and the others in this book) is how, as with albums, owners made these store-bought volumes unique and embodied through handmade covers, labels, repairs, removed and sewn-together pages, cut-out tabs in fore-edges, and things put in pockets or pasted, sewn, or wafered on, not to mention what they handwrote in them, sometimes in different ink or pencil colors.[2] They became intricate members of everyday life—carried on the body, kept near, referenced, and treasured.

Quarries and Other Common Places

The commonplace book has been, historically, a space to gather together one's favorite quotations, or, more systematically, a method for storing information from one's reading in one place.[3] As with the terms "album" and "scrapbook," archivists and historians call different types of manuscript books "commonplaces," including those volumes labeled "friendship albums" in Chapter 2.[4] I use the term for a codex in which one person has taken notes from her reading or copied out favorite quotes from other writers (although the terminology is complicated by the use of some commonplace books for additional purposes). Readers made extracts to hold onto ideas before returning borrowed books too expensive for most to own; Samuel Taylor Coleridge remarked: "as I have few books of my own, I read with a common-place book."[5] Similar to the marginal note-taking explored in Chapter 1, commonplacing was recommended as a way to embark on serious study, improve the memory, and organize research.[6] Heather Jackson points out that marginalia and commonplacing served similar functions, since the margins or flyleaves of a book could be locations to store quotes, like a notebook set alongside what one was reading.[7] Some arranged their commonplaces under alphabetical headings, while others utilized indexes or tables of contents.[8] Erasmus, John Locke, and others created systems for maintaining commonplace books, and printed ones with indexes could be purchased, such as the *Pocket Commonplace Book with Locke's Index* (ca. 1820).[9] Readers "gleaned" poetry or lines from their reading, Stephen Colclough remarks, calling their collections "excerpta, miscellanies, scraps."[10] Also known as *florilegia*, or gatherings of the "flowers" (or best quotes) of literature; *sylvae* ("forests"); table books; and memorandum (Latin for "that which ought to be remembered"), they were the foundations of encyclopedias, concordances, anthologies, thesauruses ("treasure chests"), and bibliographies.[11] Often luxury items, written in a careful, beautiful hand, commonplace books were passed down through the generations, such as Felicia Hemans's, which was given by her son, fittingly, to Elizabeth Barrett Browning.[12]

Sometimes commonplacing left behind the codex format altogether. Read and beloved text migrated out of books, and as time went on and those books disappeared, the commonplace might become what William Sherman calls "an annotated subject index to a great lost library."[13] Juliet Fleming discusses quotations written on walls and ceilings, such as Montaigne recording "54 sayings from biblical and classical sources onto the rafters of his library."[14] Other examples come from Heidi Brayman Hackel, like Lady Anne Clifford, who had her servants assist her in pinning slips of paper with sentences and sayings onto her bed and around her bedchamber, giving an added meaning to the "place" in "commonplace."[15] This living in, dwelling inside of, beloved writing could aid the author at work. An idealized fictional writer named Mavis Clare in Marie Corelli's *The Sorrows of Satan* (1895) has study walls "divided into panels, and every panel had, inscribed upon it in letters of gold, some phrase from the philosophers, or some verse from the poets."[16] In Ella Hepworth Dixon's *The Story of a Modern Woman* (1894), the main character, also a writer, saved "scraps of poetry in various tongues which she would scribble hastily on the back of some young man's visiting card and then pin up, with a slender gilt tack, on to her door."[17] George Eliot's blotter served a similar function: to have useful lines nearby or underneath what one was working on.[18] The quotes on it range from Shakespeare and Bacon to Keats, Coleridge, and Wordsworth. Four favorite lines from the "Rubaiyat of Omar Khayyam" appear here and in one of her notebooks: "The moving Finger writes and having writ / Moves on; nor all your piety and wit / Shall lure it back to cancel half a line, / Nor all your tears wash out a word of it."[19] Although the "writing" here is meant figuratively as indelible and unchangeable events set down by something like a recording angel, the idea also calls to mind Eliot's favorite theme of fragments of text that stick around forever and reappear with momentous consequences, such as the long-forgotten writing "cut in stone" in *Middlemarch* that comes "by curious little links of effect under the eyes of a scholar, through whose labours it may at last fix the date of invasions and unlock religions" or become an "opening of a catastrophe."[20] The idea for that passage in *Middlemarch* perhaps came from a snippet she wrote in one of her notebooks while she was researching the novel:

The Eugubine Tables, which contain a living specimen of the Umbrian language, were discovered in 1444 in a subterranean chamber at La Schieggea in the neighborhood of the ancient city of Iguvium (now Gubbio or Ugubio). They are seven in number and related chiefly to matter of religion. The greatest relique of the Oscan language is the Bantine Table—a bronze tablet found 1796 at Oppidum on the borders of Lucania.[21]

While not as glamorous as these "tables," commonplace books also recorded "found" writing, with the potential to hold power in the present even if hundreds of years old, to be reanimated.

Writers' commonplace books fall into a special category as workaday objects, as a step in the writing practice. The most studied ones, predominantly kept by men, include those created by Samuel Taylor Coleridge (some of them he called his "fly catchers"); Robert Southey (with *mise-en-abîme* drawings of paper on paper and published in four volumes in 1849–50); Matthew Arnold (with entries often unattributed and reworked by him); Thomas Hardy (most of them burned by himself or by his executers at his request); and Lewis Carroll (with anagrams and ciphers).[22] The Wordsworths compiled a sort of family book, with quotations written in different hands—William's, his sister Dorothy's, and others.[23] Pamela Woof speculates on the ways Wordsworth used these extracts for his own writing, especially obscure Scottish ballads.[24] As with many such volumes, including albums, parts of it fell to other purposes. Here, Dorothy started at the back of the book, upside-down, with domestic entries, such as a list of the "Linen which came from Penrith" belonging to Mary, William's wife, a recipe for making ink with gum arabic, and a rendering of the baby babble of John, Mary and William's first child. Although the mixing of poetic verse with ordinary household matters may have no more meaning than a shortage of paper, costly at the time, the combination sets the exalted art next to the day's routine, foregrounding them as both work done in the home and the notebook as an object catching different sides of the house and work life. Simon Reader, in his examination of Oscar Wilde's notebooks, argues for the usefulness of the creative jumble in the commonplace book. He considers how "facts and quotations" in the notebooks "inflect one another ... keep their distinctiveness while ... [they] reach out from their original context to confer with others across vast stretches of time, or across disciplinary protocols."[25] Hackel focuses on the act of copying out the text of others as itself turning the reader into a writer. She argues that "by transferring the read text into his or her own handwriting, the compiler appropriates and transforms the text, nearly collapsing the roles of reader and writer. This act of transcription commonly transforms the text visually, syntactically, and contextually."[26] For some writers, like Eliot, writing out lines from one's reading made those lines one's own, and allowed for digestion, absorption, a thinking through the activity of the hand, writing.[27]

The stores where notebooks were bought and their varied and personal use over time can be "read" in the objects themselves. Linda Hughes sees them as "standard commodities," but also salutary reminders of how "Victorian authorship resided not just in minds and writing hands but also in bodies that moved away from desks or tables in streets, then shops, reaching into pockets or reticules for the ready money to hand over to stationers' clerks."[28] Evidence of these shops, most of them in the City, can be found by stationers' labels intact on front pastedowns, like "Letts, Son and Steer Stationers, Account Book Manufacturers," where the novelist and journalist Charles Reade bought many of his notebooks and George Eliot at least one of hers.[29] Other Eliot notebooks came from "John Mabley, 143 Strand, 8 doors west of Somerset House, Medical and other student's note and manuscript book warehouse" (as the label reads); "Parkins and Gotto Manufacturing Stationers 25, Oxford Street"; "Creswick and Co. Stationers, 12 Gt. Portland St, Oxford St.," and surely other stores, since the majority do not carry labels.[30] Reade also bought some of his big folios at "Partridge and Cozens, Wholesale and Retail Stationers," and the Michael Fields (as they liked to call themselves) seem to have bought most of their twenty-nine journals (spanning 1888–1914) from "Partridge and Cooper, Wholesale and Retail Stationers and Account Book Manufacturers," a later evolution of the same shop, at the same addresses in the City on Fleet Street and Chancery Lane.[31] Lisa Gitelman gives a rather dizzying list of the many sorts of blank books manufactured by the end of the nineteenth century. Here is a partial rendering:

> address-books, bank-books ... blotters, card albums, collection-books, composition, exercise and manuscript books, day-books, diaries, drawing-books, fern and moss albums, herbariums, letter-copying books, note-books, pencil-books, perpetual diaries, portfolios, reporter's notebooks, scrapbooks, scratch-books, visiting books, writing-books ...[32]

Another reminder of embodiment appears with authors' modifications of these "commodities," thus turning them into singular possessions. A particularly labor-intensive change was cutting tabs into fore-edges in order to alphabetize, commonly seen in dictionaries and address books. In a large-format journal compiled from 1859 to 1894, with each page hand-divided into columns, the writer George Augustus Sala (1828–95) cut in tabs by hand. He filled the pages with handwritten excerpts from his reading, ideas for pieces he might write, and personal entries about travel and his mental and physical health (for instance, "September 3rd, 1877, In dark and dismal plight both mental and bodily"), and he pasted or pinned in with straight pins reviews of his work and other articles of interest from newspapers.[33] Periodically reading back over the journal, Sala made marginal comments and eventually devised a complicated numbering system keyed to an index at the back. Eliot made similar thumb tabs, presumably for ease of reference, the letters elegantly penned in her characteristic purple ink, in a notebook she labeled "Oriental Memoranda, arranged alphabetically."[34] The tabs have a well-used, grubby appearance, so it seems she did put them to work. She pasted newspaper articles onto the front flyleaf and tipped in more clippings, making this a sort of cross between a standard commonplace book, a scrapbook, an index, and a storage space, like a drawer. In some of her other notebooks, if she felt the need to remove pages, she cut them out carefully and then sewed the stubs together, as she did with her "Hebriac studies and miscellaneous notes" (as her paper label states), presumably to neaten the appearance, make the book whole again.[35]

Commonplace book keepers rebound them by hand, the resewing bringing them closer to the body, akin to worn and mended clothing.[36] The copious diarist and commonplace-compiler Anne Lister bought volumes with marbled-paper covers, and she re-covered them herself with leather. The visitor to the archive today can see how the leather has deteriorated on many of them, with the original covers now showing through.[37] Eliot (re)hand-bound an important, early journal that spans the years 1849–61, in which she doodles (women's fashions) and records travel, the death of her sister, what she is reading (and when aloud), when her pug arrived, why and how she began writing fiction, an account of the writing of *Adam Bede* and *Silas Marner*, and more.[38] This book went on travels with her and lasted through many years, and it shows it. The spine at some point began to come apart, and someone, likely Eliot, inexpertly re-stitched it with red thread. The original paper cover has black cloth sewn over it, again presumably by Eliot, and then the whole was varnished. This rebinding, sloppily done, led to the black bleeding onto the first and last pages, and eventually itself becoming partially undone, separating from the original binding along the spine. As with many of Eliot's notebooks, she created two beginnings by turning it around and starting again at the other end, with the ends meeting in the middle. In this one, she records the doing of this, remarking that it happened accidentally. So, about a quarter of the way through, she writes, "My journal continues at the opposite end, by mistake, as a continuation of the History of Adam Bede." (It's hard to imagine how this would happen, and it's certainly the case that she did this purposely with other notebooks.) She ends the whole with the following affectionate and sad comment on it.

> This is the last entry I am to make in my old book in which I wrote for the first time at Geneva, in 1849. What moments of despair I passed through after that—despair that life would ever be made precious to me by the consciousness that I live to some good purpose! It was that sort of despair that sucked away the sap of half the hours which might have been filled by energetic youthful activity: the same demon tries to get hold of me again when ever an old work is dismissed and a new one is being meditated. / June 19 1861.

Writing this down here, in this tattered material object that has come to represent those years and that despair, might put that demon away for good, with first recognition and then banishment. It doesn't fully. We see such melancholy in her later diaries. Even so, she went on to write other novels, recognizing the distress and sapping of the hours, but also continuing to write about and through it. The old book, like a shabby dress that has witnessed daily experiences and thus speaks of them in its wear and tear, becomes an object to keep and return to.

Reade, an obsessive keeper of journals of many sorts, also commented on his use of notebooks in the notebooks themselves, recording his method being part of that method. Reade compiled personal diaries, large albums with clipped and pasted reviews of his own work, small records of what he was reading and his opinion on it, and what he called "copy books," where he wrote drafts of his novels.[39] Some of his commonplace books, which he called "digests," are themed, like one he titled "Bonae fabulae et. vera fab" or "Good stories of man and beast," in which he pasted in newspaper articles or sheets with his handwritten notes or just handwrote anecdotes directly onto the page.[40] He used this notebook as a storehouse for ideas for articles and fiction topics, returning to it many years after its completion, marking sections "used" when they evolved into published work. Other volumes are more miscellaneous, gleanings of anything that came to hand with potential as source material. A representative brown leather journal contains subject headings with articles and handwritten notes under each, such as "Married life," with an article about a wife sale under it, along with stories of "domestic crimes."[41] "Balloon races," "Doubles," "Harlots," and "Fire" (with pictures from illustrated newspapers of actual fires), "Tremendous Stories," and "Miscellanea" all fill pages. In another notebook, he complained about his arduous routine of keeping anything promising: "Breakfast 9:30—Just skimming two newspapers ... Pasting in extracts ... Tedious work. It being almost impossible to classify them properly at once, I paste them first into a book as classifieanda. Then by degrees I may cut them out, and put them in a guard-book [a volume with tabs for attaching snippets and other paper leaves] in some order."[42] His gleaning workload became so heavy that he hired secretaries, sometimes employing two at a time.[43] Eventually he created a printed pamphlet entitled "List of Subjects entered as headings in my various guard books and solid digests," an index for all of the notebooks.[44] In Reade's novel *A Terrible Temptation* (1871), he describes the chaotic study of a writer called Mr. Rolfe, whose process is based closely on his own. Along with "loose notes to be pasted into various books and classified," there are "five things like bankers' bill-books, into whose several compartments MS. notes and newspaper cuttings were thrown, as a preliminary towards classification in books." Other types of volumes are here: "underneath the table was a formidable array of notebooks," which he distinguishes from "about twenty large folios, of classified facts, ideas, and pictures." And yet others: "a collection of solid quartos, and of smaller folio guard-books called Indexes. There was 'Index rerum et journalium'—'Index rerum et librorum'—'Index rerum et hominum'—and a lot more: indeed so many that, by way of climax, there was a fat folio ledger, entitled 'Index ad Indices.'"[45] This last sentence was probably meant to be facetious, although it is hard to tell. The rest of the description is in keeping with Reade's own multi-stage process, explained here in a tone that feels almost proud, reveling in this forest of notes. In contrast to Eliot's notebook practice, Reade's has an obsessive quality that was probably often counterproductive.

While many of Reade's commonplace books collect potential story and article ideas, others were compiled during work on specific novels, and he often described in them the stages and materials of novel making. For *Hard Cash* (1863) and *The Cloister and the Hearth* (1861) especially, he devised a complicated process involving not only notebooks but also large notecards and even a screen. In one of the large folios for *Hard Cash*, he writes, in part,

I took notes for this work in various ways:

1. I covered eight or ten large folio cards. Some of these still survive.
2. I pasted extracts from journals and Dickson's [a doctor he consulted about mental illness] works on a screen, where I could see them in one view ...
4. I took notes on the ordinary system in books.[46]

The cards and screen—distillations of text taken from the commonplace books—rearranged his notes and made them more visually accessible, similar to the quotes on walls or bedcurtains described above, but here more directly part of the writing work. Seeing his material "all in one view" values the visual quality of writing-as-process, makes it more digestible, closer to himself. They helped Reade/Rolfe concentrate, as he says in *A Terrible Temptation*:

> By the side of the table were six or seven thick pasteboard cards, each about the size of a large portfolio, and on these the author's notes and extracts were collected from all his repertories into something like a focus, for a present purpose. He was writing a novel based on facts; facts, incidents, living dialogue, pictures, reflections, situations, were all on these cards to choose from, and arranged in headed columns.[47]

Arranging blocks of text on a single "page," no matter how large, was key to Reade's method, seen also in his commonplace books, where an individual page's layout gave the constitutive parts added meaning by their side-by-sideness. His experiments with the visual aspects of text continued in his printed novels through his use of unusual typography, which John Sutherland calls "violently expressive."[48] While not as avant-garde as Laurence Sterne's *Tristram Shandy* (1759–67), with its interruptions of marbled and blank pages and its deployment of page-long dashes and asterisks, some of Reade's novels use all caps, tiny or large fonts, legalistic gothic, simulated newsprint, and pictorial cues mid-text to call attention to dramatic moments and text inserted into text, such as signs for shops or hotels.[49] He most commonly employs this device when a character reads a note or letter, as in *Griffith Gaunt; Or, Jealousy*, when Mercy, handed a small parcel, unfolds it to find a bullet and the words "I love Kate." In caps, bold, a different font, and more than twice the size of the surrounding print, the text of the note is marked as a text within a text, held in the hand and read by a surrogate reader, then the actual reader, who holds the novel in her hand.[50] In his *Put Yourself in His Place*, characters use chalk to scribble messages onto a smoky wall that are rendered on the page in italics and more than double sized.[51] In a more striking example, Reade depicts an illiterate family's attempt to "read" a letter from their son, in *The Cloister and the Hearth*, by "reproducing" the pencil sketch the letter contained, of one person taking the hand of another. "As they gazed on that simple sketch, in every turn and line of which they recognized his manner, Gerard seemed present, and bidding them farewell."[52] In Reade's attentiveness to the material support of writing, both his process and final product call attention to papery versions and "originals," as if this letter needs to be "authentically" represented on the page, just as he wanted readers to know his novels were based on "facts," emphasized in the passage above from *A Terrible Temptation*.

Eliot took notes far more studiously than Reade, whose volumes strike one as madcap and slightly unhinged.[53] Notebooks for Eliot had their own heterogeneous, recursive, organic lives.[54] What is probably the most famous of Eliot's notebooks, her "Quarry for *Middlemarch*," as she wrote on a paper label glued to its front, provides an example for how she revisited and mined them in complicated ways.[55] The volume seems to have originally been manufactured for a different usage, since she pasted her title over a word embossed in gold on the cover, which is now mostly indecipherable (see Fig. 10), although it seems to start with an "M" and have a "p" toward

Fig. 10 George Eliot's handwritten paper label on her notebook that says "Quarry for Middlemarch." Houghton Library, Harvard University, Lowell 13. By kind permission of the Estate of George Eliot

the end (possibly "Manuscript" or perhaps "March–April"?). A mixture of a commonplace and a draft notebook, it contains her research on medical current affairs from the *Lancet*, world mythology, reform bill politics, and more; some of the mottoes (as she called the epigraphs) that opened chapters; lists of *Middlemarch* dates; and chapter outlines made in preparation for writing. While the term "quarry" has other meanings, such as prey or a heap of dead bodies, Eliot seems to be referring to a rich store, and possibly a place for the heavy mining of blocks of stone, cut or blasted out of the earth and used to build or pave. It reminds us, again, of the text "cut in stone" finally uncovered by the right person in *Middlemarch*, yet it also has a somewhat ephemeral quality in that the rock will all be removed eventually, leaving a hole shaped like it. In that sense, it could seem like the notebook is the hole with *Middlemarch* built from its innards, something like the blotter is the text underneath the text being composed, or the paratext is a kind of boundary that is essential, permeable, and able to expand. Yet this isn't fully true, either. In his detailed study of the writing of *Middlemarch* and this quarry notebook, Jerome Beaty points out that some of the chapter outlines Eliot wrote in the notebook—basically lists of the events that would happen in that chapter—were written after the chapters themselves were completed. He describes a complicated method involving different sorts of lists and summaries, not just of chapters but also "elements," "motives," "sketches," "scenes," and so on, where the same connections and occurrences, like Lydgate's financial embarrassments, appear in different guises on different lists. This tells us not only that Eliot used the notebook non-sequentially, for doing things like adding to lists already started after later pages had been filled in—turning back and forth between parts of the volume—but also that it was a place to see a simplified version of parts already written, so she could envision what was to come. This is an incipient book, then (an incipient *Middlemarch*), but not in a straightforward, phylogenic way. Notebooks were not dead things for her: as we have seen, she often re-copied specific passages from one notebook to another, as with the "moving Finger" lines mentioned above, as if she wanted to try out different conversations and configurations between different quotes, or reanimate old ones.[36] Eliot's scribal work had a strong element of *doing* and *acting* for her, not of passive recording but rather a carrying forward by reading her notebooks repeatedly and then copying out into other notebooks generative text that needed further absorbing.

Paper Places

Eliot maintained a wide range of notebooks, often multiple ones simultaneously, some with more than one purpose. Except for one volume she composed when a schoolgirl, the twenty-five extant notebooks begin in 1854, approximately when her relationship with George Henry Lewes became serious and they started out on their travels.[57] She did keep notebooks before this, referring to one in an 1840 letter: "Perhaps something I wrote this morning to my useful little pocket-book (Brown's patent with a metallic pencil the marks of which are indelible) will amuse you."[58] Some of her notebooks were for learning, such as the Greek vocabulary one that Linda K. Hughes discovered in Texas Christian University's Special Collections.[59] There are travel accounts, such as a black one, bound in soft leather, containing a chronicle of her 1858 trip to Germany and then, beginning over again at the back of the notebook, recollections of her travels in Italy, 1860.[60] Others are what we today would call a diary, such as a small volume with "Diary for 1879" embossed in gold on the front, which includes some printed pages of an almanac, with information about eclipses, the phases of the moon, and more.[61] In addition to entries for most days about how she felt and what she was writing and reading, she also wrote out favorite quotations. Her dear partner Lewes had died in November 1878, just two months before she began this diary, so she charted her grief in entries such as, "Here I and sorrow sit"; "Weather still cruel, and my soul in deep gloom"; and "His presence came again." The quotations recorded here have mostly to do with mourning and loss. They seem to be remembered and beloved words, rather than what she happened to be reading just then, or research for a novel or a poem. She copied out stanzas from "In Memoriam," the poem so many grieving Victorians revered, and, toward the end, Emily Brontë's "Remembrance." Also here are lists of addresses, ships she might take somewhere, and rows of numbers (money spent? made?).[62] The quotations in this notebook, a form of commonplacing woven into an account of daily life, show the emotional purpose of writing down, a step further than just reading or even remembering. The lines of poetry recorded in these pages serve to carry them into the daily, living hours. Abbott, in her study of the notebook Eliot labeled "poetry," remarks that Eliot "worked to discover and catalyze as well as faithfully copy ideas into her commonplace books."[63] Here the catalyzation involves consolation. William Baker, quoting lines that Eliot copied down in a notebook, describes Eliot's method in the "Wordsworthian terms of the 'Commemoration holy that unites / The living generations with the dead.'"[64]

One of Eliot's travel diaries exemplifies her reliance on its materiality, as something more than a codex in which to record text, similar to her attention to the books she owned as physical carriers of relationships.[65] On the front of this small, oxblood-colored leather notebook, with a clasp to keep it closed, she affixed a paper label with "Journeys to Normandy in 1865 and Italy in 1864" handwritten on it, thus fixing its date and place (see Fig. 11).[66] On the front pastedown, a label from a stationer describes its new-fangled technology, "Improved Patent Metallic Book, the writing on these books warranted secure from erasure when written with the accompanying pen."[67] The pen, an ivory stylus, remains, pushed into its leather loop on the side. But the technology didn't seem to work well, since she traced over with ink what she wrote with it. The journal came with a built-in pocket, where a folded-up, hand-drawn map of France and a pressed flower are tucked away, the latter probably plucked somewhere in Normandy, a means to carry the place with her, pressed next to the text about her experience there. Like her copy of Wordsworth discussed in Chapter 1, this volume traveled with (or on) her, and she enclosed in it different levels of representation: textual description (recollections), drawing (mapping), and a tactile fragment of the thing

Fig. 11 One of George Eliot's travel diaries, labeled in her hand: "Journeys to Normandy in 1865 and Italy in 1864." George Eliot and George Henry Lewes Collection, General Collection, Beinecke Rare Books and Manuscript Library, Yale University, Journal 1864–5, GEN MSS 963, Box 18. By kind permission of the Estate of George Eliot

or place itself. Many of Eliot's notebooks had pockets, and her blotter has one in the back, now empty. A pocket works as a kind of extreme paratext, which furthers the idea of the volume as a container (with different "rooms") and text becoming meaningful because it is adjacent, beside, underneath, on the wall or ceiling. In another small commonplace book with miscellaneous notes, some in Greek and German, kept in 1880, the year she married John Cross, Eliot folded a minute snippet of paper and stored it in a pocket.[68] On it, she copied out a poem, written about her by her close friend Sara Sophia Hennell in 1859 that takes as its theme female rivalry that turns into loving encouragement and rejoicing for Eliot's great success.[69] Did she write out and keep this poem in this pocket for a reason, perhaps needing this support near her as she read and jotted down notes, during a momentous time of her life?

Like her quarries, these other sorts of notebooks Eliot amassed had recursive qualities. As we have seen already, she returned to them, recording in them the act of reading through her old notebooks, sometimes aloud to George Henry Lewes or close friends, not only for research when she was writing but also to review, remember, study, make changes for the future. In one of her diaries, started in 1861, she writes, "I am fond of my little old book in which I have recorded so many changes, and …. It will perhaps last me all through the life that is left to me."[70] The pages that still remained empty at this point seem to measure out the last years (or days) of her life, as she imagined it, as if turning them would show her the remaining chronology. But she would go on to fill this and other journals, and when she arrived at the end of this one, bumping up against text from over a decade ago, since she again started from both ends of the notebook, she records the date—"Dec. 31 [1877]"—and says,

> Today I say a final farewell to this little book which is the only record I have made of my personal life for 16 years and more, I have often been helped by looking back in it (I compare former with actual states of despondency from bad health or other apparent causes) … I shall record no more in this book because I am going to keep a more business-like diary. Here ends 1877.

She speaks of the "little book" as if it has some animacy, some helping agency, even more than a container for parts of her selfhood. The help she receives in reading it shapes her future self, as she, in some sense, puts herself in the book and then takes herself out of it. As with her treasured copy of *The Linnet's Life*, discussed in Chapter 1, the object holds an almost mystical sense of personal meaning. And as with Maggie and *The Imitation of Christ* or Dinah with the bible, help comes from turning and touching the pages, in finding vivid life and memory inside the volumes.

The *Middlemarch* Papers

The epigraphs that start each chapter in *Middlemarch* have a close relationship to commonplace and album culture, most coming from her reading copied into notebooks, others composed herself, that then end up in the *Middlemarch* manuscript. They stand alone, unincorporated, something like the jumble of quotes written into notebooks and albums. Their relationship to the chapter they begin is often far from obvious, thus emphasizing disparate parts that communicate through nearness on the page and in the chapter, through a sometimes mysterious association. For Eliot, as Ruth Abbott argues, referring to both Eliot's notebooks and her thinking and writing about poetry, "perceiving the separate parts of a whole is as important as perceiving their interfusion."[71] The epigraphs express Eliot's love for the heterogeneous, in particular bringing together her own separate moments of reading others' work. In his study of the way Eliot's epigraph and fiction interact, David Leon Higden remarks that "with them, she establishes a context and a sense of literary community," and he concludes that her wide reading along with observation of life around her saturated her novels.[72] This community, wrought on paper like the friendship album, creates a conversation or network of association between time periods, authors, and even genres. Eliot's reading and commonplacing do not only appear in the epigraphs, of course, but are also interfused into her story—brought to fictional life. Eliot wrote the following in a notebook, probably for research for *Romola* (1863): "Antigonus the second, when Zeno of Citium whom he admired beyond all philosophers died, said, 'The theatre of all my actions is fallen.'"[73] Then it appears again, exactly as it is written in the earlier notebook, in a circa 1868–71 notebook, now at the Folger Shakespeare Library.[74] Eliot carries the idea into book three of *Middlemarch*: "'The theatre of all my actions is fallen,' said an antique personage when his chief friend was dead" (242). The "theater" in this case is Mary Garth, who spurs on Fred Vincy's good deeds for love of her. Eliot's theater are authors and her "conversations" with them, in her notebooks and in her published works, which she then brings to other readers.

Writing and its adjuncts—script, notes, and book and album making—appear in *Middlemarch* as major plot movers and as minor details. Eve Kosofsky Sedgwick sees *Middlemarch* as "one of the definitive novels of texture," and the texture is often that of paper, books, and inscription, such as when Brooke is described as "a very good fellow, but pulpy; he will run into any mould, but he won't keep shape" (70), as if he is unfinished paper.[75] The novel is about, in part, the processes of creating, acting, and producing, especially the ways they fail, with Casaubon as an author, Dorothea as an active force for good, Lydgate as an inventor of medical advances, and many others. Much of the forward momentum of the characters' evolutions (and devolutions), as well as their domestic backdrops, is signaled through text and the materials of writing and reading. As a writer and scholar, Casaubon appears in the midst of such matter. His memory is described as *not* "the ordinary long-used blotting-book which only tells of forgotten writing" (27), which calls to mind ink-smeared sheets with mysterious bits of text, not to mention notebooks filled with text that no one ever reads. Dorothea understands "almost everything" Casaubon says as "the inscription on the door of a museum which might open on the treasures of past ages" (32–3). She is wrong, of course, as she finds out too late, after they are married. The inscription doesn't open out into a museum of the mind, but only petty little anterooms leading nowhere. Eliot probably based Casaubon in part on herself, as Seth Lerer points out.[76] Beginning her writing career as a journalist, translator, and book reviewer, Eliot learned early how to incorporate or work with the writing of others to create her own text. Her incredible pace of taking in information, not to mention her learning of languages, is noted partially in her notebooks, where she often made lists of what she was reading, sometimes on slips of paper sewn into a notebook, such as one she heads, "Read from June to Oct." (probably 1877), where she records around twenty-six books, and notes when they were read aloud.[77] What to do with all of this knowledge, how to make it something more than the translating or critiquing of others' work, more than "abundant pen scratches and amplitude of paper" (*Middlemarch* 200)? Failed writers are sprinkled throughout Eliot's work, some of them not able to move past the stage of recording research in notebooks. Others do produce but ineptly or insufficiently, such as those silly novels by lady novelists in her 1856 essay discussed in Chapter 1 and multiple fictional authors in *Impressions of Theophrastus Such*, whose careers languish or whose success comes at the cost of originality and truthfulness. In *Romola*, Bardo de' Bardi doesn't "effect anything but scattered work," such as copying manuscripts and making marginal notes, annotations, and extracts, before his death.[78] Casaubon is the most obvious example of the failed writer; Lerer describes him as "someone incapable of anything other than marginal comment."[79] Eliot worried that she too would become a "dried-up pedant" as Will Ladislaw thinks of Casaubon, an "elaborator of small explanations" (*Middlemarch* 205), or a filer of others' ideas alone, not an author who adds to the stores of the world's great ideas.[80] Casaubon uses notebooks (and pigeon holes) to "gather in this great harvest of truth" (24).

> His notes already made a formidable range of volumes, but the crowning task would be to condense these voluminous still-accumulating results and bring them, like the earlier vintage of Hippocratic books, to fit a little shelf. (24–5)

These notebooks probably contain a mix of primary source material, secondary source material from other scholars with whom he competes, and his own ideas, summaries, perhaps even outlines for the projected book. The condensation proposed here is quarry-like—extracting the best and most useful parts, to produce one volume (or perhaps a few), and then making the notebooks themselves obsolete. But his notes stay saved up in their places, scraps of reading that sit still and are never transformed into published works (except for a few pamphlets) that enter into circulation. His process becomes impacted, repetitive, and inward, rather than a moving outward into dispersal and plenitude, as with Eliot's own work when published. At some point early in their marriage, Casaubon says to Dorothea "Doubtless, my dear ... The notes I have here made will want sifting, and you can, if you please, extract them under my direction" (199). This sifting and extracting has a deadening feel to it that even Dorothea, who is no scholar or writer, questions, asking him, "all those rows of volumes—will you not now do what you used to speak of?—will you not ... begin to write the book which will make your vast knowledge useful to the world?" (199–200). They die with him—they are dead things, in a sense, as Dorothea thinks sadly as she looks at them soon after his death.

> The morning gazed calmly into the library, shining on the rows of notebooks as it shines on the weary waste planted with huge stones, the mute memorial of a forgotten faith ... Then, she lingered in the library and could not be at rest till she had carefully ranged all the note-books as she imagined that he would wish to see them. (538)

The notebooks have a corpse-like feel, as if they are relics connected to that now-dead body. Eliot fought against this weary waste, of course, with her own secular humanist project, which shines through her novels, and even back to the notebooks.

As with Dinah in *Adam Bede* and Maggie in *The Mill on the Floss*, Dorothea has a feeling toward books and paper that borders on the superstitious. When she returns from her honeymoon, her sense of her newly benumbed life manifests in "the volumes of polite literature in the bookcase [which] looked more like immovable imitations of books" (273). These call to mind the dummy books that Dickens and others created, appearing to be full of textual life but empty inside, openings not into museums but into sad little rooms that imprison, comparable to Casaubon's notebooks. Dorothea feels writing is for communicating emotion to those close to one rather than for revenge on enemies far away, as is Casaubon's project. After his death, he wants Dorothea to keep working on his book, but she refuses. She takes his instructions, which he has called the "Synoptical Tabulation for the use of Mrs Casaubon," and

> carefully enclosed and sealed [it], writing within the envelope, "I could not use it. Do you not see now that I could not submit my soul to yours, by working hopelessly at what I have no belief in?—Dorothea." Then she deposited the paper in her own desk. (539)

The sealing up, the writing inside the envelope, and the putting away in the desk have a ritual aspect to them, as if this is the way to speak to the dead, make a pact with them, rather than the living, and the means to put something away, for good, bury it.

Another character around whom paper slips and writing accrete is, curiously enough, the alcoholic, abusive Raffles, who isn't exactly illiterate but certainly doesn't write or read much. As with Casaubon, Raffles's mind is characterized using a paper and text simile, but this one from a different class and education level. With the former it is the blotting-book and the inscription of the door of the museum. Raffles describes his faulty memory for names by referring to a type of form, the sort of ephemeral paper object, mostly forgotten today, that kept printers at the time busy: "I've got my faculties as if I was in my prime, but names wear out, by Jove! Sometimes I'm no better than a confounded tax-paper before the names are filled in" (530). In contrast to this empty form, other fragments of paper connected to him have a huge importance to the plot. As in Gaskell's novels, with their scraps with partial text that become momentous evidence, in *Middlemarch* Bulstrode's reputation and whole life (and those close to him) unravel because of a fragment of paper, picked up by chance. Raffles finds that his flask "had become dangerously loose from its leather covering, and catching sight of a folded paper which had fallen within the fender, he took it up and shoved it under the leather so as to make the glass firm" (415). He later reads it, and it contains part of Bulstrode's address, providing Raffles with the opportunity to blackmail the supposedly morally upstanding Bulstrode with his dark past. Trying to contain the spread of information after Raffles falls ill, Bulstrode goes through Raffles's pockets for clues, knowing they will "carry signs in the shape of hotel-bills of the places he had stopped in" (705). Found text and scraps of paper thus become callers-up of a past, bringing alive in the present profound ethical implications, expressing Eliot's philosophy of moral responsibility to those nearest.

Rosamond, trained to attract a husband, is set into a domestic backdrop of pretty albums and paper crafts, similar to other women, like Celia, who constructs a paper man as a toy for the curate's children (49), and Dorothea, whose poor educational opportunities mean her knowledge of art is "chiefly of the hand-screen sort" (193). When the contents of a Middlemarcher's house are sold at auction, Mr. Trumbull, the auctioneer, knocks down a "collection of trifles for the drawing-room table," including a bijou,

> "a sort of practical rebus I may call it; here, you see, it looks like an elegant heart-shaped box, portable—for the pocket; there, again, it becomes like a splendid double flower—an ornament for the table"—Mr. Trumbull allowed the flower to fall alarmingly into strings of heart-shaped leaves—"a book of riddles! No less than five hundred printed in a beautiful red ..." (606)

This "trifle" is a printed version of what is found in friendship albums of the time, with its riddles, cut-outs, and shape-changing ingenuity. These sorts of things can be found on drawing-room tables in Gaskell's *Cranford*, where a "kaleidoscope, conversation-cards, puzzles-cards" sit for visitors to toy with, and in Austen's *Emma*, where a handmade book of riddles "ornamented with ciphers and trophies" is displayed on the table for visitors to leaf through.[81] In Rosamond's drawing-room callers admire a relative of these cards and trifles, a "gorgeous watered-silk" (269) *Keepsake*, a popular annual that mimicked the sorts of handmade albums explored in Chapter 2, with work by famous writers like Letitia Elizabeth Landon (L. E. L.), Lady Blessington, and Sir Walter Scott and illustrations of famous beauties.[82] Ridiculed by Lydgate as sentimental and frivolous—"I wonder which would turn out to be the silliest—the engravings or the writing here" (270)—the *Keepsake* is criticized in a similar way that Eliot uses for those lady novelists and their silly novels. The papery things that surround Rosamond are generally derided, such as her "elegant note-writing [and] private album for extracted verse" (268).[83] This album is a commonplace book, not meant to be confused with the sort that Eliot or even Casaubon kept. Still, in the case of the latter, the use both of them make of their extracts is, in the final analysis, not so different. Just as Eliot didn't want to turn into a Casaubon, she most definitely didn't want to be a Rosamond, filing verse into a silken volume as was the fashion for ladies. Mary Garth, another female character defined by documents such as a hidden will, almost burned, is one of the few successful authors in the novel. Mary and Fred Vincy succeed in writing books and having them published, and they are the opposite of inward-looking pedants. Fred's book, *Cultivation of Green Crops and the Economy of Cattle-Feeding*, is a practical guide growing out of active work on local land. Mary's book, *Stories of Great Men, taken from Plutarch*, published by "Gripp and Co., Middlemarch," has a scholarly ring to it and also sounds akin to a commonplace book, anthology, or miscellany. Yet she produces it to entertain and instruct children, as an aid to those nearest her, in contrast to Casaubon's narcissistic hoarding of his classical knowledge. More than most characters in the book, Mary has the outside standing ground so valued by Eliot—an ability to see herself as one insignificant person among other competing egos, and to accept it with humor. The fact that citizens of *Middlemarch* think that Mary wrote Fred's book and Fred Mary's gives a humorous flavor to the sorts of appropriation and lack of attribution found often in commonplace books and albums. All of these leaves and volumes remind the reader of the paper object that is *Middlemarch*, which they hold in their hands while reading, to be carefully distinguished from unfinished paper, inscriptions that lead nowhere, elegant notes, tax-papers with empty forms, or imitations of books.

Eliot said in a letter that she didn't want her novels to be read as "an assemblage of extracts," but something like this did indeed happen.[84] Leah Price explores how Eliot's own writing entered into publications similar to the *Keepsake* in Rosamond's drawing room. Price points out that Eliot had a "peculiar vulnerability to intertextual appropriation" because the "structure of her own narratives [is] punctuated with epigraphs and lapidary generalizations." This led to the publication of volumes such as the *George Eliot Birthday Book*, which includes inspirational extracts from her work and was "used to collect autographs of celebrities or inscriptions from friends."[85] Bookmarks with Eliot quotes proliferated, and anthologies such as Alexander Main's *Wise, Witty, and Tender Sayings in Prose and Verse Selected from the Works of George Eliot*, published the same year as *Middlemarch*, became popular. Price goes on to remark that "amateurism alone distinguishes the album and the birthday book from her own working notebooks of sources."[86] Another recursive process can be traced here, from Eliot's recording of her reading into commonplace books to her incorporating these extracts into her novels, then readers encountering them, and eventually her works becoming disassembled wise sayings, sometimes in albums meant to also contain handwritten autographs, verse, quotations. Heterogeneity and fragmentation win out, in part, over narrative, wholly interfused.

Scribal Publications

The sorts of writers' notebooks explored thus far have been incipient books only in a loose way. This last section moves from quarries to drafts or final versions of artworks—stronger forms of nascent books. Many nineteenth-century fiction and poetry writers used notebooks for drafts of their writing, as with Eliot's outlines for *Middlemarch*.[87] In William Wordsworth's draft notebooks, for instance, the hands of the women of the household appear, taking dictation. Extra pages are sewn in. Alfred Lord Tennyson decorated his notebooks for drafting his poems with drawings and doodles.[88] The left-hand margins in E. B. Browning's and Virginia Woolf's widen as the handwriting goes down the page, probably evidence of fast, flowing writing done without the support of a desk or table for the heel of the hand.[89] While these and many other writers treated their notebooks as utilitarian workbooks, the creators of the small sample of notebooks taken up in the final pages of this chapter didn't employ them as workspaces for drafts, but rather presented them as finished artifacts, not so much as outside standing grounds, in Eliot's sense, but rather expressions of the interior. The performative side of creative writing, drafting, and volume making emerges clearly with these case studies, as well as the integration of—and care for—the paper support for text. A close attention to date, place, and sometimes hour of composition or transcription underlines how artistic labor is an embodied activity in a present moment. Emily Brontë approached the notebook as a work akin to a final product, as did the Michael Fields, who interspersed final or almost-final drafts of poems with diary entries and commonplacing. These writers had a more highly wrought, sometimes ritualistic system that brought in the author-as-actor and her materials as central players.

Emily Brontë never explained her writing practice to anyone, as far as we know, and most of her manuscripts have gone missing, so we can only speculate using the few that survive. Before she began writing *Wuthering Heights*, much of her work was done for herself alone. She kept her two most important notebooks secret, seemingly even from her sister Anne, with whom she collaborated on the imaginary world of Gondal. Charlotte recounts how she "accidentally lighted on" one of these notebooks in October 1845 and took it away to read "alone and in secret."[90] Stirred by the verse's "peculiar music," Charlotte admitted her act to Emily, who reacted furiously to this "unwarrantable liberty," this looking into a private world. With the help of Anne, Charlotte convinced Emily to publish a handful of her poems in a collection of the work of all three sisters, under the pseudonyms Ellis (Emily), Currer (Charlotte), and Acton (Anne) Bell.[91] Next came their first novels, with Emily accepting an audience of more than just herself for *Wuthering Heights*, although still under the veil of Ellis Bell. The notebook that Charlotte found still exists—a rare survivor from the mass of missing manuscript material, possibly destroyed by Emily herself or Charlotte, after Emily's death. No drafts of *Wuthering Heights* have been located, not even the fair copy or proofs. Almost all of the juvenilia have disappeared, including a raft of stories about Gondal, referenced by both Anne and Emily in their few diaries and occasionally by Charlotte and Branwell, too, in their own youthful writings. Emily may have started work on a second novel when her sisters were writing theirs (Charlotte *Jane Eyre* and Anne *The Tenant of Wildfell Hall*); if so, it is now lost. What remains are poems written on miniature snippets of paper—to be explored in Chapter 4—and three notebooks. One of these three, now known as the Honresfeld manuscript because it was owned by the collector William Law of Honresfeld, Littleborough, near Rochdale, became unlocatable to researchers sometime in the 1930s, after a facsimile copy was made and some photographs taken, but has recently resurfaced for sale at Sotheby.[92] Another one, the earliest, from 1839, lost its original binding and some of its leaves and was rebound, probably by the disreputable collector Thomas Wise. (He also rebound the Honresfeld MA, in morocco, and one wonders if the removal of the original covers meant the loss of meaningful endpapers, flyleaves, a "title" page, etc.) Only one, which she entitled *Gondal Poems*, is still intact.

Brontë's finished drafts developed out of a process of lyric attenuation, a destruction of earlier versions, making the one left the last, and only, word. When Brontë transcribed a poem into a notebook, she destroyed its earlier form, evidenced by poems that shared single leaves or notebook pages being torn off (with bits of text remaining) or by being crossed off if removing meant losing the text of another poem. (Did Brontë destroy all drafts of *Wuthering Heights* for this reason?) Her two later notebooks, both created in February 1844—*Gondal Poems* and the other, untitled, for poems not directly related to Gondal (the Honresfeld MA)—superseded the 1839, intermediate notebook. Brontë removed poems from the earlier notebook if they were entered into the later two by cutting them out or crossing them out. While we don't know why she decided to create the two 1844 notebooks (or the earlier one, for that matter, or other ones that might have once existed), they have the feel of a body of work, proffered up, herself as the only reader. These two notebooks do not feel recursive or organic like the Eliot quarries, in the sense that they weren't meant to be mined actively for something else, changed, or later rewritten into another form, although Brontë must have returned to them repeatedly. Instead they seem like scribal publications, skipping over the usual forms of print culture. Janet Gezari comments on Brontë's process: "Where her poems were concerned, what mattered to her, as to Wallace Stevens, was not that they would survive but that she had written them."[93] Brontë gives herself all of the roles—of author, editor, and publisher—situating "her production in a field of free transgressive prediscovery," Susan Howe writes (of Emily Dickinson).[94] This doesn't seem to be the whole story, however, given her attentiveness to her notebooks as artworks.

The *Gondal Poems* notebook, the only one extant in its original form with flyleaves and title page, will be my focus (see Fig. 12). A slim booklet, the thread holding it together along the spine visible when opened, it has a scratched, worn leather binding in an oxblood color and its pages came pre-lined.[95] Brontë decorated the title "Gondal Poems" with twisting vines and flourishes, making the letters appear to be overgrown, like a gothic mansion gone to seed, or as if the words are coming alive. Above the title, she has penned "Emily Jane Brontë Transcribed February 1844," the words linked together with fancy curlicues that look something like letters themselves, but illegible. The poems are copied out in the tiny hand meant to look like published print that all of the Brontë siblings favored. She didn't put

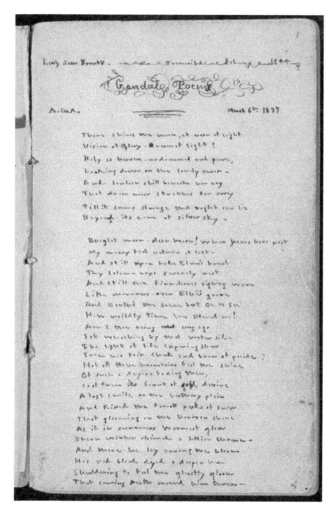

Fig. 12 First page of Emily Brontë's "Gondal Poems" notebook. © The British Library Board, Add. MS. 43483

them in the chronological order of their composition, so the presentation had some other meaning for her, one no longer obvious. Forty-five poems fill the pages, all including composition dates but two, ranging from 1841 to 1848—the year she died. They are careful fair copies except for the last two poems, which contain heavy revisions, as if her complete work became drafty as she neared the end of it. And the last poem, dated May 13, 1848, is the start of another version of the penultimate one, dated September 14,

1846.[96] The artifact as a whole, taking up many hours of a short life, has the feel of an artist's signed drawing, as with her own watercolor portrait of her dog Keeper, on the top of which she wrote, "Keeper—from life—April 24th 1838—Emily Jane Brontë" in a tiny script similar to her signature in *Gondal Poems*.[97] Or perhaps it makes more sense to compare her notebook to an artist's book?[98]

For Emily, the temporality of the *doing* of writing (or drawing) was central to her art, as it also was for Charlotte. In Charlotte's early manuscripts, she often included a date when the work was commenced and then another at the end when she had finished, in an obsessive need to locate its composition within a particular run of hours.[99] For instance, Charlotte prefaced "The Adventures of Mon Edouard de Crack," written when she was fourteen years old, with,

> I began this book on the 22 of February 1830 and finished it on the 23 of February 1830, doing 8 pages on the first day and 11 on the second. On the first day I wrote an hour and a half in the morning and an hour and a half in the evening. On the third day I wrote a quarter of an hour in the morning, 2 hours in the afternoon and a quarter of an hour in the evening, making in the whole 5 hours and a half.[100]

Emily also dated most of her poems, and when she revised them later and put them in a notebook, she generally added the date she copied them out, as we have seen with the February 1844 notebook. Sometimes she recorded a third date—when a fictional Gondal character "wrote" the poem. For instance, in the *Gondal Notebook*, one poem gives the date (and place) in the world of Gondal in the title—"Written on returning to the P[alace] of I[nstruction] on the 10th of January 1824"—and the composition date in the real world as "Jan. 14th 1839."[101] With some of the poems, like "A.G.A. to A.S.," which begins "O wonder not so far away!," she has included an "E" before the date, here May 20, 1838, as if she needs to affirm when *she* was there writing it, as opposed to when it was written by the fictional poet A.G.A. For the poem "Written in Aspin Castle," she wrote the "E" next to two dates, August 20, 1842 and February 6, 1843, presumably the initial composition, then a revision.[102] Perhaps the characters and their temporal location were so real to Emily that she needed to re-include herself and her day of composition repeatedly. Or, going further with this theory, did she feel like a character in this world, as if the writer "Emily" was something other than (or in addition to) the woman living there in Haworth at the family home? These different types of "writing time"—the "real" present of sitting down and penning the poem, the later one of transcribing it, and the pliable fantasy world, with its possibility of forever—all mattered to her. And since many of the poems were written by Gondal characters, Emily creates a world in which she is a writer among writers, or is able to inhabit different worlds as a writer, be different sorts of people who write. Most of all, she furthers the drama of the writer's lot, making it spacious and grand. Perhaps the "publication" of *Gondal Poems* happened in the imaginary world of Gondal? This did occur (fictionally speaking) in Charlotte and Branwell's Angria. Their handcrafted booklets, made when they were children, were meant to be volumes and magazines "published" in their made-up world, with handwriting mimicking print, title pages, and tables of contents.[103] In one of Charlotte's little books, the title page reads "The!!! Evening Walk, A Poem by the Marquis of Douro in Pindaric Metre, Published and Sold by Captain Tree [one of Charlotte's pseudonyms] and all other Booksellers in the Chief Glass Town, Wellingtons [sic] G[lass] T[own] ... and etc." The "author" of this poem also tells us that "the following pages are the production of my pen ... the fruit of some days labour ... having cast them unprotected on the world I leave them entirely at the public's mercy," signed "DOURO June 28 1830."[104] Charlotte and Branwell's tiny tomes advertise books like themselves and by the same authors, such as "*The Law*, in 50 vols folio, price 600 guineas; very closely printed by Sergeant Bud [one of Branwell's pseudonyms], Scrivener to Tally, Chief Genius Charlotte."[105]

Like Charlotte, then, Emily made herself a dramatic character in her own writing life, steeped in the mystery and vitality of the creative experience. While Emily never described her writing practice in words, she did depict it in drawings. In a sophisticated use of recursiveness, Emily drew a picture of herself writing on the sheet of paper she was writing, a reverse of ekphrasis—creating a visual depiction of what she writes about and how the creating happens. In a diary of "Monday evening June 26 1837," as it says at the top, Emily reported that "Anne and I [are] writing in the drawing room," and, at the bottom of the page, she sketched herself and Anne sitting at a table, with the box in which they kept their one-page diaries (labeled here "the tin box") and the diaries themselves (labeled "the papers") in front of them.[106] She began another diary, dated "July the 30th 1841," "It is Friday evening—near 9 o'clock—wild rainy weather. I am seated in the dining room having just concluded tidying our desk boxes—writing this document."[107] On the top left-hand corner of the page, she doodled another self-portrait: in profile at her portable desk on a table, penning "this document." On the top right-hand corner is a third—this time pausing, gazing out the window, the opened desk and page temporarily abandoned. Probably the most famous of her representations of herself writing ends her July 30, 1845 diary.[108] Sitting in her tiny bedroom on a little wooden stool, she has her desk box open on her lap, writing the paper on which she draws herself writing. Her dog Keeper stretches out on the rug near her, and what looks like Anne's spaniel Flossy lies on the bed. What seems to matter to Brontë here is thinking of herself (and picturing herself) in the process of putting pen to paper. It is not as an author that she represents herself—a published author, say—but as at the work of writing, a thinking about her own process similar to Gertrude Stein's idea of compositional time as a present enactment.[109] She depicts the material and physical conditions of the activity: the chair or stool she sits on, the desk and table used as writing surfaces, the paper on which she composes, the room in which the process happens, the box in which the production will go, and the creatures that people the space. These pictures also foreground the body's place in the creation of text, showing what Gerard Curtis calls an "awareness of the viscerality of the writing process."[110] Brontë cared about the performance of writing and its portrayal, including the immediacy of the act and its props. These portraits of the artist (as a young woman) have an odd dimensionality; a form of *mise en abîme*, as we saw in albums in Chapter 2, where the imaginary page depicted on the actual page might have another picture of the same sheet, as if many can be found in one. Each sheet has a clear border that seems to be overcome through this opening up of the middle, with depiction within depiction—turning the leaf into a window through which one might enter, or at least look. As we saw in Chapter 1, in *Wuthering Heights* Emily embraced this self-referential, self-conscious artistic approach that rethinks what a notebook, text, or piece of paper can be. The *Gondal Poems* notebook, then, is an enigmatic dispatch from Emily's avant-garde practice.

Writing in a very different time, the Michael Fields had a Brontë-like need to body forth themselves in notebooks. Katharine Bradley, Edith Cooper's aunt, started keeping notebooks well before their collaboration began, but when they settled into their Michael Field writing persona, their joint journal making began in earnest. They gave it the title "Works and Days," and they took turns writing in it, evident by the different handwritings switching off from one page to the next. Emma Donoghue, in her biography of Michael Field, describes how this multi-volume work "allowed them to shape petty details into a grand narrative. There were to be no secrets. Katharine and Edith used the diary to tell each other painful things as well as to reassure;

if one was away, the other would read and write in the diary as a sort of psychic phone call."[111] The "White Book," as they called their notebooks (most of them are bound in white leather), formed an integral part of their aesthetic creed to live their art, to make their daily lives dramatically vivid.[112] They had elaborate manners, wore "artistic" dresses, and filled their London house, The Paragon, with William Morris-designed furniture, gold Japanese wallpaper, eighteenth-century satinwood furniture, and book cases with lavender-velvet curtains.[113] They created rules for their formal dinner parties, on one night, for instance, only serving oysters to be eaten in strict silence.[114]

In and with the notebooks, they found space to "shape life divinely," as they put it.[115] *Fin-de-siècle* productions, their notebooks-as-artworks developed out of a self-conscious looking back on the nineteenth century. Their work has an artifice to it, a decadent scene-making that feels wholly different from the deep earnestness of a George Eliot or an Emily Brontë. On the spines and "title pages" of each volume, dates and the title "Works and Days" are penned in a special font, akin to letters turned into drawings (or calligraphy, close cousin to the fancy writing found everywhere in albums). They begin with epigraphs, often quotes from the bible, Milton, and the Romantic poets, a way to frame each year with a grand beginning. Their poems in fair copy (and occasionally drafts) are interspersed with experiences composed carefully, sometimes with titles like "Flashes of Impression." There are accounts of their travels, visits to friends and exact renderings of the conversations had there, descriptions of paintings they visited in museums (ekphrasis), copied-in letters they wrote and received, and lists of books they are reading, as well as pasted and tipped-in newspaper clippings, postcards, theater tickets, printed invitations to art openings, pressed flowers, and more. Not only do they include their original poems but they also give striking accounts of when they begin writing a new piece, such as, in the 1890 volume, "Sunday—August 24 / We have had our Carloman [a play eventually called *In the Name of Time*] papers out—our drawers are arranged to hold the great new drama—our brains begin the toil of bringing it into being."[116]

Their loving, erotic collaboration runs through the volumes, depicted not as raw facts as with some diaries but rather as a polished dreamscape, an act or performance garnering rich and changing roles for each of them, expressed by nicknames. Katharine is Michael and Edith is Field, but that is just the start. Katharine is also Sim, short for Simorg, an Eastern, all-knowing bird, also represented by a Y-shaped symbol. Edith is Henry, Hennie, Blue Bird, Puss, Pussie, Persian, and more. Their handwriting and accounts of their experiences share the page in a collage-like way. In the 1904 volume, for example, they tell of a visit from their close friends, the artists Charles de Sousy Ricketts and Charles Hazlewood Shannon, who were also a couple. Edith begins the account, starting with "Wednesday Jan. 20th / The Artists came out of the fog to dine—again not as diners should be—but they plead the frightful weather, and indeed the star Earth is getting a terrible place to live in."[117] She goes on to tell us what Michael [Katharine] is wearing: "her black striped silk Directoire with fischu of ivory net darned with green and bowed with green velvet." The menu in list format follows, and then she tells us a bit about their conversation, quoting the men here and there. She ends with, "and then a cloud came round the god, chilly and harrumphing—yet at moments vaporous as if about an altar. So he went, with cold fingers—mortally cold adieux." Katharine then picks up the narrative, in the middle of the same page: "the day after the artists have dined with us, I write to Painter. You are painting today,—you are as a bee at her honey. I can speak to you." Thus they present and create their life together, as a drama, as an act of writing, and as a gorgeous performance.

In many of their poems, the eroticism of the shared space of the page, part of a savoring of the body and soul, becomes central. In "A Girl," the addressee's soul is "a deep-wave peal / Dim, lucent of all lovely mysteries," and her face, brow, and mouth call forth nature's most seductive forms, such as forest trees and aspen-leaflets trembling in the breeze. The poem ends like this:

> Such: and our souls so knit,
> I leave a page half-writ—
>   The work begun
> Will be to heaven's conception done,
>   If she come to it.[118]

The "half-writ" page needs the other for completion and divinity. It brings the two together as do their notebooks, calling for their handwriting, knitting together their works and days.

The Michael Fields and Emily Brontë all found in their notebooks a place to make art, form identity, and to dwell. Emily preferred her poetic work to be part of her solitude, peopled only with her made-up characters. The Michael Fields needed to present their shared lives in their notebooks, to shape them into an art for themselves and, eventually, for posterity. Before they died, they instructed their friend Thomas Sturge Moore to open

"Works and Days" at the end of 1929, read it, and "publish so much and whatever parts of it I might think fit," as he put it.[119] Charles Reade's compulsive hoarding and ritualistic routine pushed him to create his library of notebooks. Like Reade's, Eliot's notebook work was meant to be processed into stories to bring into the larger world, a project she described as looking past the "conventional, human, temporary dress" of the world and considering it "in its essence and in its relation to eternity."[120]

4
Reusing, Tearing, and Folding

> "You must tell her," she continued, "that I would answer her letter, but I have no materials for writing, not even a book from which to tear a leaf."
>
> Catherine Linton (the daughter) in *Wuthering Heights*[1]

Emily Brontë's writing process involved tiny shreds of paper, often torn or cut from already-used leaves. She penned many of her poems on scraps, some probably taken from notebooks, then divided into halves, quarters, or portions even smaller.[2] Other fragments of poetry manuscript consist of bits of cardboard or sections of stationery. Some leaves had been used already, with writing or doodling filling one side, and Brontë ripping or scissoring a rectangle from them and turning them over for the blank space. Many writers of the time practiced this sort of scrimping on, parceling out, and reusing of paper because of its steep cost, especially those under discussion throughout these chapters—the Brontë siblings, for instance, and George Eliot. Yet in some cases restrictions served aesthetic purposes, often at the same time that they served thrifty ones. When Brontë scribbled a poem on the verso of a to-do list, she was recycling something that had already been recycled, since paper "is made from the rags of things that did once exist," writes Thomas Carlyle—mostly used clothing.[3] Leah Price details how cloth that had kept limbs covered became reading matter, and printed paper was then used again for food wrapping, lining, toilet paper, and more. Because of its linkage to food and the privy, Price notes, paper had a recognizable connectedness to bodies and their functions.[4] Along these same lines, Lothar Müller mentions a popular nineteenth-century joke about the morning's newspaper becoming the evening's toilet paper.[5] The manuscript has an added meaning when thought of in this way, and superstitions about the properties of paper—what it means to fold, burn, and tear it—connect to ideas about the mysteries of the skin and the alimentary.

Victorians had a daily awareness of paper's expense and the need to wring every bit of potential out of the dear substance. Industrialization and the lowering of costs due to mass production came late to paper manufacturing. Most paper mills still used the water wheel for their source of power, the steam engine not coming into wide use until the middle of the century.[6] A tax on paper, not repealed until 1860, added to the price. Yet the most important factor was the need for linen and cotton cloth as the primary materials of paper, before wood pulp came into common use as the main ingredient in the 1880s. Perennial shortages of rags made them expensive, a cost passed onto the buyers of paper. These rags began their lives not just as clothing but also bedding, drapes, old sails, ropes, and so on, and they made their way to paper mills via rag pickers and collectors.[7] Various laws, including restrictions on exports and imports of rags, were used to try to regulate this precious material, including a seventeenth-century requirement that the dead be buried in wool rather than linen, since the former wasn't good for making paper, and when cloth was buried, it went out of circulation.[8] Some have claimed that the rise in the general use of underwear contributed to the development of paper, creating as it did a new source of rags.[9] Clever inventors searched for other ingredients for paper for centuries—substances that didn't rely on the slaughter of many animals (parchment) or on an expensively produced material, like cloth. Materials such as the nests of wasps (the original paper makers), moss, hemp, bark, straw, cabbage stalks, thistle, mallow, corn husks, pine-cones, old shingles, reeds, nettles, hops, and jute had been used for experimental papermaking. One late eighteenth-century experimenter included specimens in his treatise on papermaking of a sheet made from the insides of potatoes, and, next to it, one made from potato skins.[10]

Because of paper's dearness, parcel paper, wrappers for store-bought items or things sent through the mail, wallpaper, newspapers, journals, and even discarded books had further domestic lives. The 1779 "it narrative" "Adventures of a Quire of Paper," published in *London Magazine*, charts the heterogeneous stages of paper's existence beginning with, for example, a thistle in a ditch that is woven into a piece of cambric used as a handkerchief, which wears down into a bandage and a "spitting cloth," then ends up in the "ragman's bag," who sells it to a paper maker.[11] A poet writes his poetry on the resulting sheets, but soon they are "twisted up with a half-pennyworth of tobacco for a night-man," and they eventually end their life lining the bottom of mince pies.[12] There were even attempts to "wash" the print off of paper, thus making it blank and ready for more text.[13] Albums were sometimes made from repurposed books. Ellen Gruber Garvey explores many American examples, especially such "useless" books as free governmental-issued

Patent Office reports, city directories, banking reports, and used ledgers (including plantation ledgers that list slaves owned) salvaged for new lives as scrapbooks.[14] Similar "useless" books with handsome bindings were repurposed in Britain, as well, as two examples from late in the period show: a "specimen volume" of *The Temple Dictionary of the Bible*, made to show the binding and a few pages of print, but otherwise full of blank pages, and *The Stock Exchange Year-Book 1898*.[15] Early twentieth-century Brontë scholars collected Brontë-related clippings in them, and with the former volume, chunks of pages were cut out so the volume could still be closed with many thick clippings added.

Elizabeth Gaskell's novels often detail such thrifty reuse, especially *Cranford*, with an extended discussion by the narrator that opens chapter 5 about "small economies" that involve caring about the complete lives of string, "rubber rings" (rubber bands), candle ends, and more. Miss Matty "made candle-lighters of all the notes and letters of the week" (124), and an "old gentleman" chaffs about paper being wasted:

> Envelopes fretted his soul terribly when they first came in; the only way in which he could reconcile himself to such waste of his cherished article was by patiently turning inside out all that were sent to him, and so making them serve again. Even now, though tamed by age, I see him casting wistful glances at his daughters when they send a whole inside of a half-sheet of note-paper, with the three lines of acceptance to an invitation, written on only one of the sides. (87)

There are also newspapers sewn into sheets and put down on a new carpet to protect it from the shoes of party-goers. Talia Schaffer explores the Victorian ethos of salvage crafts—how "handicraft after handicraft uses leftover scraps—shells, candle ends, bits of cotton or straw, pieces of newspaper, old glass bottles, feathers … lengths of ribbon, offcuts of dress material, stray buttons."[16] The japanner used printed paper in ornamenting boxes, screens, and the like, Lucy Peltz explains.[17] One decorative use of "waste" paper Charlotte Brontë mastered is rolled-paper work. Rolling small strips of old paper—whether letters, the cut edges of books, newspaper, food or package wrappers—into circles or other shapes, the crafter then pasted them onto surfaces, such as the covers of books or needlework boxes, forming designs. A rolled-paper tea-caddy Charlotte constructed, probably as a gift for her friend Ellen Nussey, still exists at the Brontë Parsonage Museum, faded and tattered.[18] George Eliot has an aristocratic character, Miss Assher, in *Scenes of Clerical Life*, angrily doing a similar type of paper work, called "filigree work," as a means to ignore her out-of-favor lover.[19]

Because of this rampant refeeding of paper and books into production and consumption, it was a common worry among writers that their work, whether in manuscript or published book form, would suffer a degrading form of afterlife, devaluing its supposed immortal value as a work of art. Charlotte fretted that her publishers would use the manuscript of *The Professor*, before it was ever published, to protect the inside of leather traveling trunks and butter barrels after it had been rejected by them and nine other publishers.[20] Poetry is so poor that it is rolled up to light a pipe in one of Charlotte's early writings, a means for her to poke fun at the clumsy verse written by one of her brother Branwell's characters. Harry Buxton Forman, a nineteenth-century book collector, asked others to inspect the linings of their trunks when he was searching for missing works by Percy Bysshe Shelley, William St. Clair reports.[21] Years earlier, Matthew Lewis prefaced his gothic novel *The Monk* (1796) with lines of verse that address his book directly, picturing its demise:

> In some dark dirty corner thrown
> Mouldy with damps, with cobwebs strown,
> Your leaves shall be the book-worm's prey
> Or sent to chandler-shop away,
> And doomed to suffer public scandal,
> Shall line the trunk or wrap the candle.[22]

Lord Byron worries in *Don Juan* that a man's "new portmanteau … may be lined with this my canto."[23] The fear of having one's writing turned into a device to curl women's hair was a fairly common trope. Charlotte uses it in *Shirley*, when the title character imagines that her old school copybooks had long ago become curl-papers for the servant girls' hair and is surprised to find that the man who loves her has kept and treasured them. Tennyson pictures his poem *In Memoriam* (1850) meeting this fate, along with it ending up in the bindings of new books:

> These mortal lullabies of pain
> May bind a book, may line a box,
> May serve to curl a maiden's locks[24]

Before or after publication, the writing that hopes to transcend its mere body enters back into the cycle of reuse along with other ephemeral matter.

But in some cases, papery products were deliberately recycled to make scribal productions, wedding the frugal to the artistic. When Charlotte and Branwell were children, they made miniature books and magazines by sewing together little leaves of paper and, for the covers, scraps of domestic detritus, steeping the texts in habits of household recycling. Anything available that suited their fancy went into their productions—what Virginia Jackson, writing about Emily Dickinson, calls "ready-to-hand paper."[25] Charlotte covered her earliest existing manuscript, dating from around 1826 and written for Anne, in white, gray, and blue spotted wallpaper (see Fig. 13).[26] Probably chosen because it made for a pretty book cover, perhaps Charlotte was already thinking of books as kinds of dwelling places, for later she imagines the book-as-place-to-escape for the young Jane Eyre, from the hostile household of the Reed family. Gray, light-brown, or yellow parcel paper worked as a sturdy material for book binding, and some of the parcel-paper covers of the Brontës' booklets show they had already been

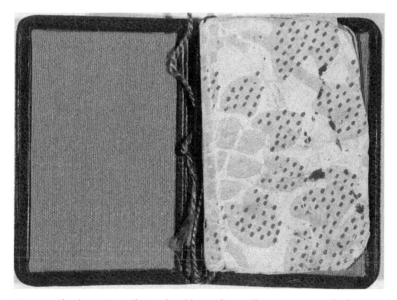

Fig. 13 Charlotte Brontë's tiny booklet with a wallpaper cover, called "There was once a little girl and her name was Anne," ca. 1826–8. Brontë Parsonage Museum, B78

used for mailing. Written on the inside of the cover of Branwell's November 1833 "The Politics of Verdopolis, A Tale by Captain John Flower," for instance, are directions for delivering a package: "Carriage Paid 110, by Red Rover, Lynn Coach, Thursday Night, March 6, 1834," giving the little text a sense of urgency and also mystery. [27] What was sent through the mail in this paper before it became a book cover? From where did it come, and what places did it travel through? Wrappers for published books that contained advertisements for other books were ripe for salvaging, as Branwell does with his "Blackwood's Magazine" of July 1829, leading us to pause over this evidence of a commercial publishing industry in a little scribal "publication," not meant for circulation except among the siblings and in the fantasy world of Angria.[28] His "History of the Rebellion" is penned on sheets for music, perhaps left over from Anne's handmade music books, in which she recorded the notes and lyrics onto preprinted music paper.[29] Blue or brown sheets that had contained salt or sugar worked as especially attractive covers, and Charlotte's "Albion and Marina" (October 1830) has "Purified Epsom Salts, SOLD BY WEST, CHEMIST & DRUGGIST, Keighley" printed on it, bringing to mind the possibility of tasting a book.[30] These volumes, magpie collections of household odds and ends, speak of the sort of ephemeral paper so common at the time but now rare indeed. They show writing evolving out of domestic rhythms, often practiced by servants and women, of food purchasing and preparation, package sending, and book buying. They were a "montage praxis," as Esther Leslie calls crafts made by hand, that used "debris and rubbish, the broken pots and torn scraps, not the high, sublime reordering of harmony in a bloodless, hands-off aestheticism."[31]

Lisa Gitelman, in her history of American and British printing houses in the nineteenth century, focuses on these sorts of "noncodex print artifacts," which made up about 30 percent of the work of printers, she estimates. She cites an 1894 list of types of "job printing," some of which was culled from earlier sources. A partial list shows us the stew of papery things writers might repurpose:

> Ball tickets, bank notices, bonds and coupons, billheads, bills of lading, bills of fare ... deposit tickets, drafts and notes, printed envelopes, election tickets ... labels, law blanks, leaflets, letter-circulars, letter headings, manifests ... pamphlets, pamphlet covers, passage tickets, programmes, price currents, policies, posters, railroad blanks ... wedding cards, and wrappers.[32]

These sorts of artifacts hardly ever end up in archives, and are therefore mostly unavailable to us today, unless they were put into an album or used to shore up a piece of literature.

Calendars appear on the full version of the above list, like the bit of calendar that served George Eliot for notes for a projected novel. The single-leaf, printed card, headed January 1876, with a grid indicating which days of the month fell on a Sunday, a Monday, and so on, was made by "Thos. De La Rue & Co. London," the same company that manufactured the album from Charlotte Brontë's school (see Fig. 14).[33] Since the company also produced diaries and other paper goods (playing cards, visiting cards, pocket calendars, and "companion memorandum books"), perhaps she received this for free as part of a promotion.[34] On the blank back side, in her characteristic purple ink, she jotted a list, headed "Mem.ᵃ" (see Fig. 15). Names of people and places are here—the Baronne de Ludwigsdorf (& Cousin Rosa), Scilly Isles, and Leicestershire Farm, for example—as well as descriptions of characters and their situations: "widow supporting herself by keeping

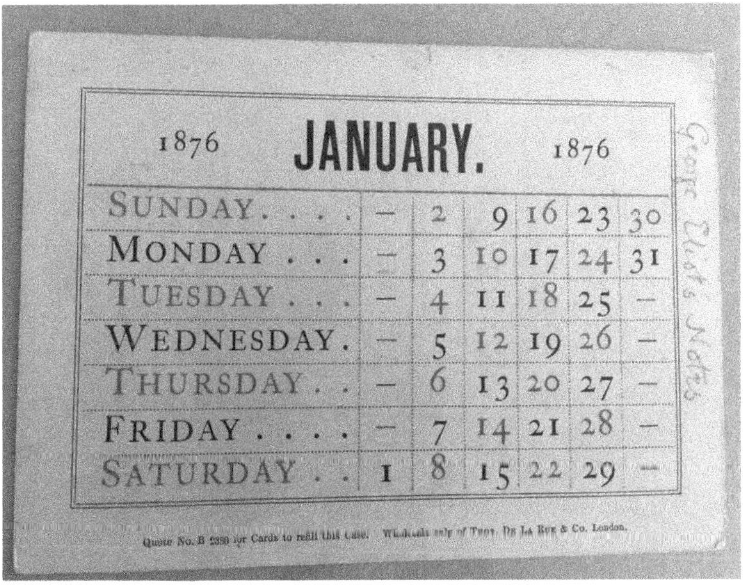

Fig. 14 Calendar card with George Eliot's notes for a novel on the verso. George Eliot and George Henry Lewes Collection, General Collection, Beinecke Rare Books and Manuscript Library, Yale University, notes 1876, GEN MSS 963, Box 23. By kind permission of the Estate of George Eliot

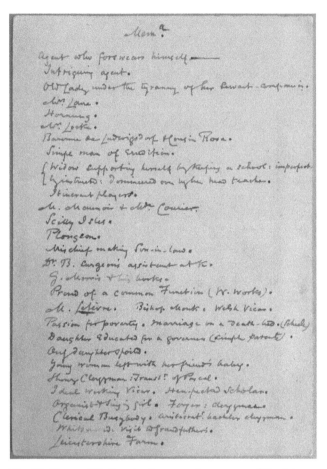

Fig. 15 George Eliot's notes for a novel, on verso of Fig. 14. George Eliot and George Henry Lewes Collection, General Collection, Beinecke Rare Books and Manuscript Library, Yale University. By kind permission of the Estate of George Eliot

a school: imperfectly instructed: domineered over by her head teacher"; "old lady under the tyranny of her servant-companion"; "showy clergyman: translator of Pascal"; and "young woman left with her friend's baby." We can only speculate as to why she wrote these ideas here and not in one of her many notebooks. Since Eliot by this time had become wealthy from her writing, paper wouldn't have been especially dear for her. One possibility: it was hung up somewhere, like Reade's large cards with details for his novels, perhaps above a desk. Or was it kept in a drawer, box, or pocket (her leather blotter had a large one) where other notes for potential novels, poems, and essays were kept? It's possible the novel would have been set in the year 1876 (and maybe partially in the month of January), so plotting out the various days of the week would make the calendar card helpful.

In a related act of adding text to an object ostensibly meant for some other purpose, Charlotte Brontë penned the six-line poem "I never can forget" on a small piece of pink card (measuring approximately 1 by 1½ inches), which she then pasted to the middle of a paper pattern, probably for a coin purse, and framed with penciled lines.[35] The undated poem is similar to conventional verse put in friendship albums or printed in keepsake albums, and Charlotte probably gleaned it from elsewhere and wrote it here.[36]

> I never can forget
> The time may pass years may fly
> And every hope decay and die
> The distant shore yet still my heart
> From love and thee can never depart
> I'll bless the hour when first we met
> For thee I never can forget.

This statement of hopeless, everlasting love reads like a dispatch from an Angrian tale of passionate (often adulterous) romance. The pattern has four flaps that fold, shutting in the poem at its heart, and a tab can be pushed through a cut-out to secure it further. As with the miniature books, this book-like object, with "covers" that close, has a secret quality, as if this ardent avowal needs to be sealed up and hidden away. The text is crafted in and onto its setting, making it a unique kind of "publication," with a narrative embedded not just in the text but in its very material. It reminds us of the much later "poem objects" created by André Breton, which bring together written text and pasted material.[37] While today this artifact is valuable as a poem on paper, in the past, before Brontë became a famous writer, it was of use to make a purse, with the scribbling an unimportant detail. Such details—with either the material support or the text being superfluous—can be threatening because of their "tendency to subvert an internal hierarchic ordering of the work of art which clearly subordinates the periphery to the center, the accessory to the principal, the foreground to the background," as Naomi Schor remarks.[38] The question arises: what then takes precedence, the work of art or the handicraft?

Emily's tiny bits of poetry manuscript also hold these qualities of both ready-to-hand waste and possibly significant choices. A small fragment of light-gray cardboard, measuring 3 by 1½ inches, clearly ripped off from a larger piece, serves for Brontë's undated poetic fragment, "She dried her tears and they did smile," about strong emotion kept secret inside of the body.[39] As a total "scribal object" (a phrase used by Virginia Jackson to describe Emily Dickinson's poetry manuscripts), the work has an extra heft with its thick substance, more like a chip than a piece of paper.[40] She tore a 3½-inch square from a piece of black-bordered mourning stationery, probably left over from when her Aunt Branwell died in 1842, for "A.S. Castlewood," dated February 2, 1844.[41] The theme of the six quatrains, about the dark night of the soul, fits well with its housing (although so many of Emily's poems would work on mourning paper).[42] The last two quatrains give a flavor of the whole:

> Dark falls the fear of the despair
> On hearts that drink of happiness
> But I was brede [sic] the mate of care
> The foster child of sore distress
> No sighs for me no sympathy
> No wish to keep my soul below
> The heart is dead since infancy
> Unwept for let the body go

The alliteration of "dark" and "despair" on the first line above, then echoed later by "distress" and "dead," are finally echoed in the paratextual black border of the paper. Further emphasizing this sense of the end of the end, on the verso Emily wrote "my task is done."

The examples explored so far have mostly involved using blank or printed paper scraps for writing (or having one's writing become a kind of domestic object or binding, as Brontë, Lewis, Tennyson, and others feared), but now I want to turn to deliberate text on text, or reusing an already-written-on manuscript or a published book (even one's own), for more writing. Robert Louis Stevenson did this with his own manuscript, penning a letter to his cousin and close friend Bob Stevenson on the back of draft pages from an early version of *Strange Case of Dr. Jekyll and Mr. Hyde*.[43] "Excuse the use of ancient scraps of MS; I have no other paper here," Stevenson wrote in the letter, although the scraps couldn't have been more than a few weeks old.[44] Stevenson was known to be careless with his manuscripts and writings more generally—most of what he wrote he started but never finished—so perhaps he really didn't have other paper, as he says, although there may be an element of bragging involved here, as in, "I'm writing so much and have been for so long, that I have all sorts of old manuscript lying about."[45] Bob, who wanted to be an artist, probably read the backs of the two pages and wondered about the story. Most of this early draft (which varies substantially from the published story) is now missing, so the fact that he sent the pages through the mail as a letter is the only thing that led to them being saved. In a curious contradiction, because Stevenson considered these pages as wastepaper, superseded in his mind by the final draft, already completed by the time he wrote this letter, they could later be salvaged, something like an old book whose spine comes apart to reveal sheets used as stiffening agents, rarer and more valuable than what the pages of the book contain.[46] Gitelman comments that "paper is a figure both for all that is sturdy and stable (as in, 'Let's get that on paper!'), and for all that is insubstantial and ephemeral (including the paper tiger and the house of cards)."[47]

Old books and manuscripts were pulled apart to bind new books, filled-up ledgers many years later became ripe for scrapbook use, and attractively bound books no longer valued for their contents became notebooks. Virginia Woolf practiced the latter craft, at the very end of the nineteenth century, at a time when paper and books had become less expensive, hence Woolf was probably not acting out of thrift. In September 1899, she went to a curiosity shop in St. Ives with her brother Adrian and looked through old books, like "eternal sermons in calf clothing all mildewed and ink stained," with the intention of remaking one into a notebook. She bought Isaac Watts's *Logic* and explained why, in its repurposed pages:

> My work—the present volume, attracted my attention firstly because of its size, which fitted my paper—and 2ndly because its back had a certain air of distinction among its brethren ... Any other book almost, would have been too sacred to undergo the desecration that I planned; but no one methought could bewail the loss of these pages.[48]

She pasted onto some of its leaves her own pages of writing (including the account of visiting the shop to buy it), cut out other pages and attached her own sheets onto the leftover nubs (similar to how a guard book is used), and kept some of the original pages as they were. As Eliot did with her "Quarry for Middlemarch" notebook, Woolf stuck a small paper label on the front and handwrote on it "Warboys. Summer Holidays 1899" (see Fig. 16). This volume is a kind of hybrid object with palimpsestic qualities; she keeps

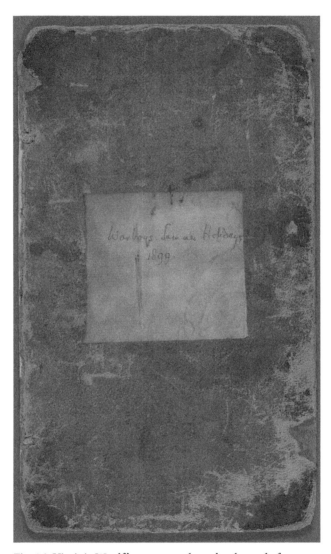

Fig. 16 Virginia Woolf's repurposed notebook, made from a copy of Isaac Watts's *Logic*. Henry W. and Albert A. Berg Collection of English and American Literature, The New York Public Library, Woolf notebook, No. 1, "Warboys, Aug. 4–Sept. 23, 1899"

enough of the Watts volume so that it is still that book, but then it's also her journal—both at the same time. One way to think of what she does here is the artistic practice of the *objet trouvé*—including a found object as part of one's original art, a practice linked to later avant-garde movements. She wants to author her text—a record of her thoughts and experience—on top of another one, a canonical text by a man about rules for reasoning properly. Woolf doesn't replace it so much as overwrite it, a kind of bold declaration of her own art, her own writing and way of being, onto an "official" version of how one should think. This was the start of Woolf's career in book making in its many forms, as well as a step toward her theories about gender and aesthetics. She wrote in 1903: "I collect books on all conceivable subjects and sew together paper books like this I write in—thick enough to hold all the maxims in the world."[49] In 1905 she obtained a silver-point press with her sister Vanessa and reported that on January 6, "all the morning I spent making a large paper book for the New Year. May its leaves bear fruit worth having!"[50] These activities culminated in founding Hogarth Press with her husband and printing her own experimental novels (not to mention writing them). From early on, then, Woolf saw writing as also about paper and sewing together books, the text embedded in its materials.

Woolf was a fan of Emily Brontë and *Wuthering Heights*, and perhaps she was thinking of the character Catherine when she filled up Watts's *Logic*.[51] Catherine tears up religious tracts, and she pens her diary and doodles in books of sermons—deliberate defiance against patriarchal religious oppression (represented by these didactic books she was forced to read by her elder brother) by placing on top a girl's story of rebellion.[52] Brontë's own writing on paper already holding text (or drawings) is harder to assign meaning to. A number of her one-sheet poetry manuscripts show evidence of reuse in that she has scribbled something unrelated upside-down or sideways in the margin or in a blank space, often in a different sort of hand (larger or in cursive rather than tiny print) and with a different implement—pen or pencil. A striking example is a messy sheet, measuring about 3¾ by 4½ inches, that holds four separate poems (or poem fragments) and also a list of Gondal characters with their ages and physical descriptions.[53] The leaf is dirty and grubby, especially along its folds, reminding us of paper's absorbency, its ability to hold onto traces of the fingers it comes into contact with. One side is mostly filled with the poem that begins, "yes holy be thy resting place," written in pencil in small print. On the verso, the four-stanza "It was night and on the mountains," in black ink and minuscule print, starts at the top and takes up about a third of one side. Upside-down to this, also in black ink and small print, is the list of Gondal names, at the very bottom (or top, when turned right side up), filling less than a quarter of the sheet. Under this list, in a larger, more flowing hand and in pencil, are two one-stanza poems, written at a slant, taking up about half of the middle of the sheet, and partially covering the last lines of "It was night and on the mountains." These two poems, "Had there been falsehood in my breast" and "I gazed upon the cloudless moon," are upside-down to that poem, and the first one is dated July 28, 1842—the only date on the sheet. Three deep, slanted folds are carefully placed so that the Gondal list and the two penciled poems can be separated from one another and foregrounded, depending on which folds are utilized. It's impossible to say what was written first, why they share a sheet, and how the folds matter. What can be said is that this is a multi-dimensional artifact, to be turned around in the hand, and to be folded to make it into something like a book, with more text on the "inside."[54] And that, perhaps, the poems (and the Gondal list) mean something more because they share a sheet; they gain something by being next to, on top of, on the other side of.

Brontë took other bits of paper that already had writing or scribbles on them and composed lines of verse on the blank side. One torn-off, 2½ by 1½-inch corner on which she scratched out in messy pencil two undated verse fragments—"Upon her aching breast" and "I gazed within thine ernest [sic] eyes"—has "domestic business" written on the verso in someone else's large, cursive handwriting, in ink, probably written either by her father or her Aunt Branwell.[55] The contrast between the texts on the front and back of the leaf is sharp. The heading for a workaday list, perhaps of things purchased for the house, servants' wages, or a shopping list, appears on one side; on the other, fierce emotions. The speaker of the second fragment gazed in those eyes and "read the sorrow brooding there / I heard thy young breast heave with sighs / And envied such dispair [sic]." Does she envy the sorrow there because she is feeling bored, stuck as she is doing domestic business?[56] Other scraps have more playful scribblings on their verso, such as "Tis moon light summer moonlight," with the pencil tracings of a compass, not to mention, just above the first line of the poem, a doodle of what appears to be a creature whose body is a coiled spring.[57] Doodles on versos and blank spaces abound on Brontë manuscripts, including a man's face on the fair copy of *Jane Eyre* Charlotte sent to her publishers.[58] Many figures adorn the back of Emily's "That dreary lake that midnight sky," for instance, including what looks like a self-portrait, in which she draws herself, characteristically, from the back, seated, looking out a big window at a mountainous landscape.[59]

In a move similar to what she has her character Catherine do when she wrote *Wuthering Heights* a few years later, Emily scavenged a large sheet with a section of a reading from the *Book of Common Prayer*, for the Fourth Sunday of Advent, roughly translated into Latin. This passage from the Gospel of John, chapter 1, verse 19, is handwritten in ink in what appears to be Emily's own hand. She then cut the sheet into smaller parts (probably four) and wrote on the verso of one section the poem "And like myself lone wholey [sic] lone," and dated it February 27, 1841.[60] In the incomplete snippet on the verso, John the Baptist is being questioned about whether or not he is the prophet, and he denies it. Emily cut it off so that it ends with, "What do you say about yourself?" His answer begins, "I am the voice of one calling in the wilderness." This has a strange resonance with the poem Emily wrote on the other side about a chained bird moaning for "liberty," to "soar away / Eternally entirely Free—," like the speaker, who also asks "for nothing further here / But my own heart and liberty." Such sentiments appear again in *Wuthering Heights* with Catherine's desire to leave her material self behind and die into the realm of nature, retiring from the "shattered prison" of her body and escaping into that "glorious world," being finally "really with it, and in it."[61] The poem works in some ways against the sacred writing on the verso and its patriarchal canonicity; it's the sort of text she has Catherine trying to escape by overwriting and ripping apart. Yet, at the same time, the questioning nature, the crying out from the wilderness, fits the mood of the poem on the back.

Emily may have had some belief in the talismanic properties of paper, which would give her salvaging added meaning. Carlyle's pronouncement about paper built on the past lives of things gives it a ghostly quality, as if it carries these spirits in it. Joanna Drucker points to the long history of magic ascribed to written language "in which the swallowing, burning, or bodily application of spells and incantations produces unaccountable effects."[62] For Charlotte Brontë, paper had this sort of enchantment, released not only by writing on it but also by burning, folding, and tipping it into published volumes. She enacted an obscure ritual—some form of bibliomancy—by taking a slip of paper, scribbling the names of Charles and Arthur Wellesley, her fictional alter-egos and pen-names, and burning it on one end.[63] Then she put it into *The Life of the Duke of Wellington*, a biography of the father of the historical individuals Charles and Arthur Wellesley. On another strip she recorded this ceremony, dating it September 25, 1829, then folding and keeping it.[64] Paper, in Charlotte's writings, is also a kind of nutrient. She tells her best friend Ellen Nussey, "your notes are meat and drink to me."[65]

She returns to this idea in *Villette*, with Lucy Snowe feeling that notes from Dr. John Graham Bretton are akin to "the wild, savoury mess of the hunter, nourishing and salubrious meat, forest-fed or desert-reared, fresh, healthful, and life-sustaining."[66] These letters—from a man she loves unrequitedly— have so much power that Lucy feels she must bury them to escape them (and to prevent Madame Beck from reading them). She buys a thick glass bottle from a junk shop, "then made a little roll of my letters, wrapped them in oiled silk, bound them with twine, and, having put them in the bottle, got the old Jew broker to stopper, seal, and make it air-tight."[67] Slipping the bottle into a hollow of an ancient pear tree, she places a slate over it, fixes it with mortar, and then covers the whole with soil. The buried letters become corpse-like, and she pictures them as a past that must be "wrapped in its winding-sheet, must be interred," in a "newly-sodded grave."[68] Brontë further imagines the paper as dead skin with the legend that an opening at the base of the tree is the "portal of a vault, emprisoning deep beneath the ground ... the bones of a girl whom a monkish conclave of the drear middle ages had here buried alive, for some sin against her vow."[69] Entombing paper might banish one's past for good, although it's also possible, especially in the case of a live burial, that putting it away preserves, lets it grow in strength.

Charlotte and Emily were well read in the gothic, especially Anne Radcliffe, and some of the plot devices in their work developed out of this reading, such as the catholic live burial just mentioned and, for Emily, the complicated story-within-a-story structure of *Wuthering Heights* with a handwritten diary found by a stranger at its heart.[70] Buried and found manuscripts and nested narratives play a central role in many gothic tales, notably Mary Shelley's *Frankenstein* (1818), Charles Maturin's *Melmoth the Wanderer* (1820), and James Hogg's *The Private Memoirs and Confessions of a Justified Sinner* (1824). In Maturin's novel, the many tales appear as material things—papers that molder, are damp, tattered, blotted, discolored, mutilated, turned into paper dolls, and often partially illegible, adding to the occlusion and chaos. A complicatedly interpolated story, *Melmoth* begins with a frame story of young John Melmoth finding a trunk in his recently deceased uncle's house that contains a manuscript written about his relative Melmoth "the wanderer" by a man who goes mad. Papery things and their lives and deaths come up often in the plot, such as legal documents used by the servants to curl their hair (again!) because they think keeping them around is bad luck, and notes swallowed after being read. Maturin relishes the material nature of writing, its connection to the vagaries of fate and mortality, and also its supernatural qualities. Stories and manuscripts decay and die as do bodies—they are lost, imprisoned, buried, swallowed, become spirits that haunt. Charlotte and Branwell both played with these ideas in their writings about Angria. In one of Charlotte's stories, "a manuscript copy of that rare work, *Autobiography of Captain Leaf*" kept in a "beautiful casket" in a "cabinet of curiosities" is "a roll of vellum, but much discoloured and rendered nearly illegible by time."[71] In the "ancient history" of the "young men," Branwell creates a scholar called Leaf (relationship to the above-mentioned Captain Leaf unclear), who must rely on manuscripts translated from the "old young men's tongue," but his tale is often interrupted because sections of the manuscript are missing or mutilated, and even though he looks in the "great libraries," he can't make them complete.[72] Hogg's *The Private Memoirs* also has as its central conceit that it is written by different hands on found manuscripts. The "editor" explains that half of it was dug out of the grave of a suicide, 100 years after his death, along with bits of his clothing and hair, all well preserved in peat. The papers, partially handwritten and partially printed (the writer of the memoirs worked in a printing press for a time, so he was able to print parts), are found in a "leathern case, which seemed to have been wrapped round and round by some ribbon, or cord, that has been rotten from it, for the swaddling marks still remained."[73] Hogg emphasizes repeatedly the materiality of his story, as if the novel is an exhumed body. The Brontës' work shared this belief in paper and books as embodied, mortal, and an integral part of the narrative written on and in it.[74]

Returning to Emily's poetry manuscripts, I want to think further about why she made them look and feel the way she did. These are, palpably, poems made using the hand to do more than write with pen or pencil: composition included cutting, ripping, doodling, and drawing. Kevin Jackson calls this sort of practice—the way one puts together a piece of writing—a "craft routine," and Brontë's was especially odd.[75] With some of these manuscripts, she tore the edges of the page to fit exactly around the already-copied poem, removing any margins.[76] With others, she packed her words onto a page too minute for her purposes, cramming on more until letters almost disappeared off the brink. She often loaded many short poems onto these minuscule leaves, crowding eight or more onto sheets measuring around 3 by 2 inches.[77] As already mentioned, she sometimes illustrated them, or doodled in their margins, with mountainous landscapes, winged snakes, flying birds, and more.[78] Others have odd symbols, like horseshoe and diamond shapes—a private language whose meaning is now lost.[79] Here "meaning appears to exist within, rather than in spite of, the sensuous elements of writing," in Juliet Fleming's words.[80] The physical matter of composition molded the text written on the page and, the other way around, the text influenced the aesthetics of the page. A way for her to get at the writing process as a form of three-dimensional making, these scribal artifacts are precursors to particular strands of modernism and the avant-garde, especially in what Peter Bürger calls their "submission to the material."[81]

The material qualities of Brontë's poetry manuscripts have received little critical attention. Never has the question Virginia Jackson asks of Emily Dickinson's manuscripts been posed of Emily Brontë's: is the "text of a poem separable from its artifact?"[82] Janet Gezari, who analyzes some of these fragments of verse in her terrific book *Last Things*, puzzles over the lack of critical writing on the early poems that were written on these single-leaf manuscripts. She calls for their redemption from "neglect as forerunners of high modernism."[83] Even feminists haven't restored them to view, she points out—in large part, she believes, because of their uniqueness. But Gezari mentions only in passing the manuscripts of the works upon which she lavishes so many lovely words. Derek Roper, in his introduction to the Clarendon edition of Brontë's poems, describes the physical nature of the manuscripts only in general, abstract terms, not ascribing any meaning to their material characteristics. Edward Chitham discusses some of these poetry manuscripts, but with little attention to their physical appearance and feel.[84] In Christine Alexander and Jane Sellar's *Art of the Brontës*, they include pictures of two drawings on Brontë's poetry manuscripts, but not the accompanying texts, giving us only a partial view of snippets that are not only visual and textual but also tactile.[85] In the same way, literary historians have largely ignored Brontë's crafted pages, packed in every part with meaning. It is worth thinking about what changes in the way we read Brontë's poems have resulted by removing them from their "historical text occasions."[86]

As already discussed, Emily's penchant for ripped-off corners of sheets—of modest allotments of writing surface—had to do, in part, with a desire to be thrifty with an expensive material. Yet this reuse didn't mean that the size and type of paper she used weren't a form of "extralinguistic" message.[87] In fact, restricted choice (and space) could enrich aesthetic decisions rather than limit them, an idea we find in many of Emily's poems. Numerous theories have been put forth to explain why the Brontës made their manuscripts so microscopic. Derek Roper and others speculate that since the worlds of Gondal and Angria began with the toy soldiers their father Patrick gave them, the manuscripts, which were written "by" the characters embodied in the toys, had to be small to match their size.[88] Another theory involves secretiveness, with the Brontë children keeping this world private among themselves by creating print too meager for adult eyes to read.[89] In terms of the poetry manuscripts under discussion here, the earliest were written in 1834, when Brontë was sixteen. While the toy bodies may no longer have been an aesthetic factor for her, Emily did continue to act out the Gondal story with Anne, and probably also on her own, speaking aloud and performing parts.[90] She records in a diary paper of 1845 that she, now twenty-seven, and Anne, twenty-five, took Gondal roles on a trip to York. Emily explains that "during our excursion we were Ronald Macelgin, Henry Angora, Juliet Augusteena, Rosobelle Esraldan, Ella and Julian Egramont, Catherine Navarre, and Cordelia Fitzaphnold escaping from the palaces of instruction to join the Royalists who are hard driven at present by the victorious Republicans."[91] Since a number of her poems are written "by" Gondal characters, the manuscripts themselves may have been props of a sort. Most of them are the right size to fit in a closed hand—and the larger ones show signs of being folded to palm size—so Brontë, in the role of a Gondal character, may have hidden them in her or his hand, in a land where spying, espionage, and secretiveness were rife. Additionally, if one were writing in prison, as so many Gondal characters are, then it makes sense to write on slender scraps—better to hide them from being taken away by prison guards, not to mention the scarcity of writing materials to be found in dungeons.

A further reason for Brontë's tactile awareness of the edge of her page (felt in the ripping and cutting) and the margins of her text (limiting them by filling them with doodles, or stripping them away so that they no longer existed) was that the gesture of peeling off was part of her creative process. Her manuscripts show what Drucker calls a "materialization of gesture."[92] Emily had a habit of periodically wanting to arrange her poems in "final" drafts (though they were sometimes revised into later and more "final" drafts). Early on, she did this by taking a fleck of a sheet and fitting as many poems as she could on the front and back, neatly penned in her "book print." Here was a sort of finished anthology or collection of her work (composed elsewhere first, perhaps in her head), and she may have had a number of these sheets at any given time that could be arranged freely, in a stack or side by side—more freely than if they had been written in a notebook or any sort of volume, since the latter forces a sort of chronology onto the collection, dictated by the order and the turning of the pages. As we saw with her notebooks, when she decided to revise a poem, she would usually destroy the first version either by severing it from its anthology sheet or crossing it out if it shared a leaf with one that wasn't to be "published" elsewhere, and thus needed to be saved. Therefore, as with the notebooks, the poems that exist only on one of the manuscript snippets can be seen, arguably, as a kind of finished product, a presentation of work, if for herself alone.[93] As Drucker writes (in relation to Mallarmé, but her words also apply to Brontë), her "attention to the space of the page *as* a space, and his [her] careful measure of the relative weight of words as forms on the page, activated dimensions of the visual poetics."[94] The fragmentary, rough-shod nature of Brontë's artifacts, her spaces, should be understood as a deliberate choice, part of the works' creative whole.

Let's consider one of these "final" poetry manuscripts, a torn fragment of paper, measuring about 3¾ by 2¼ inches (see Figs. 17 and 18).[95] The manuscript, designated E13 by C. W. Hatfield, works as a fine exemplar, since it is one of the anthology sheets, and poems were detached when they were copied out and revised into the first (1839 or intermediate) notebook. Also, at least one of the poems on the sheet is explicitly written "by" a Gondal character, lending the sheen of Gondal-land to the others on the same sheet. The two poems on this manuscript that were not excised—"I'm happiest when most away" on one side and "Weaned from life and torn away" on

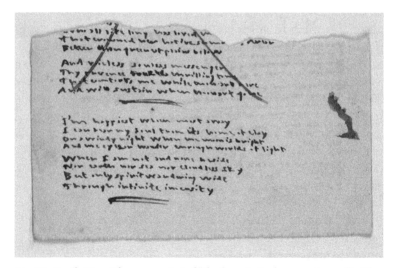

Fig. 17 Emily Brontë's manuscript of "I'm happiest when most away," with a few lines still visible from "To a Wreath of Snow / by A.G. Almeda." Henry W. and Albert A. Berg Collection of English and American Literature, The New York Public Library, E13

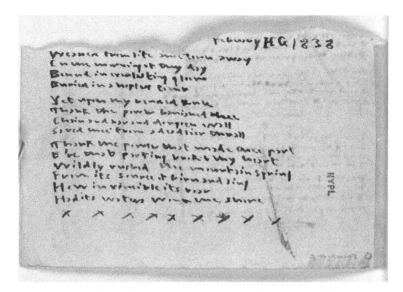

Fig. 18 Verso of Brontë's manuscript pictured in Fig. 17, with "Weaned from life and torn away." Henry W. and Albert A. Berg Collection of English and American Literature, The New York Public Library

the verso—exist on no other manuscript; these are the only versions that Brontë has given us. The paper probably came from a sheet snipped out of a notebook, which was then filled with poems. Eventually, its top half was cut adrift when some were "published" in the intermediate notebook. The poem that was once above "I'm happiest" can be identified, since she left some of its last lines on the page, crossed off. There was surely a poem severed from the verso, which would have been above "Weaned from life," but we have no way of knowing what it was. The few lines of the excised poem above "I'm happiest" had to remain because "Weaned from life" was already recorded on the verso, and it took up more space than "I'm happiest." The tops of some letters of the former have been removed—including the word "torn," which was itself almost torn. The date, "Febuary [sic] H G 1838," written on the upper, right-hand corner and higher than the lines of the poem, has been exactly traced around by the rough-edged boundary.[96] This whittling around the text—this attention to the interplay of writing and its papery setting—fulfilled Brontë's need to deliberately frame and gather her poems.

These three poems share common themes. The deleted poem, eventually called "To a Wreath of Snow / by A G Almeda—," was written "by" the character Augustus Geraldine Almeda, probably when she was imprisoned in a dungeon of the Northern College for several years.[97] Brontë dated its composition December 1837, in the 1839 notebook, so it was composed a couple of months before "Weaned from life." Given the Gondal setting of the poem just above it, "I'm happiest when most away" could also have been written "by" Augustus, and "Weaned from life" might have been written "by" her about another character, like Fernando De Samara, whom Augustus loved and then imprisoned in the Gaaldine prison caves.[98] Or they may represent particular moods or emotions that Brontë felt should be next to one another.[99] All three poems explore forms of imprisonment and intense thought about what lies outside of the prisons, a place where nature holds sway. In "To a Wreath of Snow," Augustus is in "a prison room" and the snow, a "transient voyager of heaven," blows into her "dungeon." It works as a "talisman" that pulls her out of her "sinking gloom" with its "silvery form so soft and fair / Shining through darkness" speaking of "cloudy skies and mountains bare." Here are the last two stanzas, most of which are still legible on the E13 manuscript:

> The dearest to a mountaineer
> Who, all life long has loved the snow
> That crowned her native summits drear,
> Better, than greenest plains below—
> And voiceless, soulless messenger
> Thy presence waked a thrilling tone
> That comforts me while thou art here
> And will sustain when thou art gone[100]

In the poem on the verso the speaker (Augustus?) addresses one "buried in a hopeless tomb," yet who should thank the power that banished him (her?) there, because it tore him away before his passion could develop like a mountain spring that wildly rushes "From its source of firn and ling / How invincible its roar / Had its waters won the shore."[101]

In sharing the same page with these other poems, "I'm happiest when most away" reads as a means of escaping yet another prison—or perhaps the same one—described here as the "home of clay." Being "most away" would be to let the "soul" be borne away "On a windy night when the moon is bright." Willing her own absence, even to herself, the speaker becomes "only spirit wandering wide / Through infinite immensity." Removing the other poems from the sheet brings these two closer together and eliminates any clear sequence between them. Depending on which side one reads first, the sequence ends either on the plenitude of "infinite immensity" or with the impoverishment of the removal of the movement of the wild stream.

Reading these poems together as a set of shared moments or experiences, we see that the self only reaches endlessness if there is a heavy restriction, whether the body, chain, bar, or dungeon wall. Or even just the edge of the page—if we keep ourselves attuned to these poems as part of the materiality of the snippets upon which they are written. Or—another way to think of this—if we understand the manuscripts with the poems on them as the wreath of snow or the windy night when the moon is bright, then it is the writing of the poems that works as the imaginative act that takes the speaker out of her prison. Then would the boundary of the page represent the end of the escape, with everything outside of it the prison house?

The boundaries Brontë pushed up against on her poetry manuscripts were those of her own writing or her own rending, as if each line contended for space against other lines and against the edges of the page. Another restriction or boundary can be seen with the size of her print. With Brontë's minuscule words, so very difficult to read, the writing concealed even as it revealed itself on the page. As we have seen, many of her poem drafts, both in appearance and meaning, have an inner, secretive quality, as if their very composition, the bringing of them out into the world, pushed them deeper inside. Kevin McLaughlin's words are relevant: "paper here is split: it is both a finite material support and a stage on which this finitude is exceeded. Paper is, then, the exterior surface, the material in the world, that repeatedly withdraws from what it is to support—a surface that is, as Derrida suggests, 'recessing' or 'retiring.'"[102] The gestures preserved in the physical make-up of Brontë's manuscripts are of whittling down the paper and the print, and perhaps even the idea, as if the prison encroaches and the window to freedom must be made smaller to escape notice. The carving up of the paper so that the poem just fits into its setting, or the packing of many onto a cramped sheet, also means that the whole is as small as it can be and still carry meaning. By limiting herself to the smallest of handwriting and the littlest of pages—*to these prisons*—she restricted, intensified, and concentrated as a means to increase imaginative expansion. A dual movement in Brontë's composition of poetry can be traced here. A transcendence comes from creating the poem—a way of escaping the home of clay, the prison house of the living body. But then a return to the material and the body is also required—through the cramping of the handwriting and the hand—and the sundering of the matter, the substance.

Brontë's lyric attenuation is her means of practicing the miniature sublime, or the finite sublime, cramming infinite riches into the little room of the poem and the page itself, with the other lines of verse compressing those written above, below, and on the verso. Brontë's need to contain her verse dug out the infinite from within tight constrictions. In her enlarged meaning through miniaturization, an idea that she repeated in different guises and colorings throughout her writing life appears. Gezari calls this Brontë's ability to consider "what it means to open oneself to one's own absence."[103] The more the text, or the self, disappears, the more meaning it radiates. This is imprisonment without imprisonment, or dying without dying, in which Brontë or her characters can find joy. This takes us back again to Catherine's understanding of death in *Wuthering Heights* as a new vitality and life—especially her body—as a prison. "I'm tired, tired of being enclosed here. I'm wearying to escape into that glorious world, and to be always there; not seeing it dimly through tears, and yearning for it through the walls of an aching heart; but really with it, and in it."[104] The ripping off of the poems represents a kind of violence—or perhaps a catharsis—as if the self or the body is rent. Or, to think of this another way, the torn edge implies that the writing is partial; that there is some larger, more complete expression or artifact that can never be fully seen or read, only suggested by its absence.[105] It is as if language is inadequate, as is the material, the written, the word. Composition and decomposition went hand in hand in Brontë's poetry, just as many of her poems and her novel are about disappearance unto death or obscurity, the threshold between death and life, and possible states of existence after death.

Her need to contain in order to create also involved the storage of these speck-like leaves. Brontë probably hoarded the poetry manuscripts in a little canister, just as Anne and Emily folded their diary papers, which were already quite minute, and put them in a tin box about 2 inches long, according to the early Brontë biographer Clement Shorter, who was shown the box and its contents by Arthur Nicholls, Charlotte's husband who inherited most of the Brontë manuscripts.[106] They folded their first diary paper four times to form a square, but a later paper, which is a bit larger, is folded into a triangle—both then the right size to fit in the box. We have a drawing of this now-missing box made by Emily on one of the diary papers itself. It sits on the table where Anne and Emily are writing up and drawing on that very diary paper, labeled the "tin box."[107] Roper believes that the poetry manuscripts were also kept in this box, or a similar one, which is likely.[108] Most of Emily's poetry manuscripts, excluding the three notebooks, are small enough to fit in a 2-inch-long box. Many of the larger ones—the biggest is 6½ by 3 inches—show signs of being folded into the proper size for storage in such a box. Tin boxes protected against fire, of course, but, as we have seen, aesthetic and even emotional motivations existed alongside the practical. The tin works as another limiting space—a prison or finite room. It also reminds us of a money box, with the hoarding of paper leaves instead of money—of poems that will not circulate. Or the tin stands in for a book, with the lid being the cover. A published book preserves writing, as this box preserves, yet Brontë's box also holds the qualities of a library—a space where texts are kept for posterity. Here posterity would have been, from Brontë's viewpoint, only the author herself. With this archive, the writer is the reader, the archivist, and the critic.

The fairy-sized box would have easily fit into Brontë's portable desk, which she called her "desk box." Arthur Nicholls pulled the tin box out of Brontë's desk when he showed it to Shorter.[109] These portable desks folded up and locked, so we can picture layers of containment—the wooden box with the tin inside, and then the scant sheets containing minute script.[110] The manuscript shreds at the heart of these bounded spaces feel buried, like corpses in coffins interred in the ground with just tombstones as markers, an imaginative place important to many of Brontë's poems and to *Wuthering Heights*. In the novel, Catherine's coffin, when unearthed and opened, frees meaning from flesh made paper-like from peat preservation. The preservation of poetry, then, comes from keeping it deeply buried, thus retaining its status of being solely an interior gesture. Gezari remarks that in Brontë's writing burial is a type of storage that conserves the power of the body, the memory, or the poem interred.

Emily may have thought of paper as something to add to the body, to ingest, or as a shred from the body, as intimate as a paring from her own skin. She carried writing into daily tasks, ones that tended to the body and its housings. A servant describes Brontë's scribbling on paper while ironing clothes: "Whatever she was doing ironing or baking, she had her pencil by her."[111] Brontë ends her 1845 diary paper by stating that she must rush off to her "turning"—picking out the seams of cuffs, collars, and entire dresses, reversing and re-sewing them, thus concealing the worn or dirtied side. She also announces that she has "plenty of work on hands," the "work" a reference to needlework. She includes writing in this list of tasks she hurries off to finish, probably an early drafting of *Wuthering Heights*, completed about a year later. In an earlier diary paper of 1834, written with Anne, the three sisters are in the kitchen. Emily and Anne have just peeled apples, with which

Charlotte is making a pudding. They mention that Sally Mosley is washing in the back kitchen in the same sentence as they describe the Gondals penetrating the interior of a new land. The servant Tabby grumbles that Anne and Emily are "pitter pottering" rather than peeling the potatoes, which causes Emily to exclaim, "O Dear, O Dear, O Dear I will derictly [sic]" and to exchange the pen for the peeling knife.[112] This takes us back to paper made from potatoes, reminding us of the sustaining quality of literary work, of the page and its embellishments. Moreover, potato and apple skins are barriers that keep each separate, and paring them makes them the same, causing them to lose their identity, their boundaries. Ingesting them rids them of form altogether, as they cross the boundary of the body.

Ingestion and defecation (nutriment and waste) were stages of the lives of much Victorian paper. Writers picked up these cast-offs and miscellaneous leftovers and found new ways to reuse them, transforming them into wholly singular performative works, at least for a time. Walter Benjamin's theory of the aura applies to these artifacts. Works of art, he argued, grow out of their setting in time and place and are unique to it. Impossible to reproduce, artworks are precious objects one must travel to see.[113] The manuscripts explored here sit in archives and have this auratic quality. Yet in the case of most of them, they were originally fashioned, at least in part, from waste, reminding us that they are probably only in a holding pattern, that the aura isn't forever lasting. Perhaps, horribly, the manuscript of Emily's second novel was cut up to curl someone's hair?

5
Crafting

> Probabilities are as various as the faces to be seen at will in fretwork or paperhangings: every form is there, from Jupiter to Judy, if you look with creative inclination.
> George Eliot, *Middlemarch*[1]

Emily Brontë's little poetry sheets make manifest writing as part of a continuum of handcrafts when the manuscript is looked upon as a material artifact. Cutting, ripping, folding, pasting, taping, pinning, and stitching paper were all means to revise texts and to shape books in the nineteenth century. But these same actions were also common in the practice of domestic crafts, especially those created by women. This final chapter will pick up threads from earlier chapters: the handiness of the authors under discussion, with George Eliot repairing worn notebooks with stitches; Anne Lister putting leather covers over the boards of her diaries; and Charlotte Brontë pasting a poem into a pattern for a coin purse, to name a few of many instances already detailed. Manuscripts, letters, and books with common crafts in their construction or repair studied alongside craft artifacts created by writers using ingredients usually associated with texts and the production of books take us further away from traditional ideas about "authorship" to more experimental acts, expanding conventional ideas about what a manuscript, book, page, poem, or story can be, especially when brought into a domestic scriptorium. One didn't need pen or pencil to compose text, as Victorian women knew. Embroidery on paper, pinpricks through paper, cut-out silhouettes, pincushions with text in pinheads, and needle-books inscribed or shaped like books littered Victorian parlors. Shadow writing was a device for reproducing text at home, as the novelist and naturalist Anna Atkins discovered when she handmade volumes using plants and photography, her words produced not with ink or lead but with chemicals, sunlight, and paper. Samplers with sewn words were a form of inscription so slow and laborious that the artists sometimes imbued them with the intensity of passion and meaning found at times with novels or poems. In some cases, however, the artistic process took precedence over the meaning to be found by reading text. Such handiwork evokes what Victoria Coulson calls an "aesthetic of the surface."[2] Often with these keepsakes, material texts, and handmade volumes, it is the gift between two people (or more than two) and the making of something together that holds the most significance, rather than a plumbing of depths. The needle, pin, and pen all matter here.

Cutting (and Pasting)

The fair copies (the ones sent to her publishers for printing) of Charlotte Brontë's novels echo those little books she made with Branwell when she was a child, her rolled-paper work on the tea caddy fashioned for her best friend, and the fern album she perhaps built after her honeymoon.[3] No earlier drafts of her novels exist, although two friends reported on her writing method: Gaskell, who saw some of these earlier drafts, and Harriet Martineau, who spoke to Charlotte about her work routine. Gaskell says that Charlotte scribbled with a pencil on small bits of paper "against a piece of board, such as is used in binding books, for a desk" in her miniature hand.[4] Martineau adds that Brontë's "first [draft] manuscript was a very small square book, or folding of paper," presumably similar to those Angrian productions.[5] While her fair copies are not tiny, they display complex scissor work, most notably her two final completed novels, *Shirley* and *Villette*.[6] *Jane Eyre* is by far the cleanest (although it does have a doodle). Unlike many of her contemporaries who delete sections by crossing them out, effacing them with dark ink, or scratching them off the paper surface (all of which she also does on occasion), Brontë most often cut away the bottom, top, or some middle part of a page and either left it like that or pasted on (or sometimes used a type of paper tape) part of a sheet, blank or with new text. In volumes 1 and 2 of *Villette*, she practiced the most visually radical of her revisions. She carefully snipped out, from inside a page, a word or a few words, and then just left it like that; the next page can be seen through the open rectangle. One could stick one's fingers through the gaps. These sheets with their small windows, their absences made present, appear much like other cut-paper crafts of the time, some made by Brontë herself. She scissored out patterns for lace collars, cuffs, coin purses, and needle-cases—such as a fan-shaped one, hand illustrated with a garden, urn, and fountain that was eventually owned by Elizabeth Gaskell's daughter Meta, who knew Charlotte.[7] None of these patterns took as much skill with the scissors as carving out words from the middle of a page, however.

The open-work craft-ship of the *Villette* manuscript evokes handmade valentines; paper dolls, houses, and theaters; paper-mâché; and silhouettes. In other words, considering *Villette* as a material object of its time carries it into a world of artifacts whose meaning comes from the visual and tactile rather than the textual. The sending of valentines became a commonplace pastime in 1840 once the universal penny post was instituted, and gear could be purchased at a stationer's shop and assembled, or made entirely from scratch. Hand-wrought paper lace in complex shapes and embroidery decorated valentines. Catherine J. Golden lists other stuff added to valentines: "feathers, shell, and metallic foils ... small bits of mirror, grasses, ferns, seashells, seeds, mother-of-pearl," and more.[8] Brontë's manuscript also calls to mind paper dolls, which sometimes ended up in friendship albums, like Miss Jane Edwards's, of Madeley, dated 1830–70. The dolls have watercolor-painted faces and separate dresses, all sewn into the pages (see Fig. 19).[9] Assembling two- and three-dimensional objects out of paper grew in popularity throughout the eighteenth and nineteenth centuries—dollhouses and flowers, for instance—made at home or store-bought.[10] Recipes for preparing paper-ware (eventually called paper-mâché, French for "chewed paper" and, when lacquered, "Japan-work") ran in women's magazines, beginning with the direction to "boil a quantity of slips or pieces of brown paper in common water, and pound it well in a mortar till it comes to a pumice, like rags pounded in the trough of a paper-mill."[11] The strips Brontë cut out of *Villette* would have been perfect fodder for paper-ware or the rolled-paper work she used to decorate the tea caddy she gave to her friend. In this process paper is deconstructed, taken near to its pre-existence as rags, before being forged into something new, such as needlework boxes.[12] George Eliot and Florence Nightingale both had portable desks made of paper-mâché, so "waste" paper became a base on which to write on yet more paper.[13] Silhouette cutting, practiced by professionals and amateurs alike, involved tracing the outline of an individual's face or an entire family sitting in a parlor, a type of pre-photographic portraiture, a marking of light and shadow onto paper to hold onto an ephemeral moment.[14] They were often put in albums, such as a ca. 1800 volume of white cut-paper designs pasted onto black pages, showing domestic scenes telling a visual narrative, now in the Victoria and Albert Museum.[15] Hans Christian Andersen composed stories using paper cutouts, such as his *A Fully Cut Fairytale* (ca. 1864), sometimes snipping figures—animals, humans, landscapes—out of already-written-on

Fig. 19 Hand-crafted paper dolls sewn to a page of Miss Jane Edwards's friendship album, dated 1830–70. The Jane Edwards album, © The British Library Board, Add 57724

or printed paper, such as letters and newspapers, or pasting figures onto printed pages from books or music sheets.[16] These works, like Brontë's *Villette* manuscript, rely on negative space, on what is missing, to make out meaning. When the paper object and the stages of its creation are the focus, the cut-out work of Brontë's manuscript pages tells both a story about the handiwork of writing and revision and a story of aesthetic presence. In other words, putting to one side the narrative conveyed by the text, the manuscript elucidates the cross-pollination between revision and tales made by snipping out shapes from paper to create visual messages, objects, doll bodies, and spaces.

Cut-paper decorations, toys, and silhouettes run through the writings (and lives) of the authors under discussion in these chapters, acting as metafictional commentary on the cut-and-paste craft of the manuscripts on which they are written.[17] Gaskell's novels mention many of these types of paper crafts, as Talia Schaffer has explored, such as Matty's spills for lighting candles in *Cranford* that are made of colored paper and "cut so as to resemble feathers."[18] In Gaskell's *Sylvia's Lovers*, when Philip and Sylvia marry, they have their silhouettes created by a

> wandering artist, if so he could be called. They were hanging against the wall in little oval wooden frames; black profiles, with the lights done in gold; about as poor semblances of humanity as could be conceived; but Philip went up, and after looking for a minute or so at Sylvia's, he took it down, and buttoned his waistcoat over it.[19]

Could Gaskell be making a self-deprecating joke with this wandering artist, trying to trace the characters on paper of his subjects, like a novelist would? In *Middlemarch*, Celia cuts out a paper man for the curate's children, calling attention to these types of gifts made by women's hands. Eliot did some cutting and "pasting" in the fair-copy manuscript of *Middlemarch*. While most of the many deletions and additions are done with a pen on the page, on occasion Eliot added an extra snippet of paper, cut out messily and written in her purple ink (whereas the main body of the text is in black ink), and stuck to the backs of pages with gummed wafers.[20] Celia's paper man also speaks to the novelist's work and materials more figuratively, in the sense that in *Middlemarch* Casaubon is something of a paper man, in his flatness, his inability to have an emotional, empathic interiority. In *Wuthering Heights*, "a fireplace hung with cut paper dropping to pieces" signals the decay of a house once cared for and daintily decorated, perhaps in the time of Mrs. Earnshaw (Catherine and Hindley's mother).[21] Did a young Catherine Earnshaw cut out these decorations, around the same time she was defacing her books by doodling in the margins and scratching graffiti into the windowsill in her bedroom? The paper dropping to pieces showcases the ephemerality of the writer's medium—as do all these examples—most poignant for readers today with the loss of so many paper materials related to Emily Brontë, including the manuscript of *Wuthering Heights*.

While in these novels the papery objects that are part of the plot stand in for the manuscript from which the novel is printed, with other material made of paper the influence moves the other way: book-construction becomes a commentary on the interiority effect a novel might achieve, a "place" the reader can enter into and dwell. Movable or action books (what would later be called pop-up books) are the most whimsical examples of these thick book-objects, and they proliferated in the nineteenth century.[22] The type closest to the cut-out work of *Villette* are the early "toy-books" made by Dean and Sons, the innovative publishing firm founded in 1800. In the 1840s, a series they began with *Dame Wonder's Transformations* has a picture of an "English girl" on the last page and each of the previous pages has a different outfit and a circle cut out for the face, so that the girl on the last page wears different costumes depending on which page is turned.[23] Such books were also handmade in imitation of these store-bought volumes, but with their own flourishes and inventions.[24] Peep-show books, with a hole in the front and an accordion shape that stretches back to create a three-dimensional effect with layers of scenes, seem to make literal the space and distance that a novel does imaginatively.[25] In the 1850s, Dean and Sons began publishing books that really did move when opened, with layers of pictures lifting up from the page architecturally or activated by tabs, levers, or ribbons.[26] Volumes with removable paper dolls and their clothing, or paper figures that could be slotted into different domestic scenes created in the pages of the book, share qualities with Victorian novels like *Villette*, as cut-paper objects and in terms of the world-making of the published novel when read, with its details, dress, and rooms filled by clothed characters.[27]

Stitching and Pinning

Needlework and other skills with cloth and thread inform manuscript, text, and book production, sometimes in surprising ways. Instead of employing paste or sticky wafers for attaching revised bits of papers, authors also wielded straight pins, ribbons, and sewing into the page. Marie Corelli fastened short manuscripts together with "little bows of silk ribbon."[28] Charlotte Brontë hand-stitched many paper artifacts, as we have seen with the little Angria booklets, but, later, she stitched together the few pages of a French essay.[29] Austen "pasted" with straight pins on her unfinished manuscript of "The Watsons," sticking them into patches of paper with new text and attaching them to the manuscript, thereby covering the original text.[30] Elizabeth Barrett Browning revised her 1819 poem "The Battle of Marathon," written when she was fourteen, by stitching on her emendations with thread—a "cut and sew" rather than "cut and paste."[31] Another poet who edited in this way was Dorothy Wordsworth; she composed verse in notebooks and affixed paper overlays with needle and thread or sealing wax—or sometimes both.[32] This type of revision is less permanent than Brontë's cutting out or off, or even, in some cases, the usual blacking out with ink, since the original text still exists in readable form underneath and can easily be reinstated by unpicking stitches (or unsticking wax or paste), like a Victorian needlewoman might do with an old dress to "turn" it—making it last longer by reconfiguring it so that the stained parts were hidden. In fact, librarians and curators often remove pins from manuscripts, since they cause rust and decay, and, in the best-case scenario, record where they had been and what they had held.[33] The archival researcher often encounters the tell-tale holes and rust marks of where straight pins once were, such as in Gaskell's handmade music books and George Augustus Sala's commonplace book, with the remnants of now-disappeared pins piercing and staining the page.[34] The ghostliness of these now-missing attachments echoes the haunting return to the cloth that paper once was—when it is sewn newly, paper to paper. Lothar Müller traces this confluence: "When woven products die, they are resurrected in a new form" to become paper, and thus weaving becomes a "partner in paper's potency."[35] Andrew Stauffer encourages us to "go beyond 'texts' as linguistic forms and to think about texts as something closer to textiles, woven creations of material and semantic content."[36] Taking this in the other direction, from textile to paper, Dard Hunter in his history of papermaking explores how "wove" paper earned its name because the brass screen used to form it was woven on a loom like cloth, making the paper it created look like fabric.[37] Another stage along this circular route—from rags to paper to book to rags—is clothing being used like paper, as when a man scribbled something in pencil on his starched shirt cuffs, which would disappear when they were washed.[38]

Stitching into (and pinning) paper wasn't only an editing device; it was also a means to repair and, in some cases, beautify it—as a craft. Charles Dickens describes an old book, in *David Copperfield*, "in rather a dilapidated condition ... with divers of the leaves torn and stitched across."[39] It seems likely that Dickens himself had seen, or perhaps owned, just such a book and brought it into his fiction. When Charlotte Brontë wrote love letters to the married Professor Heger, he ripped them into pieces, but his wife sewed them back together again with a loose baseball stitch.[40] Embroidery in paper was a handicraft practiced mostly by women in the eighteenth and nineteenth centuries.[41] It can be found on bookmarks and in friendship albums, such as Eliza Threipland's album, which has colored threads sewn into a page, forming flowers held in a horn with added pinpricks part of the design.[42] Eliot's close friend Sara Sophia Hennell took black thread and stitched an "A" and an "x," a kind of secret signature, into a letter she sent to Eliot.[43] In her letter in reply, Eliot said that she kissed the device "again and again and shall put it in a sacred place."[44] Occasionally, marginalia took the form of sewing into the edge of the page to mark a passage.[45] Pinpricks in paper were another craft often practiced by women, not only in friendship albums but also on bookmarks and on such paper things as needle-books, calling to mind Austen's use of pins for editing but also pins used in dressmaking.[46] Charlotte sewed together a small needle-card, made with paper covers, ribbon edging, and pink tissue paper, with thick cloth on the inside for the needles to be stuck into, for a friend named Eliza Brown.[47] Adorned with vines and flowers formed from pinpricks in the paper covers, it may have once held embroidery. Needle-cases crafted from paper and looking like little booklets with pages often became gifts handmade for the creator's close friends.[48] In terms of pure craft—setting aside text and narrative—these needle-books utilized similar skills and desires for a visually appealing object as Marie Corelli did with those bow-fastened manuscript pages.

Piercing paper with needle, pin, thread, or scissors emphasizes its porous qualities, its openness to permeation. Inversely, adding overlays, as we've seen with sewing or gumming paper on top of paper, thickens it. Part of a broader craft ethos, piercing and overlaying were often done with a sense of play and attention to the decorative. Returning to paper dolls, many store-bought sets were meant to be "dressed" with fabrics, in some cases included—in tissue, silk, or other fabrics—or with instructions for how to make the clothing at home.[49] Homemade paper dolls had clothing sewn onto them, and fashion prints in magazines were also dressed, called "tinseling," with metal foil, ribbons, leather, and feathers.[50] These artifacts sometimes ended up in albums, so, in effect, they became part of a book when attached to a page like elaborately dressed characters in novels, a paper Blanche Ingram from *Jane Eyre*.[51] Pictures or drawings of birds, treated similarly, had real feathers, glass beads for eyes, and actual grasses affixed to the page, creating the appearance of bird bodies coming off of the flat plane and giving the whole a narrative quality.[52] Sand pictures, a related craft, started with prints or drawings of buildings like cathedrals or castles, which were then decorated with glued-on sand. A house with trees and hedges all done in sand, for example, made for a friendship album, has this handwritten caption: "Drawn with Alum Bay Sand. This was the residence of the 'Dairyman's Daughter, Hale Common, Newport, 1844.'"[53] Fabric, feathers, sand—these are all means of "editing" on the page, of crafting paper and the book in unusual ways that attempt to bring domestic or natural effects to volumes, to plump them out with a material "reality." Schaffer comments on the kinship between such crafts and the one of writing: "Handicraft allows writers to work through a vision of themselves as makers: crafters of an item that might not survive, whose value is unfixed, whose circulation is uncontrollable, whose existence depends on worrisomely cheap and fragile materials, and whole reception is determined by the audience's sentiment."[54] This takes us back to both sand pictures and Austen's straight pins in "The Watsons," with their fragility and, from the point of view of Austen when she was writing her novel, the question as to their ultimate value and fate. With crafts like the needle-books and sand pictures in friendship albums, however, "value" comes from pleasure—in the act of making, giving, and showing. They draw attention to the potential pleasures of all work with paper, including writing novels.

Of these sorts of crafts, the one most linked to writing, narrative, and their production is needlework. Paper made from rags is more amenable to being sewn or embroidered than wood-pulp sheets, of course (not to mention that the pages of published books were sewn together). Yet, the adjacency of women's sewing work to handwriting, reading, and books was even broader and deeper than the editing, repairing, and handicraft already discussed. In historical and fictional accounts, women practiced needlework while others read aloud to them, so that sewing and consuming text went hand in hand. Women recorded in their diaries how, if they were reading alone, they would be writing in the margins of their books, but if they were listening to someone else reading, then they would work with the needle.[55] In Gaskell's *Cranford*, Miss Pole crochets while Mr. Holbrook reads aloud *Locksley Hall*—and Miss Matty falls asleep. Charlotte Brontë had a habit of reciting poetry while sewing with friends.[56] Nelly Dean, in *Wuthering Heights,* recounts to Lockwood the story of Catherine and Heathcliff while she does needlework, as if the tale grows as does the textile, the two emerging out of the same wellspring. Learning to write and learning to sew went hand in hand for girls in the nineteenth-century household, both seen as domestic arts.[57] Christine Bayles Kortsch traces the history of women's "dual literacy" in the "language of cloth and the language of print."[58] Gaskell taught her daughters to read and sew together, six stitches and one word every day, Schaffer tells us.[59] A young Jane Austen illustrates Bayles Kortsch's point that women writers "utilized two kinds of literacy, literacy in fabric (sewing and interpreting dress) and literacy in print (reading and writing)."[60] She made an embroidered cotton bag for her friend Mary Lloyd to hold a sewing kit (called a "housewife"), with this poem inside it:

> This little bag I hope will prove
> To be not vainly made—
> For if you thread and needle want
> It will afford you aid.
> And as we are about to part
> 'Twill serve another end,
> For when you look upon the bag
> You'll recollect your friend—Jany 1792[61]

Remember me when you sew and read, Austen says, as she might also have said about any of her published books. Another example of the intimacy of needlework with textual work: bookmarks made of materials like Bristol board—a stiffened paper punched with regularly spaced holes—were a backdrop for embroidered sayings, such as "Do not turn down the leaves but use me" and "Forget me not," and were often made as gifts.[62] These said: think of me while you read. Thus does text made with needle and thread serve to hold the place of page-and-ink text.

Embroidering a special bag to hold or protect a book, embroidering the cover of a book, or rebinding the book altogether in a handmade binding were means of treating the book as a beloved object to be adorned with handicraft.[63] The decorative surface of the book also has meaning in these cases, at times even overwhelming the substance on the inside and its seeming depth as a "place" to dive into, a plot to lose oneself in. Virginia Woolf, who had an early interest in bookbinding and letterpress printing, writes in her journal on January 15, 1905:

> Then began to read Eugenie Grandet in the 1s paper edition which I bought at Haworth Station, when I wanted to buy Charlotte Brontë! The cover got so torn in my coat pocket that I decided to bind it before reading it: so I cut it up, and sewed it strongly, and gave it a good blue paper cover, and put it in the press and it is now a nice looking and strongly bound book.[64]

The skill of remaking the book-object—that sadly doesn't hold Charlotte Brontë (the slippage between the author's actual person and her fictional writings is interesting)—replaces, at least initially, the experience of reading the inside of the book. Hand-embroidered book bindings have a long history, stretching back to the thirteenth century and earlier and becoming especially popular during the Tudor period. Princess Elizabeth in particular embroidered various religious books in the 1540s.[65] Margaret D. Stetz tells the story of George Egerton (born Mary Chavelita Dunne) rebinding a copy of her own work, *Keynotes* (1893), in green satin, hand-embroidered with purple and lavender thread to form a "G.E." (the initials of her pseudonym). She added comments in the margins and gave it as a gift to her publisher and friend John Lane—an odd act of self "re-publishing."[66] In George Eliot's *Scenes of Clerical Life*, we find local women coming together to re-cover books for the Lending Library with black canvas and to discuss goings-on about town—book binding and gossiping are linked activities. Not surprisingly, given their centrality to the craft ethos, friendship albums often had hand-embroidered covers, such as a miniature one bound in silk and sewn flowers that belonged to Julia P. Wightman.[67]

The textiles utilized for book binding were, at the start, "dress materials," Michael Sadleir argues, thus linking book making to dress making. He even speculates that the popularity of patterned fabrics for binding volumes may have originated in Edith and Kate Southey's rebinding of books belonging to their father, the Romantic poet Robert Southey, which were then seen by many visitors to their home.[68] The Southey sisters took volumes in his library with paper covers that had become shabby and worn and rebound them in fabrics from their own and their friends' cast-off dresses, including those of Sara Coleridge (the daughter of Samuel Tayler Coleridge) and Mary and Dora Wordsworth (the wife and daughter of William Wordsworth) (see Fig. 20).[69] Dora followed suit by binding her friendship album in old dress material, blue silk with a brown design of flowers.[70] The Southey sisters did this with over 1,000 of their father's books, and he called them his "Cottonian Library," a humorous reference to Sir Robert Cotton's seventeenth-century collection, which became the foundation of the British Museum. His son Charles Southey wrote that the "ladies would often suit the pattern to the contents, clothing a Quaker work of book of sermons in sober drab, poetry in some flowery design, and sometimes contriving a sly piece of satire at the contents of some well-known author by their choice of its covering. One considerable convenience attended this eccentric mode of binding,—the book

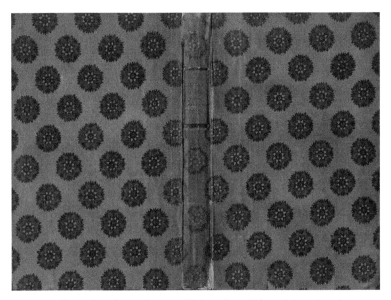

Fig. 20 Volume handbound in an old dress by Edith and Kate Southey. John Constance Davie, *Letters from Paraguay* (G. Robinson, 1805). Rare Books, Special Collections and Preservation, River Campus Libraries, University of Rochester, Rochester, NY

became as well known by its dress as by its contents, and much more easily found."[71] Said another way, there is something subversive in these daughters' re-embodying of their father's books, utilizing a kind of craft re-possession that emphasizes ordinary domestic work—sewing, making and remaking dresses—over (and placed over) patriarchal knowledge and influence.

Surface Language

Binding books with one's dresses, and those of friends, wraps texts in the domestic arts, with an emphasis on embodiment and work done collectively. Another aspect of these arts and crafts that gives text a different kind of presence involved neither ink nor paper. Readable textile art carries us away from ordinary writing and publishing meant for a reading audience and toward a space where texture and process matter more than textual meaning. For instance, pincushions with pins spelling phrases or initials were popular handmade gifts between women. One made these "sticking pincushions" by inserting the pins so that the heads formed phrases like "ever true to you" or "ever love the giver."[72] In *Villette*, Lucy Snowe makes a pincushion for her godmother Mrs. Bretton. Years later, after Lucy collapses on the street and wakes up in a room she doesn't recognize, this pincushion appears as a strange ghost from the past. "Made of crimson satin ... and frilled with thread-lace" with the letters L. L. B. formed in gold beads, Mrs. Bretton's initials, the keepsake leads to Lucy reforming ties of friendship and love, lost to her for many years.[73] Women learned to sew their initials or names into their clothing, called "marking," usually as a means to retain ownership if their possessions went astray. A record of the many things Charlotte crafted still exists, including in some cases the things themselves, such as her handkerchief with "Charlotte" embroidered on it and suede boots with her initials, reminiscent of inscriptions in books that say things like "Charlotte Brontë, her book," but with needle and thread rather than pen and paper.[74] Eliot shows an extreme self-identifying with one's textiles in *The Mill on the Floss*, when the Tullivers go bankrupt and must give up their possessions. Mrs. Tulliver mourns the loss of her many things:

> "To think o' these clothes as I spun myself," she went on, lifting things out and turning them over ... "and Job Haxey wove 'em, and brought the piece home on his back ... And the pattern as I chose myself—and bleached so beautiful, and I marked 'em so as nobody ever saw such marking—they must cut the cloth to get it out, for it's a particular stitch. And they are all to be sold—and go into strange people's houses, and perhaps to be cut with the knives, and wore out before I'm dead."[75]

It's almost as if cutting out her initials, stitched in permanently, like indelible ink, is akin to cutting her skin. Using hair for needlework, including marking, carried the body even more directly into this sort of "writing." Brontë has passionate, adulterous women in two of her early stories embellish handkerchiefs for their male lovers with their own hair, both with a coronet and, in one, with the name of the maker—"Agathe"—underneath.[76] These were meant to be erotic gestures, with the intricate difficulty of the embroidery part of the intensity of the gift. A sort of magic was ascribed to sewing certain words and shapes, such as in the case of the servant Jenny in *Cranford*, who fears being attacked until she "had sewed two pieces of red flannel, in the shape of a cross, on her inner garment."[77] Gaskell doesn't comment further on this superstitious act, but it seems like a sort of prayer for protection, similar to wearing a cross pendant around the neck. The extra effort it takes to hand-sew it might increase its efficacy, as a kind of work-like incantation, to protect the body of the wearer.

More elaborate instances of sewing symbols and text rather than handwriting them—and the time and care that it could take—gave them an extra layer of meaning, especially a gendered one.[78] In Samuel Richardson's *Clarissa*, the title character prepares for her death with many elaborate performances, including keeping her coffin in her room and using it as a desk, inscribing it, giving away her books and embroidery to favorite friends, and creating her will. The preamble to the latter, "written on a separate paper, was stitched with black silk."[79] This text (and textile) states that she is of sound mind, proven in part by the many years she has been working on her will. Clarissa doesn't explain her choice of needle and black silk over ink, but this lugubrious and slow process adds to her general worthiness—her serious, dutiful preparation for dying—and the melodramatic tragedy of her rape that (somehow) must lead to her death. Richardson may have been thinking of the Greek mythological character Philomela, the daughter of the King of Athens. Raped by her sister's husband, who then cuts out her tongue, she weaves her story in an embroidery and sends it to her sister. Procne, the sister, then pays back her husband by murdering their son and serving him the flesh for dinner. Eventually Philomela is turned into a nightingale. Embroidered writing carries a fury and power leading to action that ink-and-paper communication might wish to have.

Or perhaps Richardson was thinking, more simply, of the sampler, the sort of thing girls made during his time and later. The sampler represents an even closer connection between sewing and literacy, since it taught girls different fonts and ways of arranging words on a "page." While for much of its history the sampler was a collection of patterns and techniques professional needleworkers, often male, made to display work to clients, by the late seventeenth century they were increasingly stitched by young girls as instruction and decoration.[80] Usually a form of writing—alphabets, numbers, religious and moral quotations, and more—samplers had signatures and dates, like a manuscript or an inscription in a book. Samplers were, in one sense, an experimental form of creating text; they were attempts to think through how words and letters interact without ink or paper, to investigate from a different angle the material nature of composition. Text is textile: soft and made more slowly with the fingers and hands and then able to be felt by the fingers. But, in a different sense, sampler sewing was a rote commonplace activity, usually following a boilerplate pattern. This dual nature makes them similar to friendship albums—fashionable, ordinary, unoriginal. But they could also be creative and singular, the only trace left of a young woman with interesting ideas, now long dead.

This is especially true when the girl went on to become a famous writer, like Emily Brontë, who made two fairly unexceptional samplers. Her second and more complex one, produced when she was eleven years old, contains a good deal of text—quotes from the bible—and is signed "Emily Jane Brontë Finished this Sampler. March 1st 1829." This recording of the date and of the activity—*this* is what Brontë was doing on *that* date, finishing this piece of sewing—follows the habit in so much Brontë writing of pinning down when the performance happened. Emily's diary papers in particular, with drawings of the rooms she was writing in, along with date, time of day, weather, and more, continue this practice set up in the samplers, of saying "here I am, sewing (writing, reading, etc.)." Putting the samplers next to her manuscripts brings out the similarities, especially when her micrography, bordering on illegible, looks like stray threads worked into the page. Brontë often ended her poems with crosses that look exactly like cross-stitching, and her curling flourishes at the end of lines, as with the title "Gondal Poetry" in her notebook, match these flourishes in samplers.[81] Although *Wuthering Heights* is in so many ways not domestic (and neither is her poetry)—rather, gothic and unearthly—comparing samplers and manuscripts shows how they emerged from the same domestic scriptorium. Home crafts are cast in an avant-garde light when set next to Brontë's poetry manuscripts.

This cast light can help us reexamine other samplers of the period, especially exceptional or odd ones. Using human hair to stitch words on the sampler, for instance, showed off especially fine skill. If the hair was one's own (or from a friend or relative), then it was free, an important consideration for poor girls, for whom sewing materials, and especially writing materials such as ink, pens, and paper, were too expensive to be had. Jane Toller mentions a sampler with this stitched in black hair:

> Had I the world at my command,
> The treasures of the sea and land,
> And should I all the world bestow
> It would not pay the debt I owe.
> Eliza Yates aged 9
> Years, done at
> Sileby School 1809[82]

Musing on twentieth-century experimental pen-and-ink composition, Joanna Drucker could be commenting on this sampler: "Writing contains a record of time in the very accretion of marks which is both a record of temporal production and the trace of a time-based somatic gesture."[83] Here the somatic includes part of the body (hair instead of ink) as the text. The record of time includes at least three distinct periods: the cutting of the hair from the body, which stops its growth for good; the slow "writing" (sewing) of the text, a stretching out of writing time that makes each letter stand out in its material weightiness; and the reading of the text, which could include tracing it with the fingers.[84] Another somatic sampler, at the Victoria and Albert Museum, was stitched by one Elizabeth Parker in the 1830s. A long text, done in red cross-stitch on a white background, it represents an autobiography of Parker, a working-class woman living in Ashburnham, Sussex. She tells of being sexually and physically abused by her employer when she was working as a housemaid, paralleling both Clarissa's sewn text (she dies because she was raped) and Philomela's textile telling of her rape. Full of loneliness and thoughts of suicide, it breaks off in the middle of a sentence, saying, "what will become of my soul ...."[85] Why did she sew this rather than write it down on paper? In the same vein, why did the character Clarissa sew the preamble to her will rather than pen it? Parker begins her sampler with this sentence: "As I cannot write I put this down freely and simply as I might speak to a person whose intimacy and tenderness I can fully intrust myself and who I know will bear with all weaknesses." Bayles Kortsch speculates that when Parker states that she "cannot write," she means that she cannot write well, the sort of modest apology that many authors, especially women, begin with. Or was it, as Bayles Kortsch also observes, that she couldn't afford writing implements as a domestic servant, while stray thread and cloth would probably be readily available?[86] A third possibility: as with Clarissa's will, the sewing is a form of slow writing that becomes more significant as the hours it takes add up. It becomes an intimate form of speech rather than the colder, less embodied, writing with pen and ink.

Another sampler-maker from the period clarifies further the passion and distress behind the sewing of text, giving it an almost magical presence. Mary Frances Heaton was a music teacher admitted to the West Riding Lunatic Asylum in Wakefield in 1837 suffering from epilepsy and "delusions" of an affair with Lord Seymour, whose children had been her pupils. She remained there for thirty-six years, believing in the truth of her claims and rejecting the diagnosis of her doctors. One way she communicated her beliefs was through making samplers that detailed her experience, including

Fig. 21 Sampler made by Mary Frances Heaton, ca. 1852. Mental Health Museum, Wakefield, SR2015.323

an embroidered letter to Queen Victoria, to which she asks the Queen to "affix her seal," and another "To the British Government" (see Fig. 21).[87] Heaton ascribed a legal authority to her samplers, as if they were official documents or publications. She sewed patches and symbols on them, mimicking the seals and signatures of legally binding agreements of the time, like wills. Her belief in their efficacy, which was of course wholly unfounded, was poignant in a society where such texts carried no authority or legal weight. Her act of embroidering them signaled, to her, their official status as texts that could change real-life events, but to everyone else this signified their debased status as merely domestic ornament made by women (here, a "mad" woman). Framing the sampler as a kind of early avant-garde art (or conceptual art), we can see its "letters as potent forces for bringing the world into being."[88] Considering samplers such as these as part of a history of experimental forms of writing reshapes this history, moving it in a female-coded direction.

Shadow Writing

I end this chapter (and these chapters) with a contemplation of the artist books of Anna Atkins, who died in 1871 at the age of seventy-two. Her work brings together many ideas developed throughout these pages, and I want to revisit them here, treating Atkins as a kind of overarching case history. While her botanical volumes fit most readily into the history of albums, hence my brief discussion of her in Chapter 2, she also invented an experimental type of composition, and she hand-crafted strange and extraordinary books. But not only this, she also published four novels and a biography of her father. So, even though she is remembered (if at all) as a naturalist and a photographer, she was also a woman novelist, her productions part of literary movements in the middle of the nineteenth century. She began crafting photographic books in the early 1840s and her writing was published between 1853 and 1863, contemporary to late work by Charlotte Brontë, early work by Eliot, and the middle period of Gaskell. (Gaskell also experimented with the same kind of photography as Atkins, calling it "sun pictures.")[89] As with her contemporaries, she troubled the boundary between handicraft and the printed book.

Most of what we know about Atkins (née Children) comes from the biography she wrote of her beloved father after his death, called *Memoir of J.G. Children, including some unpublished poetry by his father and himself* (1853).[90] She published it anonymously, and her name appears only a few times in it, as part of poems her father wrote to her, making her presence as his child rather ghostly, and echoing Southey's daughters and their dresses binding his books. Atkins located and leafed through many volumes and other types of texts to compile this biography, and she is careful to record where—and on what—the bits of writing she reproduces were found. Drawing heavily on his letters, she also quotes from his marginalia, notebooks, travel journals, inscriptions on furniture and tombstones, and poems he wrote in friends' and acquaintances' albums and in his own commonplace books. Indeed, Children seemed ready to fall into verse on almost any occasion—birthdays, holidays, outings, gift-givings, job resignations, his friends' engagements (but also their dreams and the deaths of their chickens). Here is a characteristic poem, with the title "In the Mabledon Album, Whose Cover is Very Splendid":

> Album (loquitor)
> Like thee, fair Mabledon, with honest pride
> I boast a beauteous and a gay outside;
> May every page evince a nearer kin,
> And nought but purity be found within.
>
> J.G.C.[91]

He flirts lightly with the album itself, imagining its, and his own, interior might not be wholly pure. The care for its material nature (and his own, with his splendid "cover") he shows in this poem was reflected in his daughter's care for the papery traces he left behind. She tracks his travels through, in part, the places where he left his poems. Verse he wrote in an album at St. Leonard's-on-Sea appears in her biography, along with another at an inn at Capek Curig, Wales, and others, including one *about* the travel journal of her best friend and collaborator in book making, Anne Dixon, which he wrote after reading it. Long inscriptions on gravestones, some composed by her father, are recorded here, and even the dogs garnered memorial inscription that became part of the biography—for Floss, a spaniel, and one for another dog called Blucher. After Atkins married, her father wrote verse to accompany a locket in the shape of a miniature book that held his hair and that of his son-in-law—all to be worn by his daughter. It begins thus, "To Anna Atkins, With a Certain Volume Not Quite So Big as a Church Bible, From Her Old and Affectionate Father, J. G. Children, Halstead Place, March 16th, 1844," and goes on to pretend that the locket is a book and discusses its contents.[92] Hair inside a tiny book-shaped object becomes in the poem a real book with pages and plot. This interface between organic matter and the book ran through the family.

Atkins littered her novels with the sorts of book-objects and paper materials that peopled her world (and her father's). In *Murder Will Out* (1859), a man attracted to a picture of St. Geneviève hides it from prying eyes "between two blank leaves of his log-book, the edges of which were carefully fastened together by wafers."[93] He thus creates a hidden pocket inside a book, turning it into a container with some depth. In one of Atkins's books about the rich, fashionable life, written in a popular subgenre called the "silverfork" novel, she both admires and trivializes the leisured class, sometimes at the same time. A young woman in *The Colonel: A Story of Fashionable Life* (1853) attracts the proposal of a "slow minded" rich man using her album. The "huge green-morocco book, filled with every variety of calligraphy and design," is what draws him in, proving his dull-wittedness.[94] Are the readers of the novel, itself a bit like a pretty but vacuous album, meant to be compared to this dumb man? The creator of the album, Mrs. Villaroy as she's called after her marriage to the lover of her album, is labeled an "authoress" by another character, which she denies because "the utmost of my energies in literature have been one or two *pièces de société,* none of which have ever known the respectability of printers' ink."[95] Yet a rumor flies that she has written multiple novels, turning her into a quasi-authorial surrogate of Atkins, who published her books anonymously.

Atkins's book writing and book making started, however, with her experiments in photography in the 1840s. Through her father's connections as a scientist and as an employee of the British Museum, Atkins became part of a circle of early originators of photographic processes, such as Sir John Herschel and William Henry Fox Talbot, whose book *The Pencil of Nature* (1844) presented his invention of the calotype (at about the same time as Louis Daguerre, in France, developed the daguerreotype). Talbot thought his discoveries would be useful for authors—one of the plates in his book is a "facsimile of an old printed page"—to reproduce their writing, even their handwriting, at home.[96] This aspect of the early history of photography is often forgotten, overwhelmed by the more glamorous capability of freezing a moment of the visual field. But it was not forgotten by Atkins. She approached photography in part as a naturalist, who had perfected the art of drawing shells and of creating herbariums, collecting activities dear to many makers of albums. The accomplished and beautiful drawings she made of nature in its tiny particulars—the pale pink stippling on the back of a conch—remind us of the Brontë sisters' careful studies of dogs, birds, flowers, and trees.[97] In Atkins's desire to represent botanical species in all of their exact details, she mastered Herschel's cyanotype technique, which didn't require a camera or other expensive and unwieldy equipment. She brushed a mixture of ferric ammonium citrate and potassium ferricyanide onto an ordinary piece of writing paper. She dried the paper in a dark room, then arranged a spray of seaweed, fern, or feather on it and exposed it to the rays of the sun for a few minutes. Pin holes in some of the sheets show how she hung them up at some point in the process, probably for drying. Removing the plant and washing the print in water, Atkins had its shadow marked directly on the page—the part covered by the plant remaining white and the portions exposed to light becoming a rich blue.[98] She used the same plant to make multiple copies of a sheet, thus creating numerous sets to give to friends and associates to form books. Early in her process of fashioning these volumes, she hand-sewed together groups of prints before she sent them (or, in some cases, hand-carried them) to friends.[99] The traces of sewing holes and their locations on the sheets have helped curators reassemble plates that have been dis-bound and divided among multiple collections and archives.[100] Later, she sent them as individual sheets, in sets, and the receiver collated them and bound them.[101] She made these books for photography confrères like Herschel and Fox Talbot, who both owned editions of this album inscribed to them by Atkins, but also women friends such as Anne Bliss.[102] The multi-part series, called *British Algae: Cyanotype Impressions* (started in 1843), was the first book made entirely by photographic processes.

A form of painting with light, Atkins's photograms, as they were also called (or "photogenic drawings"), shared qualities with her shell pictures, as representational art of nature but also with inscription. When called photograms or photographs their linkage to writing becomes clear, with the "gram" and the "graph."[103] Atkins made her title pages, tables of contents, labels, and introductions with photogenic drawing, following through with Fox Talbot's ideas about photography as a means to reproduce writing (see Fig. 22). She sometimes did this by handwriting on a thin piece of paper, oiling it to make it transparent, then attaching it onto the photosensitive sheet. Exposed to light, the black, opaque ink became a white shadow against the blue. Other times she used delicate seaweed or ferns to form letters, and then photogrammed them, so that words are formed of the shadow of these ephemeral plants. The results feel ghostly in the sense that what is represented here is the trace of an original, as the sheets picturing the plant specimens are the trace of actual plants, now gone. The light passed around the handwriting, and that is what we see here—the absence of the letters and words on the recording surface. With other sorts of reproductive techniques, such as an ordinary photograph of a page with handwriting on it, one feels the representation of presence rather than absence. This is even true if the original sheet is now missing, as in the case of Emily Brontë's poetry notebook of non-Gondal poems (the Honresfeld manuscript), which was photographed and then lost in the 1930s.[104] In terms of Atkins's text, the referent is absence itself. (Even more ghostly is the occasional Atkins fingerprint caught in light and shadow on the edge of a print.) As such, there is a delicate sense of *mise en abîme*, in that the page with text always points

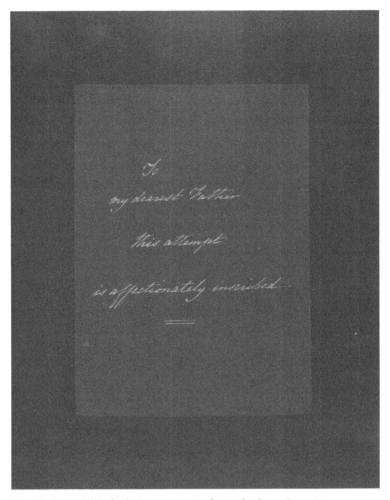

Fig. 22 Anna Atkins's photogram, part of *British Algae: Cyanotype Impressions*. Spencer Collection, The New York Public Library, Eng. 1843 93–440

to an original that is somehow on, behind, or in front of it, but never there. The letters sewn into a sampler go through the cloth, ordinary writing is ink or lead on top of paper (although perhaps absorbed into it); cyanotypy is the memory of text. This textual memory invites comparisons with Brontë's cut-out gaps in the *Villette* manuscript. While they both form "writing" from removal—of paper, plant, text—Brontë's work deletes to build, while Atkins overlays to keep the trace of the addition. In any case, they are both examples of the sometimes-complex art of writing, of the sensory manipulation of the materials of the Victorian maker.

Akin to friendship albums, cyanotypes became something women did together, and for a time they were largely female coded. After she finished the multi-year project of *British Algae*, Atkins began her collaborations with Anne Dixon (born Austen and the second cousin to Jane Austen), who was like an adopted daughter to Children and who lived with the Childrens and Atkins off and on. They made the 1854 *Cyanotypes of British and Foreign Flowering Plants and Ferns* together, moving from seaweed to a large variety of other plants. Another collaborative album branched out even further with photograms of feathers—peacock, emu, duck, parrot, partridge—lace, and skeletonized leaves. The photographer Julia Margaret Cameron, known for her pictures of famous people like Tennyson, made "My Printing of Ferns" in the 1860s using cyanotypy.[105] The important early women's rights leader Bessie Rayner Parkes (later called Madame Belloc), a poet and part of the movement for female suffrage and university education for women, created an album with peach marbled covers and calf spine and corners in 1848.[106] She included eighteen photogenic drawings of plants and of ribbons of lace. Writing to her friend and fellow radical Barbara Leigh Smith (later Bodichon), a painter, she enthused about taking impressions of ferns, and to her school friend Kate Jeavens she commented,

> I have been very much interested lately in photography, and send you some specimens of ferns and lace. The Photographic paper is easy to prepare but requires knack. If I had been a man I would have *such* a laboratory.[107]

She filled out the rest of the album with a travel diary of her trip to Antwerp and other destinations in continental Europe, turning it into a mixed-genre notebook. Her radical politics informed her experimental photography, as Atkins was a pathbreaking art-book creator.

While Atkins presents us with an obvious case for elevating material craft over textual meaning, the other authors considered here were steeped in the household arts of snipping, sewing, and pinning. Their paper work benefited from this intimate handling of matter. Some of these writers, activists, and ordinary women took traditional, gendered crafts and did something radical and new with them. Or, perhaps they made the conventional contribution, such as boilerplate samplers. Yet reading them in light of a masterful writer experimenting with materials like Emily Brontë locates them on a fresh historical trajectory. Celebrating the aesthetics of the surface, the decorative, the molecular detail, relegated so long to backwaters of literary history, places them front and center as artistic practices that in some cases developed into greatness.

Afterword

> Now, look at him, with his skin gone into lines and flourishes, just like the first page of a copy-book!
> Elizabeth Gaskell, "The Crooked Branch"[1]

Virginia Woolf admired, pulled apart, and made anew books, enchanted by their materiality, as we have seen throughout these chapters. However, she often cast aside the allure and nostalgia of dusty tomes, despite finding the tooling of the Watts's *Logik* that she uses to embed her "Warboys" notebook "resplendent today as a hundred years ago."[2] Returning to that day in September 1899—mentioned in Chapter 4—we find a young Virginia Woolf rummaging through bric-a-brac at a shop in St. Ives. She describes the stores' wares thus:

> The woman's husband scours the country for old books and old furniture of all kinds; and the results of his book finds—the modest libraries of country parsonages, sold by the widow to swell her slender purse—and chance outcasts of country gentlemen's bookshelves are all bound rudely together like so many bales of wool, and stacked upon each other in dusty corners. This, methought, was favourable hunting ground for an acute bookworm; but our minds are not married to that pursuit; we were invited to explore and untie these bales which with some difficulty we undid. … There were almost all books of the last century and in that degree to be reverenced. But such an undesirable collection I have scarcely come across. A London bookseller tries to redeem his eternal sermons in calf clothing all mildewed and ink stained by a few modern flashy novels.

Moving on to country bookstalls, she encounters "this class of work alone … an old volume of Cowper's poems, all bescrawled and underlined, otherwise I might have bought it … several remnants of family bibles—the title pages torn away from the discretion of a public book shop … a good old copy of Xenophon, possessed by three generations of Hoskings, who studied it from the year 1705 at University College, Oxford father and son and grandson."[3]

The family bibles have lost their front pages with a family's record of births, deaths, and marriages; the marks of reading so treasured by historians today make a book, to Woolf, besmirched. The inscriptions, presumably on the flyleaf, made by the generations of Hoskings, stir only mild interest in Woolf, while scholars study these traces of repeated use and reuse.

Similarly to what Woolf does among those piles of outcast things, I have sifted through a large number of heterogeneous artifacts, kept mostly in archives, throughout these chapters. But I, obviously, do not share Woolf's somewhat disdainful feelings toward old papery collections. In many ways, this book is the work of nostalgia, of a desire to preserve and understand creative processes—and the material evidence of them—mostly disappearing today. As I mentioned in the Introduction, my feelings share qualities with Jacques Derrida's "archive fever": a "repetitive, and nostalgic desire for the archive, an irrepressible desire to return to the origin, a homesickness."[4] Our time is very different from Woolf's, of course, and she functions as a transitional figure, bridging the nineteenth and twentieth centuries both in her lifetime and in her insights about nineteenth-century authors. It has become increasingly rare for writers to scribble in notebooks, write by hand on sheaves, and mark up volumes in their home libraries. Infrequently do we find pins, wafers, or sewn threads in recently created manuscripts, or even find paper manuscripts created at all. We no longer need to swallow notes. Not only are most writers and readers no longer invested in paper routines, but the remnants of these practices of the past are in some cases being destroyed. Andrew Stauffer laments the "de-accessing" of nineteenth-century books in libraries, arguing for the importance of unique copies with handwriting, pressed plants, and so much more, which can never be replaced by the scanned, electronic version.[5] His interest is mostly in anonymous or near-anonymous readers who left their marks on books, but even the paper traces of canonical authors—especially women—have suffered from neglect. For example, Woolf's "Warboys" notebook mentioned above is in many pieces at the Berg Collection at the New York Public Library. Shavings of paper are falling off the edges of the sheets, the spine hardly exists anymore, and the touch of the careful researcher causes the leaves to crumble into dust.

The decay and destruction of these volumes and paper pushes the researcher to want to surround them with theories and words, to try to hold them together. Walter Benjamin, also looking back on the nineteenth century, theorized that there is a heightened awareness and understanding of practices just as they are slipping away into the past.[6] Hence the fashion, in the last couple of decades, for book and media history and for the study of the materiality of writing and reading.[7] The increasingly dematerialized nature of writing, reading, correspondence, and friendship-album making has led scholars like me to think newly about the old culture.[8] Coming at this view of history from a different angle, Lisa Gitelman describes the term "manuscript" as a back formation, in the sense that "before the spread of printing there wasn't any need to describe manuscript as such."[9] While the artifacts I have studied in this book do not fit so neatly into this schema, we still might say that notebooks, friendship albums, marginalia, and the like only come to be defined as something odd and unique, and thus worthy of investigation and historicizing, as newer ways of doing similar things come into usage and mostly or completely replace them. They take on intermedial qualities when we look back at them from the vantage of a very different media environment.[10] Within the larger arc of the history of media (or print or paper culture), there are small, local histories to be found. For instance, the move from friendship album to photo album increasingly jettisoned handwriting, drawing, and even text. Another one: needle and thread became paste, and then eventually tape (later, post-its), as ways to edit manuscripts. A third example: inking out or scissoring out as a means to delete changed to using chemical such as liquid paper. And these examples are, of course, from before the computer and internet age. Carolyn Steedman sees the grammatical tense of the archive as the future perfect, "when it will have been."[11]

These papery things matter the most in what they tell us about the creative act—that is, once the texts they carry have been saved. More insistently, what can they tell us about masterpieces like *Middlemarch* and *Wuthering Heights*? Throughout these pages I have speculated, mused, and conjured this relationship in all of the ways I could think of. Of course it is the case, however, that ultimately mystery surrounds the making of these works, as it does the single calendar sheet that contains the notes for a novel that Eliot was never able to write. And the absence of any trace of a second novel Emily Brontë might have started before her early death cut off all creativity from that mortal body leaves us with silence. The mortality of paper, books, and the bodies that make and unmake them has been insistently central throughout these pages. I end this book on this note, and in the hope that it doesn't become curl-papers, line butter barrels, or become toilet paper before it has time to circulate, to be held by the warm hands of interested readers.

Notes

Notes to Introduction

1. Gaskell, *Cranford* (Broadview, 2010), p. 193.
2. Harriet Martineau, for instance, used brads (sometimes called split pins or eyelets) to hold together the fascicles of her 1849 holograph manuscript of "The History of the Thirty Years' Peace, 1816–1846, Book III," Pforzheimer, MISC 0658. The other types of fasteners mentioned here will be discussed in Chapter 5 and elsewhere.
3. This book builds on the work of many others, especially Leah Price's *How to Do Things with Books in Victorian Britain* (Princeton University Press, 2012); Talia Schaffer's *Novel Craft: Victorian Domestic Handicraft and Nineteenth-Century Fiction* (Oxford University Press, 2011) ; Andrew Stauffer's *Book Traces: Nineteenth-Century Readers and the Future of the Library* (University of Pennsylvania Press, 2021) ; and numerous others. These books will be brought up again and again in the following chapters.
4. Walter Benjamin, "Unpacking My Library: A Talk about Collecting," *Walter Benjamin: Selected Writings*, vol. 2, translated by Rodney Livingstone and others, edited by Michael W. Jennings, Howard Eiland, and Gary Smith (Belknap, 1999), p. 491.
5. Naomi Schor, *Reading in Detail: Aesthetics and the Feminine* (Methuen, 1987), p. 4.
6. Weaving through this book is the gendered aspect of what has been, and hasn't been, saved. Simply put: the keepsakes of women writers were less likely to be retained in archives than those of men. There are exceptions to this, of course, but generally it holds true. Just to give one example: relics of Charles Dickens's life abound, including his commode, windows from some of his residences, and three house museums. As much of a celebrity during her lifetime as Dickens, George Eliot has no house museums dedicated to her, despite the fact that at least five of the homes she lived in still stand, and only a very small number of her relics survive. See Chapter 1 for more on this.
7. Alexandra Gillespie and Deidre Lynch, editors, *The Unfinished Book: Oxford Twenty-First Century Approaches to Literature* (Oxford University Press, 2020).
8. Carolyn Steedman, *Dust: The Archive and Cultural History* (Rutgers University Press, 2002), p. xi.

9. Helena Michie and Robyn Warhol, *Love Among the Archives: Writing the Lives of Sir George Scharf, Victorian Bachelor* (Edinburgh University Press, 2015), p. 24.
10. See, for instance, Steedman, p. x, and Jacques Derrida, *Archive Fever: A Freudian Impression*, translated by Eric Prenowitz (University of Chicago Press, 1995).
11. Terry Eagleton, *The Rape of Clarissa: Writing, Sexuality, and Class Struggle in Samuel Richardson* (Blackwell, 1982), pp. 54–5.
12. Jill Liddington, *Female Fortune: Land, Gender, and Authority: The Anne Lister Diaries and Other Writings, 1833–36* (Rivers Oram Press, 1998), p. 149.
13. This was especially true of Brontë possessions like books and manuscripts. When I viewed and handled the Emily Brontë single-leaf manuscripts at the Brontë Parsonage Museum in 2016, which are wonderfully dirty, as can be seen in Fig. 1, I was told by a curator (Amy Roebottom) that they were planning on having them cleaned soon. Aaron M. Hyman and Dana Leibsohn describe a late sixteenth-century papal bull that was cleaned by conservators, which "likely took from the paper mineral traces of, the salts left by, the Indigenous body upon which this papal bull was found" (420). "Washing the Archive," *Early American Literature*, vol. 55, no. 2, 2020, pp. 419–44.
14. See Elaine Freedgood, *The Ideas in Things* (Chicago University Press, 2006).
15. Gaston Bachelard ponders "objects that may be opened. When a casket is closed, it is returned to the general community of objects; it takes its place in exterior space. But it opens! For this reason, a philosopher-mathematician would say that it is the first differential of discovery" (85). *The Poetics of Space* (Beacon, 1964).
16. I discuss this small sheet further in Chapter 4.

Notes to Chapter 1

1. From "commonplace notebook," GEN MSS 963, Box 20, Beinecke Library, Yale University. See also Joseph Wiesenfarth, *A Writer's Notebook 1854–1879, and Uncollected Writings* (University of Virginia Press, 1981).
2. Walter Benjamin, *Walter Benjamin: Selected Writings*, vol. 2, translated by Rodney Livingstone and others, edited by Michael W. Jennings, Howard Eiland, and Gary Smith (Belknap, 1999), p. 133.
3. Gèrard Genette defines "paratext" as the frame around a printed text—the author's name, the table of contents, footnotes, the title, and the like—and he sees it as "more than a boundary or a sealed border"; it is "a threshold ... a zone between text and off-text" (1–2). *Paratexts: Thresholds of Interpretation*, translated by Jane E. Lewin (Cambridge University Press, 1987). For more about paratexts, see Denis Duncan and Adam Smyth, editors, *Book Parts* (Oxford University Press, 2019).

4. Karen Sánchez-Eppler, "Marks of Possession: Methods for an Impossible Subject," *PMLA* vol. 126, no. 1, 2011, pp. 151.
5. William Sherman, *Used Books: Marking Readers in Renaissance England* (University of Pennsylvania Press, 2008), p. 56.
6. Clifford included notes in her own hand and those of her servant, to whom she dictated them. She also kept notes about whether she read alone or someone read aloud to her, and the date and location of the reading. See Heather Jackson, *Romantic Readers: The Evidence of the Marginalia* (Yale University Press, 2005), Chapter 2, and Stephen Orgel, *The Reader in the Book: A Study of Spaces and Traces* (Oxford University Press, 2015), pp. 149–50. See Deidre Shauna Lynch on Currer, *Loving Literature: A Cultural History* (University of Chicago Press, 2015), p. 137. For women's lack of legal rights to make wills, see Pat Jalland, *Death in the Victorian Family* (Oxford University Press, 1996), p. 295. Sheila Liming explores late nineteenth- and early twentieth-century American women's attempts to collect books and keep them together in *What a Library Means to a Woman: Edith Wharton and the Will to Collect Books* (University of Minnesota Press, 2020).
7. Samuel Richardson, *Clarissa* (Penguin, 1986), p. 1415. In Deborah Lynn Pfuntner's dissertation, she discusses examples of women creating catalogues of their books, such as Sarah Ponsonby and Eleanor Butler (the same-sex couple known as the "Ladies of Llangollen"), who created a list of their 895 books split into sections such as "Gardening," "Novels and Tales," and "In the Boudoir." These books were dispersed after their deaths in an auction. They used different ink colors to indicate when books were the gifts of friends and when they were given by their authors. "A Catalogue of Our Books," MS 22980C, National Library of Wales. "Romantic Women Writers and Their Commonplace Books," Dissertation at Texas A&M University, 2016, pp. 167, 187–8.
8. William Baker, in *The Libraries of George Eliot and George Henry Lewes* (University of Victoria, 1981), estimates that approximately 10,000 volumes were inherited by Charles Lewes from Eliot, the majority of which are now untraceable (11). Text on doors is significant as being, somewhat like graffiti, writing that has left the more traditional confines of paper and the codex. A quote from *Middlemarch* (Penguin, 1994) is relevant here: "Almost everything he had said seemed like ... the inscription on the door of a museum which might open on the treasures of past ages" (32–3).
9. George Eliot, *Romola* (Penguin, 1996), p. 55. Future citations will be in-text.
10. William Baker, *The George Eliot-George Henry Lewes Library: An Annotated Catalogue of Their Books at Dr. Williams's Library, London* (Garland, 1977), p. xiii.
11. Ibid., p. xiv.
12. Even the full library would be only a portion of Eliot's reading, since she was an avid user of the British Museum reading room and other libraries.

13. The manuscript auction catalogue for this sale is at the Brontë Parsonage Museum (hereafter BPM), SB:349.
14. David Gilson, "Jane Austen's Books," *Book Collector* (1974), lists eighteen books with Austen's autograph (30-8), and Deirdre Le Faye, "New Marginalia in Jane Austen's Books," *Book Collector*, vol. 49, no. 2, 2000, pp. 222-6, describes two more.
15. Jane Austen, *Jane Austen's Letters*, edited by Deirdre Le Faye (Oxford University Press, 2011), pp. 77, 92.
16. See Bruce Graver, "Lucy Aiken's Marginalia to *Biographia Literaria*," *European Romantic Review*, vol. 14, no. 3, 2003, pp. 323-43 and Janice Broder, "Lady Bradshaigh Reads and Writes *Clarissa*: The Marginal Notes in Her First Edition," *Clarissa and Her Readers: New Essays for the Clarissa Project*, edited by Carol Houlihan Flynn and Edward Copeland (AMS Press, 1999), pp. 97-118. Bradshaigh read the book in serial form and wrote to Richardson in the hope that she could influence the way it would end. In her rewrite, Clarissa escapes being raped, and she lives out her life with her friend Anna Howe. Eliot wrote in her journal about Robert Browning showing her E. B. Browning's bibles (now at Burke Library, Columbia University) and her annotations in the Greek dramatists. See *The Journals of George Eliot*, edited by Margaret Harris and Judith Johnston (Cambridge University Press, 1999), p. 126. See Kate Flint, *The Woman Reader: 1837-1914* (Clarendon, 1993), for accounts of many women readers who approached the task with intellectual and political intent, such as Frances Power Cobbe, who kept synopses and tables of Greek philosophers and other subjects of study (pp. 223-30). Jackson, *Romantic Readers*, discusses the marginalia of the other women mentioned here.
17. Henry Chorley, *Memorials of Mrs. Hemans* (Saunders and Otley, 1836), p. 108. Quoted in Jackson, *Romantic Readers*, p. 176. The British Library holds a collection of books that once belonged to Sarah Sophia Banks (1744-1818), a fan of archery and chess and the sister of the botanist Joseph Banks, with many of her marginal notes, extra-illustrations, added indexes, and more.
18. Leah Price discusses the celebration of reading with one's body by women in the late nineteenth century, like the New Women writers. See *The Anthology and the Rise of the Novel: From Richardson to George Eliot* (Cambridge University Press, 2000), p. 126.
19. Anne Boleyn scored passages of Tyndale's *Obedience of a Christian Man* with her fingernail for the king's later reading. See Heidi Brayman Hackel, *Reading Material in Early Modern England: Print, Gender, and Literacy* (Cambridge University Press, 2005), p. 205. Roger Stoddard, in *Marks in Books, Illustrated and Explained* (Harvard University Press, 2005), discusses marginal marks that don't have ink, which he calls "pressed blind without pigment" (2).

20. Sheridan, *The Rivals*, 1.2 (Crowell, 1884), p. 11. See Kevin Jackson, *Invisible Forms: A Guide to Literary Curiosities* (Thomas Dunne, 2000), p. 163, where he explores other references to fingernail markings.
21. Edward Mangin, *An Essay on Light Reading, as it may be supposed to influence moral conduct and literary taste* (James Carpenter, 1808), p. 3. A much later, fictional example comes from Arthur Machen, *The Three Imposters* (1895; Aegypan Press, 2005). The character Joseph Walters remarks about men who practice the "degrading occupation" of "befouling the fair margins of the fairest books with idle and superfluous annotation ... more pitiable still is a masterpiece spluttered over with the commentator's pen" (169).
22. See Hackel, *Reading*, p. 137, for a discussion of pinpricks as a form of marginalia. Sherman describes marginalia marked by a red silk thread sewn through the page (xvii) and pricks used to mark passages (4) in *Used Books*.
23. Jackson, *Romantic Readers*, pp. 77–9. Pamela Woof studies one of Dorothy's marginal notes in Withering's book. Dorothy scribbled next to the entry for the Common butterwort: "in great abundance all round the Grasmere Fells. This plant is here very ill described" (15). See *Dorothy Wordsworth: Wonders of the Everyday* (Wordsworth Trust, 2013). Another example of a book about plants in which the owner added real plants is a 1559 edition of Rembert Dodoens's *De Stirpium Historiae Pemptades Sex* with inscriptions from 1808, which was probably when the plants were added. Harvard Houghton, NC5. D6673.553b.
24. This book is now at the BPM. See also Ivy Holgate, "A Pilgrim at Haworth—1879," *Brontë Society Transactions*, vol. 14, no. 1, 1961, pp. 29–37.
25. Charles Lamb, "Detached Thoughts on Books and Reading," *London Magazine*, vol. 6, 1822, pp. 33–6. Virginia Woolf wrote in her journal of 1917 that Leonard Woolf and Desmond MacCarthy went to the London Library and looked up the word "fuck" in the slang dictionary. They "were saddened and surprised to see how the thumb marks of members were thick on the page" (82). *The Diary of Virginia Woolf*, edited by Anne Olivier Bell, vol. 1 (Harcourt, 1977).
26. George Eliot, *The Mill on the Floss* (Norton, 1994), p. 223. Future citations will be in-text. The feather is tipped into Browning's *Biblia Greaca*, CB31 1825 Thompson Case, Burke Library, Columbia University. Eliot used a pressed leaf as a bookmark in her copy of Friedrich Heinrich Wilhelm Gesenius's *Student's Hebrew Grammar from the Twentieth German edition of Gesenius' Hebrew Grammar* (1869), at the Dr. Williams's Library, London. In the Yale Beineke can be found a lock of hair, in the Thomas Hardy collection, tipped into *Jones' Series of Engravings*. Another fictional example: in Wilkie Collins's *The Dead Secret* (Bradbury and Evans, 1857), Sarah Leeson visits the grave of her former love, Hugh Polwheal, and picks a few leaves of grass and puts them in a little book of Wesley's *Hymns*, a gift from the deceased. See p. 38.
27. For Leigh Hunt, see "A Centre That Would Not Hold: Annuals and Cultural Democracy," *Nineteenth-Century Media and the Construction of Identity*, edited by Laurel Brake, Bill Bell, and David Finkelstein (Palgrave, 2000), p. 57;

Peter Stallybrass, "Books and Scrolls: Navigating the Bible," *Books and Readers in Early Modern England: Material Studies*, edited by Jennifer Anderson and Elizabeth Sauer (University of Pennsylvania Press, 2002), p. 46.

28. See William Sherman, "Toward a History of the Manicule," *Owners, Annotators, and the Signs of Reading*, edited by Robin Myers, Michael Harris, and Giles Mandelbrote (Oak Knoll, 2005), pp. 19–44. Charlotte Brontë often used manicules. See, for instance, those she drew in Murray's *English Grammar* and in Emily's "Gondal Poetry" manuscript to indicate which poems to include in the three sisters' first published volume.

29. Bacon, "Of Studies," *The Essays or Counsels, Civill or Morall*, edited by Michael Keirnan (Oxford, 1985), p. 153; Sherman, *Used Books*, p. 84.

30. Letter to Samuel Taylor Coleridge, October 11, 1802. *The Letters of Charles Lamb*, edited by Sir Thoma Noon Talfours (Edward Moxon, 1841), p. 62.

31. Geoffrey Batchen, *Forget Me Not: Photography and Remembrance* (Princeton Architectural Press, 2004), p. 48.

32. Andrew Stauffer, "Poetry, Romanticism, and the Practice of Nineteenth-Century Books," *Nineteenth-Century Contexts*, vol. 34, no. 5, 2012, pp. 336, 340. See also Andrew Stauffer, *Book Traces: Nineteenth-Century Readers and the Future of the Library* (University of Pennsylvania Press, 2021).

33. In Leah Price's exploration of multiple acts of "non reading," she focuses on the book as an object that Victorians not only wrote in but also hid behind, sniffed, used for the storage of herbs, and ripped up for toilet paper, food wrappings, and shelf or trunk linings. This chapter takes a different tack in considering the physical volume as fodder for the writing of George Eliot, Charlotte Brontë, Emily Brontë, and others. See *How to Do Things with Books in Victorian Britain* (Princeton University Press, 2012).

34. The notebooks that George Eliot filled with extracts from her reading will be discussed further in Chapter 3.

35. Quoted in Jackson, *Romantic Readers*, p. 61. See also Avrom Fleishman, "George Eliot's Reading: A Chronological List," *George Eliot—George Henry Lewes Studies*, no. 54/5, 2008, pp. 1–76.

36. Jackson, *Romantic Readers*, p. 33.

37. Flint, *The Woman Reader*, p. 93.

38. For a discussion of the importance of handwritten indexes, see Sherman, *Used Books*, p. 9. A few examples of the many volumes once in Eliot's library in which she added scholarly manuscript, including indexes: *The Meditations of Aurelius* (1764); Samual Beal's *The Romantic Legend of Sakya Buddha From the Chinese Sanskrit* (1875); Eusebe Salverte's *Des Sciences occultes ou Essai sure la magie* (1829); Wollstonecraft's *A Vindication of the Rights of Woman* (1792). These books are all held at the Dr. William's Library, London. See William Baker, *The George Eliot-George Henry Lewes Library*.

39. See Le Faye and Austen's *Juvenilia*, edited by Peter Sabor (Cambridge University Press, 2006), pp. 316–48.
40. Sabor describes these marginalia: pp. 316–18.
41. Eliot, "Silly Novels by Lady Novelists," *George Eliot: Selected Essays, Poems, and Other Writings*, edited by A. S. Byatt and Nicholas Warren (Penguin, 1990), pp. 140, 148. Woolf, writing in ca. 1907, also castigates those who wreak "vengeance on the margin," although her annotators are mostly male. She says: "certain passages are inscribed with dates, and a whole botanical collection is returned to the library, pressed between the leaves." Quoted in Amanda Golden, "Virginia Woolf's Marginalia Manuscript," *Woolf Studies Annual*, vol. 18, 2012, pp. 116–17.
42. Thackeray, "Confessions of George Fitz-Boodle: Men's Wives, Mr. and Mrs. Frank Berry," *Fraser's Magazine*, vol. 27, 1843, p. 359.
43. Jackson, *Romantic Readers*, pp. 39, 58.
44. Dickens, "Our English Watering Place," *Household Words*, vol. 3, no. 71, 1851, pp. 433–6.
45. *Grammar*; Bonnell 45, BPM.
46. In her novel *Shirley*, Charlotte Brontë presents a fictional version of this sort of defacing. Shirley, whom Charlotte based on her sister Emily, doodles "little leaves, fragments of pillars, broken crosses, on the margin" (410) of Bernardin de Saint-Pierre's *Fragments de l'Amazone*. Her tutor comments that she did this with his Racine—she "traced" her "mark" on every page.
47. One bible, a gift from her father's friend the Reverend W. Morgan, is at the Morgan Library, 17949 E108B, and another is a *New Testament in Latin* (bb4, BPM). Her *French Dictionary* and Murray's *English Grammar* are at the BPM, bb43 and Bonnell 44.
48. Anne's book is at the BPM, bb127, as is the Robert Southey book: *The Remains of Henry Kirke White*, vol. 1 (Vernon, Hood, and Hessey, 1810); E2016.2.
49. Price gives many examples of this, but I'll add a few further notable ones. Published cookbooks sometimes included blank pages at the end for the reader to record her own recipes. One example of this usage, from America, is a copy of *Cookery for Beginners* by Marion Harland (D. Lothrop Co., 1884). "Christin Johnson / Dec. 25th 1893 / Rockford, Ill" is inscribed on the flyleaf, and she has added in by hand many recipes on blank pages, including for Devil's Cake, Cranberry Pudding, and Sunshine Bake. Rare Books 641773, Huntington Library. A copy of William Morris's *The Earthly Paradise* (Reeves and Turner, 1891) has so many reviews of the poem, pictures of Morris clipped from newspapers, advertisements for the book and the MS for sale, and other stuff, pasted in or handwritten, that the book has become a sort of Morrisiana scrapbook. Rare Books, 607074, Huntington Library.
50. Other acts of composing in margins include Byron's "Lines Written in 'Letters of an Italian Nun and an English Gentleman; by J.J. Rousseau: Founded

on Facts'" and "Lines Written on a Blank Leaf of 'The Pleasures of Memory.'" Burns's poems of this type are even more elaborate: "Lines Written Under the Portrait of Robert Fergusson, the Poet, in a Copy of that Author's Works Presented to a Young Lady in Edinburgh. March 19th, 1787" and "Written on a Blank Leaf of one of Miss Hannah More's Works, Which a Lady Had Given Him"—often including not just that the poem was written in the blank spaces of a particular book, but who gave the book to whom (and when). John Hamilton Reynolds, Keats's great friend, wrote a sonnet called "To Keats—On Reading his Sonnet Written in Chaucer."

51. Le Faye describes this 1780 book, "New Marginalia," 225. The poet Anna Seward (1742–1809) filled the margins of her copy of William Cowper's *The Task* (J. Johnson, 1785) with comments on his poetry, her political thoughts, and lines of verse by others (Milton especially), but also her original poems, seemingly inspired by Cowper's verse. C.71.c.22, British Library.
52. See James L. Persoon, "Hardy's Pocket Milton: An Early Unpublished Poem," *English Language Notes*, vol. 25, no. 3, 1988, pp. 49–52.
53. Frank N. Owings, *The Keats Library* (Keats-Shelley Memorial Association, 1978), pp. 21, 31, 35, 55. See also Jackson, *Romantic Readers*, p. 186.
54. Sylvia Brown and John Considine, *The Spacious Margin: Eighteenth-Century Printed Books and the Traces of Their Readers* (University of Alberta Press, 2012), p. 28.
55. See Juliet Fleming, *Graffiti and the Writing Arts in Early Modern England* (Reaktion, 2001) and her discussion of these sorts of textual graffiti.
56. Eliot's Blotter, British Library, AD MS 59866. Eliot sometimes used her knees as a writing surface. For instance, in a letter to Thomas Clifford Allbutt of November 1, 1873, she writes: "your suggestions about lessening the inconveniences of writing could not come to a more appreciative person. I have for the last three years taken to writing on my knees, throwing myself backward in my chair, and having a high support to my feet. It is a great relief not to bend, and in this way at least I get advantage from the long-sightedness which involves the early need of glasses" (450). *The George Eliot Letters*, edited by Gordon S. Haight, vol. 5 (Yale University Press, 1954–78).
57. Fleming, pp. 10, 20. In Elizabeth Gaskell's *Ruth*, a poesy ring that belonged to Miss Benson's grandmother is given to Ruth to wear so that she appears to have been married. Miss Benson says, "it's very broad; they made them so then, to hold the posy inside: there's one in that: Thine own sweetheart / Till death doth part" (120). Elizabeth Gaskell, *Ruth* (Penguin, 2004).
58. Lynch, *Loving Literature*, p. 231. She points to a poem carved in marble in Matthew Lewis's *The Monk*; one in stone in Ann Radcliffe's *The Mysteries of Udolpho*; and other examples. Writing rings, popular during the Renaissance, were made of a diamond set in high bevels with one point outwards for scoring glass. In John Donne's 1635 "A Valediction of My Name, In the

Window," the speaker uses a diamond to write on a glass window. Christina Lupton gives many examples of eighteenth-century graffiti, much of it written in actual windows using a "diamond pen," but she also points to an exchange Moll Flanders has with a lover by inscribing it with a diamond ring into a window, in Defoe's novel. See *Knowing Books: The Consciousness of Mediation in Eighteenth-Century Britain* (University of Pennsylvania Press, 2012), chapter 5.

59. The family home in Charlotte Yonge's *The Daisy Chain* (Macmillan, 1870) has two large windows with "panes of glass scratched with various names and initials" (2), probably a means for Yonge to show that the house is old and well-lived-in by a large family.

60. George Eliot, *Adam Bede* (Wordsworth, 1997), p. 3.

61. Journal 1854–1861, GEN MSS 963, Box 15, Beinecke. This notebook is transcribed in *The Journals of George Eliot*, edited by Margaret Harris and Judith Johnston (Cambridge University Press, 1998).

62. Thomas Carlyle carved a few lines of verse on the window of his Edinburgh lodgings in Moray Street. The window is now at Carlyle's House museum in London. The lines read "Little did my mother think / That day she cradled me, / What land I was to travel in, / Or what death I should die." Tennyson penciled his autograph on a wall in Shakespeare's home, as did Walter Scott and many others. See Robert Bernard Martin, *Tennyson: The Unquiet Heart* (Oxford University Press, 1980), p. 252 and Alison Booth, *Homes and Haunts: Touring Writers' Shrines and Countries* (Oxford University Press, 2016), p. 211. In the cottage where Robert Burns was born, the furniture, walls, and fixtures gathered so many autographs much of it had to be replaced. See Nicola Watson, *The Literary Tourist: Readers and Places in Romantic and Victorian Britain* (New York: Palgrave, 2008), p. 69 and Booth, pp. 86 and 192.

63. Poets the Brontës read also cared about the writing surface, such as Byron and his "Lines Inscribed Upon a Cup Formed From a Skull" and "Lines in the Traveller's Book at Orchomenus," and Wordsworth and his "Lines written with a pencil, upon a Stone in the Wall of the House (an out-house), on the island at Grasmere." Letitia E. Landon had a poem entitled "Lines Written Under a Picture of a Girl Burning a Love-Letter," and Burns wrote many poems with such titles as "Lines Written on a Banknote," "Lines Written on a Window at the King's Arms Tavern, Dumfries," and more. Watson describes how Burns was given a diamond stylus by the Earl of Glencairn for glass inscribing, and two windows he inscribed are at the Robert Burns Birthplace Museum. *The Author's Effects: On Writer's House Museums* (Oxford University Press, 2020), p. 276, n. 44.

64. "From a D.W. in the N.C." was published as "A Death Scene" in the poetry book published by Charlotte, Anne, and Emily during their lifetimes.

65. *The Poems of Emily Brontë*, edited by Derek Roper and Edward Chitham (Clarendon, 1995), pp. 175–6.

66. Brontë continues here a tradition already established in the gothic novel of utilizing poems incised into glass or stone to increase a sense of haunting and absence in the one who finds them. By the time Eliza Parson's *The Castle of Wolfenbach* was published in 1793, verse incised in glass had become a kind of gothic shorthand for the horrors of torture and imprisonment. A servant explains to the young hero Matilda that a castle is haunted by saying, "there are bloody floors, prison rooms, and scriptions, they say, on the windows, to make a body's hair stand on end" (3). Matilda feels compelled to investigate the "horrid inscriptions," as she calls them, and finds that an abused wife, presumably long dead, carved them with a diamond to lament being imprisoned by her husband. She addresses the reader, here Matilda but also us, directly: "Would you be happy, fly this hated room, / For here the lost Victoria meets her doom."
67. In this sense, they have qualities of an epitaph on a tomb, since one has to travel there to see the thing itself, which generally marks the place—of a grave or of one's imprisonment. Such writing continues the early seventeenth-century tradition of the term "epigraph" signifying an "inscription of just about any sort on just about any durable surface," such as on coins, tombs, or public monuments. Sherman, *Used Books*, p. 23.
68. Eliot, *Middlemarch*, p. 412.
69. See also Garrett Stewart, "Reading Feeling and the 'Transferred Life': *The Mill on the Floss*," *The Feeling of Reading: Affective Experience and Victorian Literature*, edited by Rachel Ablow (University of Michigan Press, 2010), pp. 179–206 and Nicholas Dames, *The Physiology of the Novel: Reading, Neural Science, and the Form of Victorian Fiction* (Oxford University Press, 2007).
70. Emily Dickinson pressed a flower in her copy of *The Mill on the Floss* (Tauchnitz, 1860) between pages 50 and 51. The book is now at the Houghton, Harvard, EDR 123.
71. Eliot gave a copy of this book to a close friend, signing it, "Mary Ann Evans, February 1849, to S. Hennell, January 1851."
72. Lynch, *Loving Literature*, p. 118.
73. Dickens, *Great Expectations* (Penguin, 1996), p. 334.
74. George Eliot, *Adam Bede*, p. 27. Eliot took notes on this practice in one of her notebooks: "Drawing of Lots, and divination of God's will by opening the Bible at hazard and reading the first text the eye fell on—both practiced by Wesley." From "commonplace notebook." GEN MSS 963, Box 20, Yale Beineke. See also Wiesenfarth.
75. Eliot, *Adam Bede*, p. 133. For more on the practice of opening a book at random and hoping that "the first verse your eye comes to will illuminate the course of your life," see Michael Olmert, *The Smithsonian Book of Books* (Smithsonian, 1992), p. 23.
76. Sherman, *Used Books*, pp. 8, 13.

77. Fleming, p. 13. To give a different example of using a bible to make a vow, Robert Louis Stevenson signed the following statement, written in the hand of his wife Fanny in a bible now at the Yale Beinecke: "I, Robert Louis Stevenson hereby vow and swear in the sight of god not to sell the collected stories for less than two hundred pounds (£200) down; item—not to partake of any meal in any club or family dwelling other than the monument. Robert Louis Stevenson." While this has a facetious quality, especially given Stevenson's agnosticism, it still points to a tradition (Ip St48 Zz853B, Beinecke).

78. The Brontës also gave books as gifts, such as a copy of *Imitation of Christ*, with "M. Branwell, July 1807" inscribed in it, plus, on the flyleaf, "C. Brontë's book. This book was given to me in July 1826 [by her mother]. It is not certainly known who is the author, but it is generally supposed that Thomas a Kempis is ..." (Morgan Library). In one of her bibles, Charlotte records in German that it was given to her by her beloved professor: "Herr Heger hat mir dieses Buck gegeben / Brussels Mai 1843" (Morgan). In a copy of the *Book of Common Prayer*, Charlotte has written "Emily Jane Brontë / from her sister C. Brontë / Febr 1st 1842" (1837: bb225, Bonnell 53, BPM). In Felicia Hemans's *Songs of the Affections and other poems*, Charlotte has written "Miss M.M. Nussey / with Miss Brontë's / kind regards / Decbr. 5th 1842" (1841; bb31, BPM).

79. Charlotte Brontë, *Villette* (Harpers, 1900), p. 345.

80. Anne Brontë, *Agnes Grey* (Penguin, 1989), p. 45.

81. John Frost, *Bingley's Practical Introduction to Botany*, 2nd ed. (Baldwin, Cradock and Joy, 1827), 2004/47.9, BPM; Susanna Harrison, *Songs in the Night* (Baynes, 1807); bb30, BPM.

82. Charlotte Brontë, "History of the Year," March 1829; Bonnell 80 (11) BPM.

83. Charlotte Brontë writes about this in a letter, remarking that the majority of her mother's belongings were "swallowed up in the mighty sea." *The Letters of Charlotte Brontë*, edited by Margaret Smith, vol. 1 (Oxford, 1995), p. 240.

84. MS in Southey, vol. 1, E2016.2, BPM. See also Kathryn Crowther, "Charlotte Bronte's Textual Relics: Memorializing the Material in *Villette*," *Brontë Studies*, vol. 35, no. 2, 2010, pp. 131–2.

85. Olmert, p. 9.

86. For more on relic culture and nineteenth-century literature, see Deborah Lutz, *Relics of Death in Nineteenth-Century Literature and Culture* (Cambridge University Press, 2015).

87. Stephen Nichols, "On the Sociology of Medieval Manuscript Annotation," *Annotation and Its Texts*, edited by Stephen A. Barney (Oxford University Press, 1991), p. 46.

88. Brown and Considine, p. 83.

89. Another volume that became a many-layered memorial: a first edition of John Keats's poems with his autograph initials to his friend Charles Cowden Clarke, a poet for whom Keats wrote a poem printed in this volume. When Clarke

died, his wife added handwritten notes, wafered in drawings and newspaper articles, and recorded her bequeathing of it to a mutual friend. She writes in it about losing her husband and imagining him shaking hands with Keats in heaven. Morgan Library 16265.
90. Jackson, *Romantic Readers*, p. 171.
91. Ibid., p. 179. Another example: "In 1811 Eliza Hawtry made her daughter a present of Thomas Gisborne's *Familiar Survey of the Christian Religion*, with extracts from other edifying books copied into the back flyleaves." "'Marginal Frivolities': Readers' notes as Evidence for the History of Reading," *Owners, Annotators, and the Signs of Reading*, edited by Robin Myers, Michael Harris, and Gilles Mandelbrote (British Library, 2005), p. 142.
92. See Baker, *The George Eliot-George Henry Lewes Library*.
93. Lynch writes about the "queer intimacy" of loving reading between Lady Eleanor Butler and Sarah Ponsonby (the Ladies of Llangollen). The former kept a journal keeping track of the books she read aloud to her "Beloved." *Loving Literature*, p. 56.
94. Gillian Silverman, *Bodies and Books* (University of Pennsylvania Press, 2012), p. 19.
95. In Madame de Staël's *Corinne*, for instance, Byron announced his love for the book's owner, Teresa Guiccioli. See Jackson, *Romantic Readers*, pp. 174–5, 182.
96. Such as Hennell's *Christianity and Infidelity: An exposition of the arguments on both sides* (1857). Hennell has written, on the flyleaf: "Dr. Pollian / ab Achate suo fido- / Feb 22nd 1857."
97. Quoted in Baker, *The George Eliot-George Henry Lewes Library*. When Eliot was translating Feuerbach from German to English, she sent drafts to Hennell, who provided comments.
98. Stauffer, p. 413.
99. This bible is at the Morgan Library, 17769, E106B. Written on the first page is "To Anne Brontë with the love and best wishes of her Godmother Elizabeth Firth," then, in what appears to be Patrick Brontë's hand, "Oct 1823 / Remember, my dear child, frequently to read this book, / with much prayer to God— / and to keep it all your / lifetime, for the sake of the donor / P. [?] Brontë."
100. Sherman, *Used Books*, p. 83.
101. E. B. Browning's bible, Burke Library, Columbia. See also Anthony Elia, "An Unknown Exegete: Uncovering the Biblical Scholarship of Elizabeth Barrett Browning," *Theological Librarianship*, vol. 7, no. 1, 2014, pp. 8–20. Robert Browning reported that E. B. Browning "would join my name to hers in all the books that belonged to her" by writing a "Robert" in front of "Elizabeth" in the volumes in her library, a sort of romantic bibliomancy. Quoted in *Works and Days: From the Journal of Michael Field*, edited by T. Sturge Moore and D. C. Sturge Moore (Murray, 1933), p. 15.

102. Baker, *The George Eliot-George Henry Lewes Library*, p. 71.
103. Ibid.
104. Wordsworth, *The Prelude* (Moxon, 1851), Yale Beinecke, GEN MSS 963, Box 56. Eliot also treasured rose leaves from Wordsworth's garden. *Letters*, vol. 1, p. 99.
105. Writing about the reading experiences of the American Mary Austin, Silverman finds something similar to Eliot's experience I describe here. She posits that Austin fuses "the materiality of the geology textbook with that of her immediate vicinity, as if *Old Red Sandstone* and the 'rock quarry' that surrounds her are somehow coextensive. The book, in other words, appears not just about the earth, but *of* it, deeply entwined with her physical environs" (44).
106. One other example, of many, of Eliot date marking: in John Locke's *An Essay Concerning Human Understanding* (1828), she wrote, "Reread Dec 1876 / Marian E. Lewes." See Baker, *The George Eliot-George Henry Lewes Library*.
107. Marcel Proust, *Swann's Way*, translated by C. K. Scott Moncrieff and Terence Kilmartin (Modern Library, 2004), p. 3.
108. Yale Beinecke, GEN MSS 963, Box 56.
109. In a related type of reverence for relics, Eliot planned to have the letters George Henry Lewes wrote to her buried with her. Diary for 1879, MSS Eliot, G., Berg Collection.
110. Carol Jacobs, "*Wuthering Heights*: At the Threshold of Interpretation," *Boundary 2: A Journal of Postmodern Literature and Culture*, vol. 7, no. 3, 1979, p. 53.
111. Maggie Berg, *Wuthering Heights: The Writing in the Margin* (Twayne, 1996), p. 39.
112. U. C. Knoepflmacher writes that "Lockwood acts as the reader's prime agent. His initial willingness to partake of a reality peopled by characters totally alien to his previous experience becomes congruous with that of any reader who ventures into the book" (10). He points to the difficulty Lockwood has gaining "access to its interior," even at first in crossing the threshold of Wuthering Heights. Lockwood is like other readers in that Brontë "determine[s] their fitness as trespassers into the verbal structure that bears the name of the house into which Lockwood has stumbled" (11). *Emily Brontë: Wuthering Heights* (Cambridge University Press, 1989).
113. Emily Brontë, *Wuthering Heights* (Broadview, 2007), p. 50. Future citations in-text. For female readers and reading closets, see Hackel, especially pp. 40–1.
114. James Kavanagh, *Emily Brontë* (Basil Blackwood, 1985), p. 26. See also Jacobs, p. 50.
115. For more on Catherine's marginalia, see Seth Lerer, "Devotion and Defacement: Reading Children's Marginalia," *Representations*, vol. 118, no. 1, 2012, pp. 126–53.

116. A later example of defacing religious books is found in Robert Louis Stevenson's *Strange Case of Dr. Jekyll and Mr. Hyde* (Norton, 2020), where the Satanic Hyde "annotates" a "pious work" "with startling blasphemies" (40).
117. Silverman posits that books are something like prosthetics, "at once a foreign object and an integral part of the reading subject" (13).
118. This title comes from Isaiah 59:17: "He put on righteousness as a breastplate, and a helmet of salvation on His Head; and He put on garments of vengeance for clothing and wrapped Himself with zeal as a mantle." Brontë's use of it here is ironic, of course, since Catherine doesn't want religion to protect her, but rather she wants to be protected from religion—at least the kind force-fed her by the servant Joseph. Ripping the cover of the book is to remove its "helmet."
119. William Scruton and J. Hambley Rowe, for instance, clipped images of places important to the Brontë story and pasted them into *The Temple Dictionary of the Bible*, edited by Rev. W. Ewing (Dent, 1909), removing some pages so the thickened ones would fit between the boards; TA.198, BPM.
120. Berg, p. 24.
121. Charlotte Brontë, *Jane Eyre* (Norton, 2016), p. 101.
122. Woolf, "The Countess of Pembroke's Arcadia," *The Second Common Reader* (Mariner, 2003), p. 40.
123. Or letters, as when the daughter Cathy in *Wuthering Heights* secrets forbidden missives in between the pages of a volume so she can read them while pretending to peruse the book in the presence of censorious adults.

Notes to Chapter 2

1. Constance Wilde's album, British Library, Add 81755.
2. Patrizia Di Bello sees albums as poised "between being a reading practice and a writing practice." *Women's Albums and Photography in Victorian England* (Ashgate, 2007), p. 25.
3. Richard Menke, *Literature, Print Culture, and Media Technologies, 1880–1900: Many Inventions* (Cambridge University Press, 2019), p. 19.
4. See Leah Price, *How to Do Things with Books in Victorian Britain* (Princeton University Press, 2012) for discussions of the book as object.
5. Ellen Gruber Garvey calls this "a performance of archivalness" (20) on the part of the makers, in *Writing with Scissors: American Scrapbooks from the Civil War to the Harlem Renaissance* (Oxford University Press, 2012). Deidre Lynch writes of the album-maker as following the "impulse to treasure, amass, embalm" (90), but she also points to an appreciation of "dispersal and diversion" (99). "Paper Slips: Album, Archiving, Accident," *Studies in Romanticism*, vol. 57, no. 1, 2018, pp. 87–119. See also *Loving Literature: A Cultural History* (University of Chicago Press, 2015), pp. 140–4.

6. Anne Brontë made a handwritten songbook, circa 1843–4, to name just one of hundreds of these nineteenth-century albums. Brontë Parsonage Museum, Bonnell 133.
7. There are four volumes of music books owned by Gaskell at the Manchester Central Library, MS f 823.894 C1. This quote comes from volume 1. In Austen's *Emma*, Emma's protégée Harriet Smith sends to her friend Elizabeth Martin "two songs which she had lent Elizabeth to copy." *Emma* (Longman, 2006), p. 39.
8. Jenny Uglow mentions this commonplace book, which seems to now be missing. *Elizabeth Gaskell: A Habit of Stories* (Faber and Faber, 1993), p. 42.
9. Gaskell's Autograph Collection, the John Rylands Library, ENG. MS 731–4.
10. According to Pamela Corpron Parker, the autograph letters were once bound, but at some point most of them were taken out of their original albums and put in plastic sheets in binders. "Woman of Letters: Elizabeth Gaskell's Autograph Collection and Victorian Celebrity," *Material Women, 1750–1950: Consuming Desires and Collecting Practices*, edited by Maureen Daly Goggin and Beth Fowkes Tobin (Ashgate, 2009), pp. 265–78.
11. Gaskell to Mrs. Spencer, undated 1856, *Further Letters of Mrs. Gaskell*, edited by John Chapple and Alan Shelston (Manchester University Press, 2000), p. 163.
12. Gaskell to George Hope, February 13, 1849. *The Letters of Mrs. Gaskell*, edited by J. A. V. Chapple and Arthur Pollard (Mandolin, 1997), p. 796. She also wrote to a friend, "to think you will really touch this bit of paper! It has suddenly struck me as so odd and strange" (*The Letters of Mrs. Gaskell*, p. 743).
13. Clare Pettitt, "Topos, Taxonomy and Travel in Nineteenth-Century Women's Scrapbooks," *Travel Writing, Visual Culture and Form, 1760–1900*, edited by Mary Henes and Brian Murray (Palgrave, 2015), pp. 21–41. See also James Secord, "Scrapbook Science: Composite Caricatures in Late Georgian England," *Figuring It Out: Science, Gender, and Visual Culture*, edited by Ann B. Shteir and Bernard V. Lightman (University Press of New England, 2006), pp. 164–91, and Lynch, "Paper Slips: Album, Archiving, Accident," pp. 94–5.
14. Susan Stewart says that souvenirs show us the "capacity of objects to serve as traces of authentic experience." *On Longing: Narratives of the Miniature, the Gigantic, the Souvenir, the Collection* (Duke University Press, 1993), p. 135.
15. See Lisa Gitelman, *Paper Knowledge: Toward a Media History of Documents* (Duke University Press, 2014) for more about this absent history. See also Sharon Marcus, who writes that "today, the albums preserved in rare book collections often sit neglected, yellowing and crumbling, but these underused sources have a rare capacity to communicate the passionate feelings that celebrities aroused over a century ago." *The Drama of Celebrity* (Princeton University Press, 2019), p. 18. See also Sharon Marcus, "The Theatrical Scrapbook," *Theater Survey*, vol. 54, no. 2, 2013, pp. 283–307.

16. Samantha Matthews details the disdain leveled at friendship albums in the nineteenth century because they were female-coded. "Albums, Belongings, and Embodying the Feminine," *Bodies and Things in Nineteenth-Century Literature and Culture*, edited by Katharina Boehm (Palgrave Macmillan, 2012), pp. 107–29. William St. Clair also discusses this in *The Reading Nation in the Romantic Period* (Cambridge University Press, 2007), p. 225.
17. Gaskell to Harriet Carr, Sept. 1, 1831. *Further Letters*, p. 7.
18. See these friendship albums, for example: Mary Pearson's, Harry Ransom Humanities Research Center, University of Texas, Austin; Lady Frances Winckley Shelley's, Pierpont Morgan Library, MA 500; Emeline Creator's, Firestone Library, Princeton University, C0199, no. 260; and Hannah Ostwain Brigg's, Harry S. Page Collection, Manchester Metropolitan University, Special Collections, #108. In Austen's *Emma*, Harriet Smith and Emma create a related volume, a book of riddles "ornamented with ciphers and trophies." They ask friends to add to it, and it sits open on the table for visitors to look at. *Emma*, p. 54.
19. Jane Nelson's album, British Library, Add. MS 63784.
20. Roe Head Album, Brontë Parsonage Museum, C109.
21. Anne Wagner's album, 1795–1834, Carl H. Pforzheimer Collection of Shelley and His Circle, New York Public Library, BND-MSS (Wagner, A.).
22. Maggie Strickland album, 1893–1902, Fales Library, Bobst Library, New York University, series 4, Box 8, folder 4. Another album with an acrostic addressed to the album owner is Elizabeth Wake Bridson's, Manchester Metropolitan University, #64.
23. Wagner album, Pforzheimer Collection, BND-MSS (Wagner, A.). Another example, of many, of albums that have poems about friendship is Mary Lupton's ca. 1822–5 album, HM 82836, Huntington Library. Gaye Smith writes about a type related to friendship albums, what might be called "memorial albums," that contain things like cut-paper memorial cards, paintings of funeral urns, and wreaths, commemorating a death. "Sentimental Souvenirs: Victorian Scrap Albums from the Sir Harry Page Collection," *Catalogue of an Exhibition Held at the Holden Gallery* (Manchester Polytechnic Library, 1989), pp. 10–14.
24. Matthews, "Albums, Belongings, and Embodying the Feminine," p. 107. Writing about an offshoot of friendship albums—published "Keepsake" albums and similar titles, like "Books of Beauty"—Heather Glen argues that the poetry printed in them mirrors the proto-feminist language of *Jane Eyre*, especially images about soaring into infinity and the eternity of space, speaking not of confinement to women's "proper sphere" but "of freely aspiring subjectivity; not of rational self-management; but of soaring, transcendent desire." *Charlotte Brontë: The Imagination in History* (Oxford University Press, 2002), p. 112.
25. Edith May Southey's album, Bristol Central Library, SR91, fol. 68. Another example: on a page from a now-disassembled album, snippets from Leigh

Hunt, Percy Bysshe Shelley, and John Keats are let into the page. Hunt wrote on the page that the hair was "given to dear William and Mrs. Story, October 2, 1850, Kensington." Keats-Shelley Museum, Rome. In Dora Brown Dick's album, a small bouquet of flowers is sewn onto a page and wrapped around with hair. Princeton University Special Collections, C0199 no. 290.

26. Langford writes about photo albums, but the point holds also for these earlier ones; *Suspended Conversations: The Afterlife of Memory in Photographic Albums* (McGill-Queens University Press, 2001), p. 5.

27. Constance Classen explores this idea in "Touch in the Museum," *The Book of Touch*, edited by Constance Classen (Berg, 2005), pp. 275–6.

28. Eve Kosofsky Sedgwick writes about texture in this way in *Touching Feeling: Affect, Pedagogy, Performativity* (Duke University Press, 2003), p. 14.

29. Todd S. Gernes, "Recasting the Culture of Ephemera," *Popular Literacy: Studies in Cultural Practices and Poetics*, edited by John Trimbur (University of Pittsburgh Press, 2001), p. 109.

30. Brontë Parsonage Museum, BS15, BS177. Her father Patrick also wrote a poem in this album, signing it, "To Miss Thomas, have composed hastily, and offhand—but they may serve as a kind memento. P. Brontë, A.B., Incumbent of Haworth, near Bradford, Yorkshire." In 1845, Charlotte penned a poem in German from memory into a Miss Rooker's album and one in French—"Le Jeune Malade," by Charles Hubert Millevoye—into her friend Ellen Nussey's album. In 1846, Branwell Brontë contributed sketches and verse to the album of one Mary Pearson, of Halifax, now at the Ransom Center, MS-0526. E. B. Browning penned a few lines of *Aurora Leigh* in an acquaintance's album, signing it with her name and "Casa Guidi—June 1858," locating the place of writing as her house in Florence. Archives of American Art, Smithsonian, D0064.3.

31. As far as we know, Charlotte never made a friendship album. She did write a piece of juvenilia that she called "The Scrap Book. A Mingling of Many Things Compiled by Lord C.A.F. Wellesley," in 1835. It has the feel of a notebook in which an important person living in Angria (Charlotte and Branwell's imaginary land) has copied in historical keepsakes like a "Speech of his Grace the Duke of Zamora," a letter, a poem, and a couple of articles "extracted" from (made-up) journals. *An Edition of the Early Writings of Charlotte Brontë*, edited by Christine Alexander, vol. 2, part 2 (Blackwell, 1991), pp. 295–377.

32. Charlotte Brontë, *Shirley* (Oxford, 2008), p. 284.

33. A related type of poem was one written in a kind of visitor's book, also sometimes called an album, such as Lord Byron's September 14, 1809 "Lines Written in an Album, at Malta" and Felicia Hemans's "Lines Written for the Album at Rosanna," written about (and in) a writer's house in the county of Wicklow.

34. Maggie Strickland album, 1893–1902, Fales Library, series 4, Box 8, folder 4.

35. Ibid., folder 5.

36. Charles Lamb's "In the Album of Lucy Barton" takes the white page as its theme. It begins, "Little Book, surnamed of white, / Clean as yet, and fair to sight, / Keep thy attribution right. / Never disproportion'd scrawl; / Ugly blot, that's worse than all; / On the maiden clearness fall!" *Album Verses* (Moxon, 1830), p. 3.
37. Agnes Kitching's album, Manchester Metropolitan, #55. Many of the canonical Romantic poets wrote at least one of these album poems, and Charles Lamb collected a whole volume of his, calling it *Album Verses*. William St. Clair explores these sorts of album verses as a subgenre, p. 225. One could use manuals with verse to copy into albums, with selections to be used as "a ready means of supplying an appropriate line, verse or other matter," such as Charles A. Lilley, *Selections for Autograph and Writing Albums* (Charles A. Lilley, 1879), p. 2.
38. Matthews, "Albums, Belongings, and Embodying the Feminine," p. 121.
39. Roland Barthes, "Masson's Semiography," *The Responsibility of Forms*, translated by Richard Howard (University of California Press, 1991), p. 153. Johanna Drucker's words seem relevant here: "the act of inscription makes identity visible." *Figuring the Word: Essays on Books, Writing and Visual Poetics* (Granary Books, 1998), p. 229.
40. A. J. G. Lockhart wrote a poem in Dora Wordsworth's album in which he describes the volume being taken off of the bookshelf in order for him to write in it. F. V. Morley, *Dora Wordsworth: Her Book* (Houghton, 1925), p. 77.
41. Roe Head Album (1831–40), Brontë Parsonage Museum, C109. The album and some of its fancy pages have "De La Rue and Co. London" stamped on them. This company is still in operation, and George Eliot also bought their paper goods (see Chapter 4). For more information on the girls who contributed, see Christine Alexander, "Charlotte Brontë, Her School Friends, and the Roe Head Album," *Brontë Studies*, vol. 29, no. 1, 2004, pp. 1–16.
42. See Thad Logan, *The Victorian Parlour* (Cambridge University Press, 2001).
43. Harry S. Page, who collected more than 200 Victorian albums, remarks on the prevalence of the *"tromp l'oeil* effect," "Collecting Victoriana," *Manchester Review*, vol. 8, 1958, p. 164.
44. Eliza Threipland's album, 1812, Kislak Center for Special Collections, University of Pennsylvania, Ms. Coll. 1044.
45. For a drawing of visiting cards with text on them, see Margaret Strickland's ca. 1890s album, Fales Library, series 4, box 8, folder 5. For drawings of envelopes, see the Georgina Berkeley album 1866/71 (discussed and pictured in Elizabeth Siegel, Patrizia Di Bello, Marta Weiss, et al., *Playing with Pictures: The Art of Victorian Photocollage* [Art Institute of Chicago, 2009]). For drawings of tombstones, paper peeling up on the edges, and so on, see the miniature friendship album in the Julia P. Wightman Collection, Pierpont Morgan Library 251021, ca. 1804, and the E. T. Wilson album, Manchester Metropolitan University, #2. While there are many albums of the period with cut-paper silhouettes attached

to the pages, in some cases the real thing has been replaced with drawings of cut-paper silhouettes. See, for instance, Eliza Dennis Denyer's album at the British Library, Add. MS. 6895: 1800.
46. Pettit, p. 25. See also Lynch, "Paper Slips," pp. 99–100.
47. Drucker, *Figuring the Word*, p. 59.
48. Jed Rasula and Steve McCaffery, *Imagining Language: An Anthology* (MIT, 2001), p. 201. Tim Gaze defines asemic writing as "anything which looks like writing, but in which the person viewing can't read any words" (1). *Asemic Movement*, 1 January 2008. http//isuu.com/eexxiitt. Peter Schwenger points to its "unexpected focus on the material configurations of the markings on the page" (2). He also describes asemia this way: "writing is evoked at the same time that we are estranged from it … it is open-ended, based in wonder and in wondering" (7, 17). *Asemia: The Art of Writing* (University of Minnesota Press, 2019).
49. Brontë Parsonage Museum, E10.
50. School notebook, GEN MSS 963 Box 24, George Eliot Collection, Beinecke Library, Yale University.
51. Strickland, Fales Library, box 8, folder 5. In Agnes Kitching's album, there is another micrographic Lord's prayer. Harry S. Page collected many examples of Victorian micrography, some from disassembled albums, Manchester Metropolitan University, #7a.
52. Charlotte Brontë's miniature Lord's Prayer, Brontë Misc., Box LF, HM 33702, Huntington Library.
53. Barthes, "Masson's Semiography," p. 155.
54. Juliet Fleming, *Graffiti and the Writing Arts in Early Modern England* (Reaktion, 2001), p. 22.
55. Stewart, p. 38.
56. For more on miniature books, see Stewart, pp. 40–4, and Price, *How to Do Things*, especially pp. 19–28.
57. Morgan Library, 251021. Another miniature album, from 1832–62, belonged to Sophy Horsley and is pictured and discussed in Anne C. Bromer and Julian Edison, *Miniature Books: 4,000 Year of Tiny Treasures* (Abrams, 2007), p. 30.
58. Such as David Bryce and Company's *The Thumb Autograph Book, with Gems of Thought from Classical Authors* and Oxford University Press's *The Thumb Notebook*. See Louis W. Bondy, *Miniature Books: Their History from the Beginnings to the Present Day* (Sheppard Press, 1981), pp. 105 and 118. Florence Nightingale used tiny (2¾ by 4 inches) notebooks and almanacks, such as one at the British Library, Add. MS 45, 848, as did Fanny Burney, such as a commonplace book of consolatory extracts made when her sister died in 1800, measuring 3½ by 2½ inches. HM 293, Huntington Library.
59. Charlotte's is *A Threefold Cord; on a Precept, Promise, and Prayer, from the Holy Scriptures for Every Day in the Year* (Printed for the Religious Tract Society,

n.d.), Brontë Parsonage Museum. Emily's is Isaac Watts, *Psalms of David*, Pierpont Morgan Library, 17948. An especially poignant miniature bible, from America, was carried by a soldier during the Civil War. Most of its blank spaces are filled with penciled-in text, in some cases recording the death of a friend in battle. Attached to the front pastedown is a tintype of a child. Rare Books 254626, Huntington Library.

60. Kate E. Brown points out that the original meaning of "miniature" was "ornamented," and she explores the contradictory nature of miniature books: their "tiny size does not collapse but rather expands the time of reading" (and making). "Beloved Objects: Mourning, Materiality, and Charlotte Brontë's 'Never-Ending Story,'" *ELH*, vol. 65, no. 2, 1998, p. 405.

61. Doris V. Welsh, *The History of Miniature Books* (Fort Orange Press, 1987), pp. 33, 44.

62. Elizabeth Edwards and Janice Hart, editors, *Photographs Objects Histories: On the Materiality of Images* (Routledge, 2004), p. 11. See also Langford, pp. 91, 102.

63. Gerard Curtis, *Visual Words: Art and the Material Book in Victorian England* (Ashgate, 2002), p. 209. Curtis writes: "When the door was closed, the room became effectually sealed off from the outside world ... with Dickens surrounded by text as he wrote."

64. Nineteenth-century examples of these are pictured in Mindell Dubansky, *Blooks: The Art of Books That Aren't* (Dubansky, 2016), pp. 4–20. Giving a new meaning to the idea of a volume's interiority, an 1825 miniature book called *La Lantern Magique* (Marcilly) has removable colored illustrations that "when held against the light reveal different subjects ... for example le *sorcier*, the sorcerer, produces a beautiful lady previously invisible behind a curtain" (Bondy, p. 160). Many versions of what looked like a book, but when opened revealed a small library of miniature books, were produced in the nineteenth century. See Welsh, p. 95.

65. Dubansky, pp. 4–5, 17–21.

66. Charlotte Brontë's "housewife," Brontë Parsonage Museum, H149.

67. October 20, 1849, quoted in Uglow, 173. This desk may be the elaborate one once owned by Gaskell now at the Brontë Parsonage Museum, LI.2005.7.1.

68. See Lothar Müller, *White Magic: The Age of Paper*, translated by Jessica Spengler (Polity Press, 2014), p. 124, for examples of storing MSS in drawers and other places. See Lutz, *Brontë Cabinet: Three Lives in Nine Objects* (Norton, 2015), chapter 6, for boxes and desks. Wayne Burns discusses Charles Reade's writing methods in *Charles Reade: A Study in Victorian Authorship* (Bookman, 1961), p. 186.

69. The scrapbooks are part of the Monk's House Papers, University of Sussex, B16.f, volumes 1, 2, and 3. See Hermione Lee, *Virginia Woolf* (Vintage, 1997), pp. 630–1.

70. These will be discussed at greater length in Chapter 3.
71. Gaskell to Elizabeth Holland, December 2, 1838 and Gaskell to Marianne Gaskell, June 19, 1855. *The Letters of Mrs. Gaskell*, pp. 38 and 351.
72. Gaskell to Charles Eliot Norton, December 7, 1857. *The Letters of Mrs. Gaskell*, p. 488.
73. Gaskell to Edward Thurstan Holland, January 19, 1859. *The Letters of Mrs. Gaskell*, p. 524.
74. Gaskell to Eliza Fox, April 26, 1850 and Gaskell to Charles Eliot Norton, January 19, 1860. *The Letters of Mrs. Gaskell*, pp. 110 and 597.
75. Gaskell to Charles Eliot Norton, February 1, 1864. *The Letters of Mrs. Gaskell*, p. 725.
76. Gaskell to John Ruskin, February 1865. *The Letters of Mrs. Gaskell*, p. 748.
77. See Lynch, "Paper Slips."
78. Gaskell, *Cranford* (Broadview, 2010), p. 58. All subsequent citations will be from this edition and in-text.
79. Andrew Miller, *Novels Behind Glass: Commodity Culture and Victorian Narrative* (Cambridge University Press, 1995), p. 101. Tim Dolin, "*Cranford* and the Victorian Collection," *Victorian Studies*, vol. 36, no. 2, 1993, p. 193. See also Margaret Case Croskery, "Mothers Without Children, Unity Without Plot: *Cranford's* Radical Charm," *Nineteenth-Century Literature*, vol. 52, no. 2, 1997, pp. 198–220.
80. Talia Schaffer, *Novel Craft: Victorian Domestic Handicraft and Nineteenth-Century Fiction* (Oxford University Press, 2011), p. 61.
81. In another example, Gaskell has the core tale of "The Grey Woman" come from "a bundle of yellow MSS" (290) the narrator in the frame story acquires, then translates (from the German) and abbreviates. We, as readers, then read this "translation." *Gothic Tales* (Penguin Classics, 2000).
82. Another example from *Cranford* is a bit of folded paper with many seals calling the female community to a secret meeting to help out Matty financially.
83. Gaskell, *North and South* (Norton, 2005), p. 334.
84. Gaskell, *Wives and Daughters* (Penguin, 1996), pp. 278–9.
85. Marcus, *Between Women: Friendship, Desire, and Marriage in Victorian England* (Princeton University Press, 2007), p. 4.
86. Sometimes autographs were collected in other ways than in an album, such as on a fan. A wooden autograph fan with signatures from composers like Brahms and Johann Strauss is at the Rose Museum, Carnegie Hall. Another American one, with each spoke of the fan made up of a print of a soldier boy and, on the verso, signatures of friends, is in the Huntington Library, Zelda Walker Gaudin collection of valentines and greeting cards, ephZWG [UNCATALOGED], Paper Dolls, box 10.
87. Constance Wilde's album, British Library, Add 81755. Other nineteenth-century autograph albums of this type: Harriott Cuff White's album, Wellcome

Library, MS.5508; Jane Edwards's, British Library, Add 57724; Mary Hunt Millais's album, Morgan Library, MA 7601; and Jane H. Barge's album, Morgan, MA 7358.1-57.
88. For the history of autograph collecting, see Samantha Matthews, "Reading the 'Sign-Manual': Dickens and Signature," *Dickens Quarterly*, vol. 19, no. 4, 2002, pp. 232–42, and Müller, pp. 207–212. Susan Pearce remarks in her history of European collecting that historical objects and relics were "used as material witness to the truth of historical narratives." *On Collecting: An Investigation into Collecting in the European Tradition* (Routledge, 1995), p. 116.
89. Pascoe, *The Hummingbird Cabinet: A Rare and Curious History of Romantic Collectors* (Cornell University Press, 2006), pp. 3, 4.
90. Elizabeth Fay, *Fashioning Faces: The Portraitive Mode in British Romanticism* (New Hampshire University Press, 2010), p. 145.
91. Müller, p. 210. For more about handwriting during the period more generally, see Peter J. Capuano, *Changing Hands: Industry, Evolution, and the Reconfiguration of the Victorian Body* (University of Michigan Press, 2015), chapter 7.
92. George Eliot's close friend Sara Sophia Hennell avidly collected autographs, and Eliot often sent them to her, obtained initially when she edited the *Westminster Review* and then later through her own fame. Eliot wrote her on September 22, 1856, for instance, "Shouldn't you like an autograph letter of Currer Bell's? I hope to get you one by and bye, when Mrs. Gaskell returns the letters that have been sent to her" (263). She presumably refers to correspondence between George Henry Lewes and Charlotte Brontë, sent to Gaskell when she was writing her biography of Brontë. *The George Eliot Letters*, edited by Gordon Haight, vol. 2 (Yale University Press, 1954).
93. Hemans to Rose Lawrence, late July, 1830. *Felicia Hemans: Selected Poems, Letters, Reception Materials*, edited by Susan J. Wolfson (Princeton University Press, 2000), p. 511. Yet she gave Dora Wordsworth, William Wordsworth's daughter, a small album as a present, beginning it with her own contribution, a tribute to Rydal Mount, the Wordsworths' home. Then Dora collected contributions from her father's friends and associates, including Coleridge, his son, and his daughter. Pamela Woof discusses this album in "The Uses of Notebooks from Journal to Album, from Commonplace to Keepsake," *Coleridge Bulletin*, vol. 31, 2008, p. 17. See also Morley, *Dora Wordsworth: Her Book*. Robert Southey wrote this poem in Dora's album:

> This is a little Book; the less,
> The better it must be.
> (Dear Dora, what I think of it,
> I fairly say to thee.)

> A smaller, or a prettier Book
> I would not wish to see: ...
> I only wish it had been full
> Before it came to me.
> He signed it "Cats' Den [his office], 1 Oct. 1830."

94. Harriet Martineau, *Autobiography*, edited by Linda Peterson (Broadview, 2007), p. 219. In Martha Browne's album there are autographs from both Hemans and Martineau. British Library, Add. 73082.
95. Parker, pp. 265–78.
96. Gaskell to Frederic Chapman, February 25, 1860. *Further Letters*, p. 206.
97. Gaskell to Elizabeth Holland, December 2, 1838. *The Letters of Mrs. Gaskell*, p. 39.
98. Gaskell to Henry A. Bright, March 14, 1854. *Further Letters*, p. 108.
99. Curtis also describes how thousands of people queued outside a bookshop in order to see one manuscript page of a Dickens novel. See pp. 9, 25.
100. Gaskell to Mrs. Susan Deane, May 7, 1855. *Further Letters*, p. 136.
101. Müller discusses the materiality of letters and their history, and quotes from *Clarissa*, the famous epistolary novel in which the papery presence of letters is much dwelt on, especially ones wet with tears and kissed. See pp. 108–13.
102. See Schaffer, p. 77, for more on letters in *Cranford*.
103. Moreover, albums with autographs of the famous were often disassembled in order for individual letters or pages to be sold. For example, a page from an autograph album with scraps of paper with signatures of Charlotte Brontë, Elizabeth Gaskell, and other female writers has been removed from its album and framed with a lithograph of Elizabeth Gaskell. As of February 2020, it is for sale by Raptis Rare Books for $12,500, with the lithograph misidentified as Brontë. Another example is the manuscript leaf that contains Dickens's 1844 poem "Two verses written for Christiana Weller's [aft. Thompson] album," which was pulled off the page—tear marks on the back attest to this—and the album itself seems to have gone missing. HM 17518, Huntington Library.
104. Gaskell to someone unidentified, September 2, 1857. *Further Letters*, p. 171. Other snippets (of many) from, or still in, autograph albums: part of a letter to William Whewell, January 13, 1851 and to Sir Rutherford, February 21, 1857. *Further Letters*, pp. 52–3 and 170.
105. Gaskell to Amelia Strutt, May 18, 1850. *Further Letters*, p. 48.
106. Autograph Album, Brotherton Collection, Special Collections, Leeds University, MS 19c Gaskell/2. The 1817–73 album of Emma Isola Moxon, the wife of the publisher Edward Moxon, is a special case in that it contains autograph poems by most of the canonical authors of her lifetime, including Wordsworth, Tennyson, and Lamb. Houghton Library, Harvard University, MS Eng 601.66.

Albums that contain MSS of famous authors are often disassembled so the valuable MS can be sold or displayed separately, such as with the album created by Annie Fields (1834–1915), from which a fragment of Keats's "Hyperion" was removed and bound into a collection of his autograph poems. The album: MA 925, Morgan Library. The Keats MS is MA 342, Morgan Library. The title page of Austen's manuscript for *Susan* (published as *Northanger Abbey*) was cut up so that only a few lines remain, then pasted into an album. Realizing its value, someone cut it out of the album (but included part of the page it was pasted to) and eventually an autograph dealer sold it to the Morgan Library (MA 1958 [1]). This is the only part of the manuscript that survives.

107. *Mary Barton* (Norton, 2008), p. 205. Further citations will be from this edition and in-text.
108. Jonathan H. Grossman, *The Art of the Alibi: English Law Courts and the Novel* (Johns Hopkins University Press, 2002), p. 131. Another important scrap is the piece of letter Harry Carson rips off to draw a caricature of the working men, in their presence, adding a quote from Shakespeare. He twists it up and throws it toward the fire. One of the working-class men discovers it and is angered by his lack of respect for them, and then it is used to draw lots as to whom will murder Carson.
109. Grossman, p. 131.
110. Mary Jesup Docwra's album, Brontë Parsonage Museum, E.2006.2 Another album that has a business letter written by Patrick Brontë along with a snippet that says, "Believe me / Yours sincerely / CBrontë" is at the Fales Library, Box 21, folder 16b. Margaret Smith was able to reconstitute some of Brontë's cut-up letters when she put together her collection of Charlotte's correspondence. For example, she located five fragments of a June 9, 1849 letter Brontë wrote to her father in five different archives: the Morgan Library in New York; the private collection of Mrs. Karen Bicknell; the Ransome Humanities Center at the University of Texas; Trinity College, Dublin; and the Brontë Parsonage Museum in Yorkshire. *The Letters of Charlotte Brontë: With a Selection of Letters by Family and Friends*, vol. 2 (Oxford University Press, 1995), p. 218.
111. Gaskell to George Smith, May 31, 1855. *The Letters of Mrs. Gaskell*, p. 345.
112. Gaskell to unknown correspondent, August 23, 1855 and Gaskell to George Smith, October 10, 1855. *The Letters of Mrs. Gaskell*, pp. 369 and 371.
113. Gaskell to George Smith, July 25, 1856. *The Letters of Mrs. Gaskell*, p. 398.
114. Brontë, C., Holograph, Henry W. and Albert A. Berg Collection of English and American Literature, New York Public Library, miscellaneous manuscript material.
115. Gaskell to Mary Taylor, circa August 1855. *Further Letters*, p. 140.
116. Gaskell to Ellen Nussey, July 9, 1856. *The Letters of Mrs. Gaskell*, p. 394.
117. Gaskell to George Smith, December 1856. *The Letters of Mrs. Gaskell*, p. 426.

118. Diana Scarisbrick, *Ancestral Jewels* (Deutsch, 1989), pp. 67–8. One of these hair rings can be seen at the Victoria and Albert Museum.
119. British Library, Ashley MS 5022. The book and most of the manuscripts in it are dated 1822, but the volume was probably bound later.
120. Wise also put together a volume of Elizabeth Barrett Browning's *Sonnets from the Portuguese*, with her and Robert Browning's hair bound into the cover, and, in an edition of Robert Browning's *Reading Sonnets*, he had Browning's hair put under glass into the front cover. British Library, H843.
121. Mary Ann Evans, *Original Letters*, edited by Roland Stuart (London, 1909), British Library, Add MS 37952. A volume called *A Memento of George Gordon, Lord Byron, Countess Guiccioli, and Lady Caroline Lamb* has locks of hair of all of these three, ivory miniatures of them set into the pages, and even the envelopes in which the hair was originally kept. Kislak Collection, University of Pennsylvania, MA Coll. 386, "Collected Papers," Box 2, 1807.
122. Fleming, p. 133. In a similar sort of recursiveness, pamphlets about making paper out of jute were made out of paper made of jute, according to Dard Hunter, *Papermaking Through Eighteen Centuries* (Rudge, 1930), p. 73. Another example: a selection of poems by Robert Burns bound using part of the barn roof of Mossgiel while Burns lived there is called *The Scottish Keepsake*. The Museum of Edinburgh, HH1223/49. A volume like this gives added meaning to Stephen Orgel's comments, "the book is not simply a text; it is a place and a property." *The Reader in the Book: A Study of Spaces and Traces* (Oxford University Press, 2015), p. 5.
123. Bound by the master binder Zaehnsdorf, a Hungarian who established his London business in 1842. Now at the John Hay Library, Brown University.
124. The volumes, at the Boston Athenaeum, are entitled *The Highwayman: Narrative of the Life of James Allen alias George Walton*. See Oliver Robinson, "Bound for Glory: The Macabre Practice of Book Bindings Made of Human Skin," *Rare Book Review*, vol. 33, 2006, pp. 29–31. Other examples of books bound in the skin of criminals include a volume kept at the Bristol Royal Infirmary, bound in "the true skin of John Horwood." It tells the story of Horwood's murder of a little girl and his trial, execution, and dissection in 1821. "Human Skin as Binding," *Bookworm: An Illustrated Treasury of Old-Time Literature*, Jan. 1, 1891, p. 148. At the Moyse's Hall Museum, in Bury St. Edmunds, Suffolk, a number of relics of the famed "Murder in the Red Barn" of Maria Martin in 1827 by William Corder are on display, including an account of the trial proceedings bound in the executed murderer's skin.
125. See Lucy Peltz, "Facing the Text: The Amateur and Commercial Histories of Extra-Illustration, c. 1770–1840," *Owners, Annotators, and the Signs of Reading*, edited by Robin Myers, Michael Harris, and Giles Mandelbrote (Oak Knoll, 2005), pp. 91–135.

126. Sherman describes Ruskin as an extreme practitioner of extra-illustration. William Sherman, *Used Books: Marking Readers in Renaissance England* (University of Pennsylvania Press, 2008), pp. 87–105.
127. *Further Letters*, p. 209.
128. Mary Russell Mitford, *Rienzi: A Tragedy*, 4th ed. (John Cumberland, 1828). 11779aaa58, British Library. Tennyson, *In Memoriam* (Moxon, 1865). This book also has extra leaves bound into it, on which the reader has written extensive notes. C.194 a.693 1-3, British Library.
129. A June 17, 1886 postcard John Addington Symonds wrote to Arthur Symons from Davos-Platz, Switzerland was removed by archivists from J. A. Symonds's *Fragilia labilia* (privately printed in 1884), a presentation copy from Symonds, with an inscription that says, "Arthur Symons from John Addington Symonds." HM 59565, Huntington Library.
130. Langford, p. 41.
131. For the Queen's seaweed album, see Logan, *The Victorian Parlour* (Cambridge University Press, 2001), p. 124. For more of the Queen's albums, see Jonathan Marsden, editor, *Victoria and Albert: Art and Love* (Royal Collection Trust, 2010), pp. 185 and 355. An earlier example of a personal album is that of John Evelyn, the British intellectual, who created a page where he attached snippets of his own hair during three stages of his life. A pasted-in piece of paper says, "My hair at 40: 50: 70—80. This year: 1700," then his initials. Ransom Center.
132. Private collection, described in the 2019 auction catalogue of Marlborough Rare Books, London. I thank Liz Denlinger, curator of the Pforzheimer Collection, for alerting me to this.
133. Florence Nightingale Museum, FNM: 0600 and FM 0601.1-2.
134. Anonymous souvenir album, Brontë Parsonage Museum, E 2013.2.
135. Langford, p. 44.
136. See Carol Armstrong and Catherine de Zegher, editors, *Ocean Flowers: Impressions from Nature* (Princeton University Press, 2004) and Andrea Di Noto and David Winter, *The Pressed Plant: The Art of Botanical Specimen, Nature Prints, and Sun Pictures* (Stewart, Tabori and Chang, 1999).
137. Charlotte Brontë's fern album, Brontë Parsonage Museum, bb238. Since some of the pages of the album have a watermark of 1869, they were not all made by Brontë. It's possible Brontë arranged the ferns on some of the pages, and others were arranged by members of the Bell family, and then the leaves were bound into an album later, a common practice at the time. It's also possible that Brontë only collected and pressed the ferns, and they were made into an album later, by the Bell family. The album came from Frances Bell whose aunt was Arthur Nicholls's second wife, the Mrs. Nicholls referred to here. She gave it to Frances, who then handed it down to her niece, Mrs. Marjorie Gallop. It was donated to the BPM by her descendants. Christopher and Nigel Gallop, "Recent Acquisitions," *Brontë Society Transactions*, vol. 21, no. 4, 1994, p. 156.

138. Album of British Mosses, 1854, MS Coll. 1151, Kislak Collection, University of Pennsylvania. See also the anonymous "Album of beautiful seaweeds, souvenir de Torquay," 1860, Kislak Collection, MS. Coll. 1150, which also contains the wing of a flying fish, some ferns, watercolors of the area, and some pasted-in botanical prints.
139. Quoted in S. P. Rowlands, "An Old Fern Collection," *The British Fern Gazette*, vol. 6, no. 10, 1934, p. 261. She also included two quotations.
140. Quoted in Rowlands, p. 261.
141. The Stovin album given to Nightingale is at the Florence Nightingale Museum, FNM 1072. The other volumes mentioned here are also at the Florence Nightingale Museum, FNM 0773, FNM 0077.
142. Gaskell to Parthenope Nightingale, October 17, 1854. *The Letters of Mrs. Gaskell*, p. 313.
143. Quoted in Larry J. Schaaf, *Sun Pictures. Catalogue 10. British Paper Negatives, 1839–1864* (Hans P. Kraus, Jr., 2001), p. 35. See Chapter 5 for more on Atkins.
144. Schaaf, p. 36. Fern collecting was a major fad in the middle of the nineteenth century, and one could buy volumes with real ferns pressed into them, such as William Gardiner's *A Selection of British Ferns and Their Allies* (1850) and Jane Patison's *Gleanings Among the British Ferns* (1858). Some were regional, such as J. J. Flintoft's *Complete Collections of the British Ferns and their Allies in the English Lake District* and *The Ferns of Wales* (1858) by Edward Young. Other volumes about ferns had special pages, left blank, for real specimens to be attached. These volumes and others like them are discussed in Sarah Whittingham, *Fern Fever: The History of Pteridomania* (Frances Lincoln, 2012), pp. 69–86 and David Elliston Allen, *The Victorian Fern Craze: A History of Pteridomania* (Hutchinson, 1969), pp. 52–3.
145. See Geoffrey Batchen, *Forget Me Not: Photography and Remembrance* (Princeton Architectural Press, 2004) and Siegel et al., *Playing with Pictures*.
146. Di Bello, p. 72.
147. Ibid., p. 75.
148. See Siegel et al., *Playing with Pictures*.

Notes to Chapter 3

1. JOURNAL 1861–77 Jul–Dec, GEN MSS 963, Box 17, Beinecke Library, Yale University. This notebook is transcribed in *The Journals of George Eliot*, edited by Margaret Harris and Judith Johnston (Cambridge University Press, 1998).
2. Leah Price's work on books as objects has been important to the development of this argument, especially *How to Do Things with Books in Victorian Britain* (Princeton University Press, 2012).

3. For histories and discussions of commonplace books, in addition to the sources cited below, see Heather Jackson, *Marginalia: Readers Writing Books* (Yale University Press, 2001); Susan Stabile, "Female Curiosities: The Transatlantic Female Commonplace Book," *Reading Women: Literacy, Authorship, and Culture in the Atlantic World, 1500–1800*, edited by Heidi Brayman Hackel and Catherine E. Kelly (University of Pennsylvania Press, 2008), pp. 217–44; and Ann Blair, *Too Much to Know: Managing Scholarly Information Before the Modern Age* (Yale University Press, 2010).
4. David Allan explores the different uses of the term (see his chapter 2), but he himself confuses matters by calling friendship albums commonplace books, especially page 142. *Commonplace Books and Reading in Georgian England* (Cambridge University Press, 2010).
5. Samuel Taylor Coleridge, *Collected Letters*, edited by E. L. Griggs (Oxford University Press, 1956–71), vol. 1, p. 323. Anne Lister records in her diary how she wrote out extracts in her commonplace book before returning books: "made an extract or 2 from Lord Byron's Childe Harold and the lyrics at the end of the book in readiness to take it back." Quoted in *I Know My Own Heart: The Diaries of Anne Lister 1791–1840*, edited by Helena Whitbread (New York University Press, 1988), p. 49.
6. Jane Austen, in *Pride and Prejudice* (Penguin, 2003), pokes fun at this seriousness, with Mary, the too-studious sister, "a young lady of deep reflection" who reads "great books, and make[s] extracts" (9).
7. Heather Jackson, "'Marginal Frivolities': Readers' Notes as Evidence for the History of Reading," *Owners, Annotators, and the Signs of Reading*, edited by Robin Myers, Michael Harris, and Gilles Mandelbrote (British Library, 2005), pp. 137–53. Heidi Brayman Hackel writes that "commonplace books are the logical and radical extension of marginalia," *Reading Material in Early Modern England: Print, Gender, and Literacy* (Cambridge University Press, 2005), p. 137.
8. Anne Lister often wrote in her diary about how she created indexes for her four volumes of extracts. Here is one example of many: "In the evening, writing out the rough draft of an index to the 3rd vol. of my journal." Quoted in *I Know My Own Heart*, p. 17. Some of George Eliot's notebooks were organized under alphabetical headings (such as PFMS [MISC 0710], Carl H. Pforzheimer Collection of Shelley and his Circle, New York Public Library) and had tables of contents, such as PFMS (MISC 0711), Pforzheimer. For Lister, see also William St. Clair, *The Reading Nation in the Romantic Period* (Cambridge University Press, 2004), p. 226.
9. Lucia Dacome, "Noting the Mind: Commonplace Books and the Pursuit of the Self in Eighteenth-Century Britain," *Journal of the History of Ideas*, vol. 65, no. 4, 2004, pp. 603–25.

10. Stephen Colclough, "'A Grey Goose Quill and an Album': The Manuscript Book and Text Transmission, 1800–1850," *Owners, Annotators, and the Signs of Reading*, p. 157.
11. Earle Havens, *Commonplace Books: A History of Manuscript Books from Antiquity to the Twentieth Century* (University Press of New England, 2001), pp. 9–10. Leah Price, in *The Anthology and the Rise of the Novel: From Richardson to George Eliot* (Cambridge University Press, 2000), investigates the relationship between commonplaces and anthologies.
12. This inscription is on its flyleaf: "Mrs. Browning, in token of admiration and respect from Charles Hemans, Rome, May 25th 1854." MS Eng 767, Houghton Library, Harvard University. See also Allan, pp. 29–34. Another of Hemans's commonplaces was "Given to M.L. Bosomworth by a friend of Mrs. Hemans, June 1851," as it says on the front pastedown, Acc. 2566, Liverpool City Library. Hemans also had one of her commonplace books published: *Young Woman's Companion, or Female Instructor* (1835). In Samuel Richardson's *Clarissa* (Penguin, 1986), the title character bequeaths hers, when she is preparing herself for death: "I desire Mrs Lovick to accept of ... a copy of my book of *meditations*, as I used to call it; being extracts from the best of books; which she seemed to approve of ... As for the book itself, perhaps my good Mrs. Norton will be glad to have it, as it is written all with my own hand" (1417).
13. William Sherman, *Used Books: Marking Readers in Renaissance England* (University of Pennsylvania Press, 2008), p. 129.
14. Juliet Fleming, *Graffiti and the Writing Arts in Early Modern England* (Reaktion, 2001), p. 48. A seventeenth-century tester bed at Shibden Hall, Anne Lister's house in Halifax, has text painted around the top that says, "All within this earthly vale, by nature and by kind, are nought else but vain and vile. By this day I find the tender babes young of age whom nature hath now wrought by dint of death and destiny to the first form be brought."
15. Hackel, p. 38. The eighteenth-century American preacher Jonathan Edwards was said to have pinned to his coat slips of paper with ideas that came to him while he was out walking or riding. If ideas came to him while he was in bed, he pinned the jotted notes to the bed hangings. I thank Marion Rust for alerting me to this. See Wilson H. Kimnach and Kenneth P. Minkema, "The Material and Social Practices of Intellectual Work: Jonathan Edwards's Study," *The William and Mary Quarterly*, vol. 69, no. 4, 2012, p. 683.
16. Marie Corelli, *The Sorrows of Satan* (Valancourt Books, 2008), p. 171.
17. Ella Hepworth Dixon, *The Story of a Modern Woman* (Broadview, 2004), p. 96.
18. Eliot's Blotter, ADD MS 59866, British Library. See the transcription of the blotter in *George Eliot Blotter: A Commonplace Book*, edited by Daniel Waley (The British Library, 1980).
19. She copied out these lines again around 1875 when she was researching *Daniel Deronda*. "Miscellaneous Notes," MS 711, Pforzheimer. Transcribed in William

Baker, *Some George Eliot Notebooks: An Edition of the Carl H. Pforzheimer Library's George Eliot Holograph Notebooks*, vol. 3 (Universtät Salzburg, 1985).

20. Discussed at greater length in Chapter 1. George Eliot, *Middlemarch* (Penguin, 1994), p. 412. All subsequent quotes will be from this edition and in-text.

21. Notebook of George Eliot, M.a. 13–14, Folger Shakespeare Library. See the transcription of this notebook in *George Eliot's Middlemarch Notebooks: A Transcription*, edited by John Clark Pratt and Victor A. Neufeldt (University of California Press, 1979).

22. For Coleridge, see Jillian M. Hess, "Coleridge's Fly-Catchers: Adapting Commonplace-Book Form," *Journal of the History of Ideas*, vol. 73, no. 3, 2012, pp. 463–83; *The Notebooks of Samuel Taylor Coleridge*, edited by Kathleen Coburn and M. Christensen, 4 vols (Princeton University Press, 1980–90); and *Coleridge's Notebooks: A Selection*, edited by Seamus Perry (Oxford University Press, 2002). For Southey's notebooks, see Havens, p. 58. For Arnold's commonplace books, see *The Note-Books of Matthew Arnold*, edited by Howard Foster Lowry, Karl Young, and Waldo Hilary Dunn (Oxford University Press, 1952). For Hardy, see *Thomas Hardy's "Facts" Notebook: A Critical Edition*, edited by William Greenslade (Routledge, 2004); *The Literary Notebooks of Thomas Hardy*, edited by Lennart A. Björk, 3 vols (Macmillan, 1985); and *Thomas Hardy's "Studies, Specimens &c." Notebook*, edited by Pamela Dalziel and Michael Millgate (Oxford University Press, 1994). The Carroll commonplace book is at the Harry Ransom Humanities Research Center, University of Texas, Austin. An exception from the early twentieth century are Virginia Woolf's sixty-seven "reading notebooks," published in *Virginia Woolf's Reading Notebooks*, edited by Brenda Silver (Princeton University Press, 1983).

23. Wordsworths' Commonplace Book, MS26, Dove Cottage, Grasmere. Both Wordsworths keep a range of notebooks. See, for instance, Helen Boden's facsimile version of Dorothy Wordsworth's travel journals, *Her Write His Name: The Continental Journals, 1798–1820* (Thoemannes Continuum, 1995).

24. Pamela Woof, "The Uses of Notebooks from Journal to Album, from Commonplace to Keepsake," *Coleridge Bulletin*, vol. 31, 2008, pp. 1–18. In another mixed-use notebook, Dorothy Wordsworth composed her own poetry, quoted others, kept household accounts, recorded her travels, and more. Commonplace Book DCMS 120, Jerwood Centre, Grasmere. In her dissertation, Deborah Lynn Pfuntner discusses this notebook at great length. See chapter 2, "Romantic Women Writers and Their Commonplace Books," Texas A&M University, 2016.

25. Simon Reader, "Social Notes: Oscar Wilde, Francis Bacon, and the Medium of Aphorism," *Journal of Victorian Culture*, vol. 18, no. 4, 2013, p. 463. See also his "Oscar Wilde's Notebook on Philosophy," *Canadian Journal of Irish Studies*, vol. 36, no. 2, 2010, pp. 21–31. Joseph Bristow and Rebecca N. Mitchell write about another Wilde notebook in *Oscar Wilde's Chatterton: Literary History, Romanticism, and the Art of Forgery* (Yale University Press, 2015).

26. Hackel, p. 182.
27. As David Allan puts it, commonplacing "automatically enhanced readers' intimacy with what they copied" (112).
28. Linda K. Hughes, "George Eliot's 'Greek Vocabulary' Notebook (c. 1873) as Commodity and Rare Artefact," *Cahiers: Victorienns et Edouardiens*, vol. 84, 2016, http://cve.revues.org/2973, paragraph 3. Jackson also discusses stationers in *Romantic Readers*, p. 33.
29. One of Charles Reade's notebooks is a "Letts Extract Book prepared for the reception of various scraps from various sources." LL. No. 37, London Library. Eliot's Letts notebook: Journal 1854–79, GEN MSS 963, box 20, Beinecke. Their addresses at the time were 8 Royal Exchange and 24 Queen Street. The company, founded in 1796, is still making notebooks today.
30. Two of her notebooks have the Mabley label in them: one is a notebook for *Romola*, ca. 1860, Add MS 70, 768, British Library, and the other is Journal 1858–60, GEN MSS 963, Box 16, Beinecke. Eliot lived at 142 Strand, right next door to Mabley's, from 1851 to 1853. The Parkins one is a notebook for *Daniel Deronda*, PFMS (MISC 0718), Pforzheimer. Eliot wrote some of her MSS on Parkins and Gotto paper according to Jerome Beaty, *Middlemarch, from Notebook to Novel: A Study of George Eliot's Creative Method* (University of Illinois Press, 1960), pp. 12–15. The Creswick, called by Eliot "Interesting Extracts," is Ms. M. a. 14, Folger. For the latter, see William Baker, "The Other George Eliot Notebooks at the Folger Shakespeare Library: A Survey," *The George Eliot, George Henry Lewes Newsletter*, no. 12/13, 1988, pp. 1–6.
31. For example, Reade's commonplace books, LL no. 16 and LL no. 19, London Library, have the same stationer's label. Michael Field journals, Add MS 46776–46804, British Library. Anne Lister bought some, possibly all, of the notebooks she filled with her diary at her local Halifax stationer, Whitley and Booth, on Crown St, according to receipts at the Calderdale Archive, Halifax, where her diaries now reside, and according to the diary itself, where she says, "Called at Whitley's, the booksellers, to pay for a blank book." Quoted in *I Know My Own Heart*, p. 2. Elizabeth Barrett Browning bought blank books from the wonderfully named Serendipity Shop, 46 Museum St., London, W.C., as well as stationers in Boulogne, France.
32. Lisa Gitelman, *Paper Knowledge: Toward a Media History of Documents* (Duke University Press, 2014), p. 21. Another term is "version notebook," mentioned in Robert Louis Stevenson's *Strange Case of Dr. Jekyll and Mr. Hyde* as the type of notebook Dr. Jekyll uses to comment on his experiments. This was usually for school exercises for versions—that is, language translations—so Jekyll uses it in a way not intended by its makers. Havens lists index books, waste books, day books, entry books, account books, and more. See p. 65. Oxford University Press published a tiny blank book called *The Thumb Note Book* in 1896.

See Louis W. Bondy, *Miniature Books: Their History from the Beginnings to the Present Day* (Sheppard Press, 1981), p. 118.
33. Commonplace book, 1859–94, MA 390, Pierpont Morgan Library. Havens describes a hand-tabbed commonplace book made by Robert Clifford in circa 1706, p. 81.
34. PFMS (MISC 0710), Pforzheimer. See the transcription of this notebook in Baker, *Some George Eliot Notebooks*, vol. 4 (Universtät Salzburg, 1985) and Jane Irwin, editor, *George Eliot's* Daniel Deronda *Notebooks* (Cambridge University Press, 1996).
35. PFMS (MISC 0707), Pforzheimer. Transcribed by Baker, vol. 1.
36. Talia Schaffer explores the rebinding of books as a domestic handicraft practiced by women. See *Novel Craft: Victorian Domestic Handicraft and Nineteenth-Century Fiction* (Oxford University Press, 2011), pp. 16–17.
37. See, for instance, Anne Lister diary, SH:7/ML/E/13, 1830, Calderdale Archive.
38. Journal 1854–61, GEN MSS 963, Box 15, Beinecke. Transcribed in Harris and Johnston.
39. For discussions of Reade's notebook keeping, see Malcolm Elwin, *Charles Reade* (Russell and Russell, 1969), especially pp. 67, 140, 220, and 289, and Wayne Burns, *Charles Reade: A Study in Victorian Authorship* (Bookman, 1961), pp. 172–91, 209–12. Also see E. G. Sutcliffe, "Charles Reade's Notebooks," *Studies in Philology*, vol. 27, no. 1, 1930, pp. 64–109. Reade describes writing his novel *Peg Wolffington* in "copy books" in his diary. Quoted in Charles Reade and Compton Reade, *Charles Reade, Dramatist, Novelist, Journalist, a Memoir*, vol. 1 (Chapman and Hall, 1887), pp. 321–2. Reade kept letters written to himself and put them in an album, although it wasn't exactly an autograph collection, since it was just another example of his drive to keep everything and stick it in a book. But he did sometimes send out autographs, as can be seen in his references to this in his notebooks (Sutcliffe, p. 88).
40. LL no. 17, London Library. Sutcliffe describes this notebook, dating it circa 1860–1 and 1871, p. 83.
41. LL no. 19, London Library.
42. Quoted in Elwin, p. 289.
43. Burns, p. 209.
44. Burns, p. 191. Violet Paget (Vernon Lee) was another enthusiastic notebook keeper, mostly of ideas and drafts of her articles and fiction. She also created indexes of her notebooks, which were themselves notebooks. More than thirty of them are at the Colby College Special Collections and Archives.
45. Charles Reade, *A Terrible Temptation* (Collier, 1900), p. 99.
46. Commonplace Book, LL no. 16, London Library.
47. *A Terrible Temptation*, p. 99.
48. John Sutherland, *The Stanford Companion to Victorian Fiction* (Stanford University Press, 1989), p. 523.

49. For instance, in *The Double Marriage, or White Lies* (Chatto and Windus, 1891), a hotel has large letters written on it, which Reade has printed in enlarged text and all caps (p. 16).
50. *Griffith Gaunt; Or, Jealousy*, vol. 3 (Chapman and Hall, 1866), p. 49.
51. In one case, it says, "*Why overlook the Handlers?* MARY," with the signature in all caps. *Put Yourself in His Place* (Fields, Osgood, and Co., 1870), p. 28.
52. *The Cloister and the Hearth*, vol. 2 (Trübner and Co., 1862), p. 140.
53. Eliot's research notebooks are comparable in some ways to Florence Nightingale's, some of which were commonplace books in the more general sense (such as Add MS 45, 848, British Library), others diaries (such as Add MS 45, 847, British Library, which is a "Gentleman's Pocket Daily Companion," 1877), and still others pocket-sized, looking like little wallets with clasps, which she carried on her while traveling, taking research notes for her books (such as Add MS 45848, 1836, British Library).
54. An Eliot notebook that was recursive in a different way from the other ones discussed in this chapter is titled by her: "Copy of Fragmentary Notes in Various Books." She created this notebook, which has now lost its covers, when she was preparing Lewes's final book for publication after his death. Here she copied some of his notes, in her purple ink, from his collection of notebooks, a form of highlighting and consolidated from many into one. HM 12995, Huntington Library.
55. "Quarry for Middlemarch," Lowell 13, Harvard Houghton. Transcribed in Anna Theresa Kitchel, editor, *Quarry for Middlemarch* (University of California Press, 1950). See also Beaty.
56. Baker traces other examples of Eliot copying from one notebook to another; see especially vol. 1, p. 36, note 1. Ruth Abbott comments on this repetitiveness in Eliot's notebooks: "it seems that one thing she particularly wanted to do with these notes was to write them out several times, in several orders and contexts ... The kinds of learning that happen through writing seem to have been as important to Eliot as the kinds of learning that happen through reading." See "George Eliot, Meter, and the Matter of Ideas: The Yale Poetry Notebook," *ELH*, vol. 82, no. 4, 2005, p. 1184. The notebook she writes about is 963, Box 21, Beinecke.
57. Eliot's twenty-five notebooks exclude the single-leaf card with notes for a novel discussed and pictured in Chapter 4 (Fig. 14) and the blotter covered in notes, at the British Library, explored in Chapter 1.
58. Letter to Maria Lewis, March 13, 1840. *The George Eliot Letters*, edited by Gordon S. Haight, vol. 1 (Yale University Press, 1954–78), p. 42.
59. See Hughes.
60. Journal 1858–60, GEN MSS 963, Box 16, Beinecke. Transcribed in Harris and Johnston.

61. Diary for 1879, Berg Coll MSS Eliot, G., Henry W. and Albert A. Berg Collection of English and American Literature, New York Public Library. This notebook is transcribed in Harris and Johnston.
62. Nancy Henry discusses this mixing into the notebooks of Eliot's finances; see *George Eliot and the British Empire* (Cambridge University Press, 2002), pp. 2, 5, and 80.
63. Abbott, p. 1204.
64. Baker, vol. 1, p. 6. The quote comes from Eliot's notebook, MS 707, Pforzheimer.
65. See Chapter 1 for a sustained discussion of this.
66. Journal 1864–5, GEN MSS 963, Box 18, Beinecke. Transcribed in Harris and Johnston.
67. She used other notebooks with advanced technology, like one with a label that says, "Henry Penny's Patent Improved Metallic Books," MISC 0707, Pforzheimer.
68. Notebook, 1880, GEN MSS 963, Box 22, Beinecke. Transcribed in Harris and Johnston. In a pocket in one of the notebooks she used for her *Middlemarch* research is a memorial card with a picture of one Valère Joseph Hayman (1844–69). Notebook of George Eliot, M.a. 13–14, Folger Shakespeare Library. Transcription Pratt and Neufeldt.
69. The poem begins, "Dear Friend, when all thy greatness suddenly / Burst out, and thou wert other than I thought, / At first I wept—for Marian, whom I sought, / Now passed beyond herself, seemed lost to me." Hennell wrote the poem when Eliot confessed to her that she was the "George Eliot" who wrote *Scenes of Clerical Life* and *Adam Bede*. The books were immensely popular and much speculation went into identifying their true authorship. Hennell, herself a published author, was at first envious of Eliot's great success. See Gordon Haight, *George Eliot: A Biography* (Penguin, 1986), p. 288.
70. Beinecke, JOURNAL 1861–77 Jul–Dec, GEN MSS 963, Box 17. Transcribed in Harris and Johnston. She also writes in this notebook, poignantly, "I do not feel very confident that I can make anything satisfactory of Middlemarch," and, in 1870, "suffering from headache and depression ... I look into this little book now to assure myself that this is not unprecedented."
71. Abbott, p. 1189. In a similar vein, Sally Shuttleworth explores Eliot's use of Spencer's "universal principal of development from homogeneity to heterogeneity." *George Eliot and Nineteenth-Century Science: The Make-Believe of a Beginning* (Cambridge University Press, 1984), p. 149.
72. David Leon Higden, "George Eliot and the Art of the Epigraph," *Nineteenth-Century Fiction*, vol. 25, no. 2, 1970, p. 131.
73. PFMS (MISC 0708), Pforzheimer. Transcribed by Baker, vol. 2. Baker discusses the difficulty of dating this notebook in vol. 1, pp. 8–11.
74. Notebook of George Eliot, M.a. 13–14, Folger. Transcription Pratt and Neufeldt.

75. Eve Kosofsky Sedgwick, *Touching Feeling: Affect, Pedagogy, Performativity* (Duke University Press, 2003), p. 35.
76. Seth Lerer, *Error and the Academic Self* (Columbia University Press, 2002), p. 105. Nancy Henry explores possible real-life models for Casaubon. *The Life of George Eliot: A Critical Biography* (Wiley-Blackwell, 2012), pp. 193–8.
77. PFMS (MISC 0707), Pforzheimer. Baker transcribes this list in vol. 1, pp. 316–17, and since her handwriting is hard to make out in some entries, the exact number of volumes is an estimate.
78. George Eliot, *Romola* (Penguin, 1996), p. 53.
79. Lerer, p. 105.
80. Letter to John Blackwood, November 12, 1873. *Letters*, vol. 5, pp. 458–9.
81. Gaskell, *Cranford* (Broadview Press, 2010), p. 127 and Austen, *Emma* (Longman, 2006), p. 54.
82. For a history of these gift books, see Lorraine Janzen Kooistra, *Poetry, Pictures, and Popular Publishing: The Illustrated Gift Book and Victorian Visual Culture, 1855–1875* (Ohio University Press, 2011).
83. Comparable to the bit of letter Raffles picks up, the "tiny bit of folded paper" (804) Rosamond puts in Will Ladislaw's saucer mends the budding romantic relationship between Will and Dorothea, leading to their eventual marriage.
84. Letter to John Blackwood, *Letters*, vol. 5, p. 458.
85. Price, *The Anthology*, pp. 105, 124.
86. Ibid., p. 128.
87. There are other sorts of notebooks that I don't discuss here, in the interests of time and space. One could be called "idea notebooks," where impressions, stray thoughts, and random sketches are recorded. Thomas Hardy's "Memoranda, I" notebook is this sort, transcribed in *The Personal Notebooks of Thomas Hardy*, edited by Richard H. Taylor (Columbia University Press, 1979).
88. Sally Bushell discusses these notebooks in *Text as Process: Creative Composition in Wordsworth, Tennyson, and Dickinson* (University of Virginia Press, 2009). For other important notebooks of drafts of the period, see *Thomas Hardy's "Poetical Matter" Notebook*, edited by Pamela Dalziel and Michael Millgate (Oxford University Press, 2009); *The Complete Notebooks of Henry James*, edited by Leon Edel and Lyall H. Powers (Oxford University Press, 1987); Percy Bysshe Shelley's notebooks, *The Bodleian Shelley Manuscripts: A Facsimile Edition*, edited by Donald H. Reiman, 23 vols (Garland, 1986–2002); and Mary Shelley, *The Frankenstein Notebooks*, edited by Charles E. Robinson, 2 vols (Routledge, 2016). Dante Gabriel Rossetti buried, and then later retrieved, one of his poetry notebooks in the coffin of his wife Elizabeth Siddal. See Jan Marsh, *Dante Gabriel Rossetti: Painter and Poet* (Phoenix, 2005), pp. 374–7. Another type of "draft" notebook is a fair copy meant to be presented to another, such as D. G. Rossetti's "Kelmscott Love Sonnets," an 1874 notebook presented to Jane Morris, Ms Eng Poet d. 43, Bodleian, Oxford.

89. See, for instance, Browning's first draft of *Aurora Leigh*, MS Browning D49, Wellesley College Library Special Collections. For Woolf, see, for instance, her travel and literary notebook, Add MS 61837, British Library.
90. Anne composed a poetry notebook with poems dating 1840–5 that looks handmade. Bon 134, Brontë Parsonage Museum.
91. Charlotte described finding one of Emily's poetry notebooks and convincing her to publish the joint poetry book to her publisher and eventual friend W. S. Williams in a letter of September 1848. *The Letters of Charlotte Brontë*, edited by Margaret Smith, vol. 2 (Oxford University Press, 1995), p. 119. She gives another version of the finding in her "Biographical Notice of Ellis and Acton Bell," published in an 1850 edition of *Wuthering Heights*, *Agnes Grey*, and a selection of her sisters' poems, by Smith, Elder & Co.
92. Derek Roper details the history of the notebooks and other MSS in his introduction to *The Poems of Emily Brontë* (Clarendon, 1995), pp. 1–29. A facsimile of this notebook was published in 1934, in volume 17 of The Shakespeare Head edition of the Brontës' writing, *The Poems of Emily Jane Brontë and Anne Brontë*, edited by Thomas Wise and John Alexander Symington (Shakespeare Head Press, 1934). As of July 2021, the notebook is still in private hands and unavailable to researchers.
93. Janet Gezari, *Last Things: Emily Brontë's Poems* (Oxford University Press, 2007), p. 80.
94. Susan Howe, *The Birth-Mark: Unsettling the Wilderness in American Literary History* (Wesleyan University Press, 1993), p. 147.
95. Emily Brontë notebook, Add. MS. 43483, British Library. This notebook may have been rebound. Derek Roper writes in 1996 that it has a "red paper cover bearing the price 6d." *Poems of Emily Bro*ntë, p. 15. When I handled it in 2016, its binding was a worn, red leather, and there was no visible price. The binding was quite delicate; it was coming apart along its seams, which makes me think it is original, although this is only speculation.
96. The penultimate poem was written after the manuscript of *Wuthering Heights* had been sent off to publishers in July 1846, and she worked on the final poem after *Wuthering Heights* had been published in December of 1847. For speculation about the dates of drafts and revisions, see Edward Chitham, *The Birth of Wuthering Heights: Emily Brontë at Work* (St. Martin's, 1998), especially pp. 142–3.
97. E6, Brontë Parsonage Museum.
98. Brontë's notebook can be compared to Jane Austen's three vellum-bound notebooks, given to her by her father, started when she was eleven or twelve and finished when she was seventeen. They imitate published books, with tables of contents and illustrations made by her sister Cassandra. The second and third volumes are at the British Library, Add MS 59874 and Add 65381. The first is at the Bodleian, MS Don. E. 7. See Claire Tomalin, *Jane*

Austen: A Life (Vintage, 1999), p. 68. Lewis Carroll made the original version of his Alice story into an illustrated fair-copy notebook for Alice Liddall and her sisters, called "Alice's Adventure Under Ground" (at the British Library, Add MS 46700). Only later did he revise and publish it. In this case and that of the Austen notebooks, these "editions" were made for close friends and the family circle, whereas Emily's were only for herself. Christina Rossetti created an illustrated fair-copy notebook of *Sing-Song: A Nursery Rhyme Book* (British Library, Ashley MS 1371), and wrote after the title page, "Rhymes dedicated without permission to the Baby who suggested them."

99. In another example of the temporal marking of work, Christina Rossetti dates most of the poems in her notebooks of fair copies. Six are at the British Library, Ashley MS 1364 (1–6); nine are at the Bodleian, MS DON. E. 1–9; one is at the Ransom Center, University of Texas, MS-3623; and others are in private hands. Some of her notebooks were broken up and the separate pages sold by her brother William Rossetti after her death. See, for instance, the autograph MS of "Uphill" that also includes the conclusion of "At Home." The unscrupulous collector and forger Thomas Wise eventually owned it, and he included a letter from W. M. Rossetti when he sold it on to Henry Huntington. On mourning stationery, it says in part: "Christina Rossetti, from the time when she first began writing verse, was in the habit of transcribing them into little notebooks, giving the dates of composition. The leaf which contains 'Up-hill' (along with the conclusion of 'At Home') comes out of one of these notebooks. It was purchased from me, soon after Christina's death, by Mr. F.H. Evans," HM 6066–6067, Huntington Library. See also *The Complete Poems of Christina Rossetti: A Variorum Edition*, vol. 3, edited by R. W. Crump (Louisiana State University Press, 1990), pp. 3–6.

100. *An Edition of the Early Writings of Charlotte Brontë: The Glass Town Saga, 1826–1832*, edited by Christine Alexander, vol. 1 (Shakespeare Head Press, 1987), p. 134.

101. Anne Brontë also made poetry notebooks in which she recorded and arranged final drafts, and some of them had Gondal dates and were "signed" by Gondal characters, such as Zerona. See, for instance, MSS HM 2576 at the Huntington Library.

102. In the case of "From a Dungeon Wall in the Southern College," she has written "E.J.B. Nov. 11, 1844" and then "J.B. Sept. 1825." The former date is when she wrote it, the latter the initials of the imaginary writer who wrote it and when, in Gondal time.

103. Charlotte wrote a "Catalogue of My Books" that lists all of the micro-tomes she had written thus far, presenting herself not only as a widely published author but also as having an extensive library (large enough to be worth cataloguing), something she could never afford in the real world.

104. Victor Neufeldt, *The Poems of Charlotte Brontë* (Garland, 1985), pp. 396–7. Another title page reads, "The Search after Happiness, A Tale by Charlotte Brontë, Printed by Herself and Sold By Nobody." *An Edition of the Early Writings of Charlotte Brontë*, vol. 1, p. 42.
105. *An Edition of the Early Writings of Charlotte Brontë*, p. 69.
106. Anne and Emily Brontë, diary paper, June 26, 1837, Brontë Parsonage Museum.
107. Emily Brontë, diary paper, July 30, 1841. MS believed to be in private hands, but a facsimile can be found in Clement Shorter, *Charlotte Brontë and Her Circle* (Hodder and Stoughton, 1896).
108. Emily Brontë, diary paper, July 30, 1845. MS believed to be in private hands, but see the facsimile in Shorter.
109. Stein writes, "The time of composition is the time of composition," in "Composition as Explanation." Quoted in Steve McCaffery and Jed Rasula, editors, *Imagining Language: An Anthology* (MIT Press, 2001), p. 6.
110. Curtis sees this as a Victorian phenomenon but also, seemingly, a male one, since his arguments center on Dickens, Ruskin, and Thackeray. *Visual Words: Art and the Material Book in Victorian England* (Ashgate, 2002), p. 15.
111. Emma Donoghue, *We Are Michael Field* (Absolute, 1998), p. 47.
112. *Works and Days: From the Journal of Michael Field*, edited by T. D. C. Sturge Moore (Murray, 1933), p. 326.
113. *Works and Days*, p. 12.
114. Donoghue, pp. 106–8.
115. *Works and Days*, p. 21.
116. Michael Field, "Works and Days," 1890, Add MS 46778, British Library. Most of these diaries have been digitized and transcribed on the excellent website "The Diaries of Michael Field," https://michaelfielddiary.dartmouth.edu/home.
117. Fields, 1904, MS 46793, British Library.
118. Quoted in Donoghue, p. 12.
119. Introduction to *Works and Days*, p. xv.
120. Letter to Martha Jackson, October 20, 1840. *Letters*, vol. 1, p. 70.

Notes to Chapter 4

1. Emily Brontë, *Wuthering Heights* (Broadview, 2007), p. 281.
2. For example, E2, held at the Henry W. and Albert A. Berg Collection of English and American Literature, New York Public Library (hereafter Berg), which begins "Tis evening now the sun descends," has no date and measures 1 by 2 inches. Brontë's poetry manuscripts are designated by letters and numbers following a system created by C. W. Hatfield. See Hatfield, editor, *The Complete Poems of Emily Brontë* (Columbia University Press, 1941).

3. Thomas Carlyle, *The French Revolution: A History*, vol. 1 (Chapman and Hall, 1872), p. 26.
4. See Leah Price, "Getting the Reading Out of It: Paper Recycling in Mayhew's London," *Bookish Histories: Books, Literature and Commercial Modernity, 1700–1900*, edited by Ina Ferris and Paul Keen (Palgrave, 2009), p. 154, and *How to Do Things with Books in Victorian England* (Princeton University Press, 2012), pp. 27–9. See also Talia Schaffer, *Novel Craft: Victorian Domestic Handicraft and Nineteenth-Century Fiction* (Oxford University Press, 2011), pp. 17–19. More generally, see Andrew Stauffer, "Ruins of Paper: Dickens and the Necropolitan Library," *Romanticism and Victorianism on the Net*, no. 47, 2007; Kevin McLaughlin, *Paperwork: Fiction and Mass Mediacy in the Paper Age* (University of Pennsylvania Press, 2005); Deborah Wynne, "Reading Victorian Rags: Recycling, Redemption, and Dickens's Ragged Children," *Journal of Victorian Culture*, vol. 20, issue 1, 2015, pp. 34–49; and Claire Wood, *Dickens and the Business of Death*, Cambridge University Press, 2015, especially pp. 147–51.
5. Lothar Müller, *White Magic: The Age of Paper*, translated by Jessica Spengler (Polity Press, 2014), p. 198.
6. D. C. Coleman, *The British Paper Industry, 1495–1860: A Study in Industrial Growth* (Clarendon, 1958), p. 195.
7. For more about rags and linen in paper, see Andrew Stauffer, "Legends of the Mummy Paper," *Printing History*, vol. 8, 2010, pp. 21–6, and Richard Menke, "*New Grub Street*'s Ecologies of Paper," *Victorian Studies*, vol. 61, no. 1, 2018, pp. 60–82.
8. Coleman, 66n. Eliot brings this law into a conversation between characters in *The Writings of George Eliot: Scenes of Clerical Life* (Houghton Mifflin, 1907), with the boring chatterbox Lady Assher speaking about the burial of her husband in the late eighteenth century: "To be sure, you must have woolen dress, because it's the law, you know; but that need hinder no one from putting linen underneath" (193).
9. André Blum, *On the Origin of Paper*, translated by Harry Miller Lyndenberg (Bowker, 1934), p. 35.
10. Dard Hunter, *Papermaking Through Eighteen Centuries* (William Edwin Rudge, 1930), pp. 54–63. He discusses Jacob Christian Schäffer's six-volume treatise on papermaking, which includes the potato pages, published between 1765 and 1771.
11. "Adventures of a Quire of Paper" ran in three parts as an anonymous serial in *London Magazine*, vol. 48, 1779, August, pp. 355–8; September, pp. 395–8; October, pp. 448–52.
12. "Adventures of a Quire of Paper," p. 450. See Price, "Getting the Reading Out of It," and Christina Lupton, *Knowing Books: The Consciousness of Mediation in Eighteenth-Century Britain* (University of Pennsylvania Press, 2012),

chapter 2, for more about this story and many other examples of these kinds of it narratives.
13. Müller discusses this and mentions a 1774 booklet called "An Invention for Making New Paper from Printed Paper by Entirely Washing Out the Printing Ink," p. 135.
14. Ellen Gruber Garvey, *Writing with Scissors: American Scrapbooks from the Civil War to the Harlem Renaissance* (Oxford University Press, 2012), pp. 52–9.
15. William Scruton and J. Hambley Rowe reused the red hardback edition of *The Temple Dictionary of the Bible*, edited by Rev. W. Ewing (Dent, 1909), Brontë Parsonage Museum, TA.198. Horsfall Turner created the Stock Exchange album: Brontë Parsonage Museum, SB:2288.
16. Schaffer, pp. 120–2.
17. Lucy Peltz, "Facing the Text: The Amateur and Commercial Histories of Extra-Illustration, c. 1770–1840," *Owners, Annotators, and the Signs of Reading*, edited by Robin Myers, Michael Harris, and Giles Mandelbrote (Oak Knoll Press, 2005), p. 91.
18. Brontë Parsonage Museum, H34. According to Juliet Barker, *Sixty Treasures: The Brontë Parsonage Museum* (Brontë Society, 1988), this was a gift for Ellen. For a history of these paper crafts, see Jane Toller, *The Regency and Victorian Crafts* (Ward Lock, 1969), pp. 36–46.
19. *Scenes of Clerical Life*, p. 215.
20. Charlotte Brontë to George Smith, February 5, 1851. *The Letters of Charlotte Brontë*, edited by Margaret Smith, vol. 2 (Oxford, 1995), p. 573.
21. William St. Clair, *The Reading Nation in the Romantic Period* (Cambridge University Press, 2004), p. 219.
22. Matthew Lewis, *The Monk* (Grove Press, 1952), pp. 33–4.
23. Lord Byron, *Don Juan* (Penguin, 1996), 2.16. See Andrew Stauffer, "Byron, the Pyramids, and 'Uncertain Paper,'" *Wordsworth Circle*, vol. 36, no. 1, 2005, pp. 11–15.
24. Alfred, Lord Tennyson, *Tennyson's Poetry*, edited by Robert W. Hill, Jr. (Norton, 1999), 77.5–7. For many eighteenth-century examples of literature becoming things like "food for mice, fuel for fires, wrapping for oranges ... and tails for kites," or authors imagining them becoming these things, see Lupton, pp. 55–6 and all of chapter 2.
25. Virginia Jackson, *Dickinson's Misery: A Theory of Lyric Reading* (Princeton University Press, 2005), p. 46.
26. "There was once a little girl and her name was Anne," c. 1826–8. Brontë Parsonage Museum, B78.
27. Brontë Parsonage Museum, Bonnell 141. Another of Branwell's handmade books, "An historical narrative of war of encroachment," from 1833, has an address written in a different and larger hand, on the inside of the parcel-paper cover. MS Eng 869, Houghton Library, Harvard University.

28. MS Lowell 1(9), Houghton, Harvard. Leigh Hunt writes about the wrappers around Cooke's edition of the British poets "containing lists of other poets." *Autobiography* (Archibald Constable and Co., 1903), p. 86.
29. Brontë Parsonage Museum, BS112.
30. Charlotte's "Albion and Marina," Oct. 1830, Wellesley College Library. One of her volumes of "The Young Men's Magazine" and "Visits in Verreopolis" have covers made from Epsom Salts wrappers, stamped "J. West, Chemist and Druggist." Charlotte's "Search After Happiness" booklet and the "Blackwood's Young Men's Magazine," December 1829, both have "brown sugar-paper wrappings," according to the British Library catalogue descriptions. Ashley MA 156 and Ashley MS 157. Branwell's "Battell [sic] Book" has a cover of blue paper, cut from a sugar bag, according to Victor Neufeldt. It is at the Brontë Parsonage Museum, BS 110. For Charlotte's juvenilia, see Christine Alexander, editor, *An Edition of the Early Writings of Charlotte Brontë, 1826–1832*, vol. 1 (Shakespeare Head Press, 1987). For Branwell's, see Victor Neufeldt, *The Works of Patrick Branwell Brontë*, vols 1–3 (Routledge, 2015).
31. Esther Leslie, "Dreams, Toys, and Tales," *Crafts*, vol. 146, 1997, p. 31.
32. Lisa Gitelman, "Print Culture (Other Than Codex): Job Printing and Its Importance," *Comparative Textual Media: Transforming the Humanities in the Postprint Era*, edited by N. Katherine Hayles and Jessica Pressman (University of Minnesota Press, 2013), pp. 189–90.
33. Notes 1876, GEN MSS 963, Box 23, Beinecke Library, Yale University.
34. From their advertisement in the back of *The Laws of Piquet*, edited by "Cavendish" (a pseudonym), (Thomas De La Rue and Co, 1881), showing that they were also publishers of books.
35. Coin purse pattern, Brontë Parsonage Museum, C36. This artifact is pictured in Christine Alexander and Jane Sellars, *The Art of the Brontës* (Cambridge University Press, 1995), p. 267.
36. One example of a similar poem, called "Stanza" by E. H. Hays, in *The Pocket Magazine of Classic and Polite Literature*, vol. 6 (Oxford University Press, 1820), p. 51, contains these lines:

> Yes, time may pass, and years may fly,
> And every hope may withering die …
> From hope and thee can ne'er depart;
> I'll bless the time when first we met …

37. Steve McCaffery and Jed Rasula, editors, *Imagining Language: An Anthology* (MIT Press, 2001), p. 203.
38. Naomi Schor, *Reading in Detail: Aesthetics and the Feminine* (Methuen, 1987), p. 20.
39. "She dried her tears and they did smile" (no date, 3 by 1½ inches), E19, Berg.

40. Another example is the MS of "Alcona in its changing mood," dated September 6, 1839, which is a thin cardboard-like substance, perhaps heavy package-wrapping paper. Bonnell 127, Brontë Parsonage Museum.
41. "A.S. Castlewood," dated February 2, 1844, E20, Berg. Undercutting somewhat the seriousness of the whole artifact is a doodle of a man's head in the margin, wearing an oddly shaped hat. See Roper, pp. 145–6 for the full poem.
42. Charlotte handmade a number of paper patterns for collars and cuffs, and one of the latter is done on a piece of mourning paper. See *The Art of the Brontës*, pp. 265–7.
43. October 1885, C0171 (no. 117), Rare Books and Special Collections, Princeton Library.
44. *The Letters of Robert Louis Stevenson*, edited by Bradford A. Booth and Ernest Mehew, vol. 5 (Yale University Press, 1995), p. 133. See p. 128, n. 2, for more about when Stevenson started writing the novella.
45. See Claire Harman, *Myself and the Other Fellow: A Life of Robert Louis Stevenson* (Harper Collins, 2005), pp. 108–9.
46. See, for example, an x-ray technique used to reveal medieval manuscripts in the spines of early modern books, described in Jason Daley, "X-Rays Reveal 'Hidden Library' on the Spines of Early Books," *Smithsonian Magazine*, June 6, 2016. https://www.smithsonianmag.com/smart-news/x-rays-reveal-hidden-library-spines-early-books-180959317. D. C. Coleman writes about the process of making pasteboard from "the shavings and cuttings of books" (33). H. L. Jackson details the life of a used book, eventually ending up as curl-papers, luggage liners, and so on. *Romantic Readers: The Evidence of the Marginalia* (Yale University Press, 2005), p. 34.
47. Lisa Gitelman, *Paper Knowledge: Toward a Media History of Documents* (Duke University Press, 2014), p. 3.
48. Woolf notebook, No. 1 "Warboys, Aug. 4—Sept. 23, 1899," Berg. This notebook is transcribed in Virginia Woolf, *A Passionate Apprentice: The Early Journals 1897–1909*, edited by Mitchell A. Leaska (Pimlico, 2004); see especially pp. 159–60.
49. *A Passionate Apprentice*, p. 177.
50. Ibid., p. 217. Another notebook, from 1919, has signs of being built from the cannibalization of another book or pamphlet. On the inside cover is part of what looks like the title page of James Brown Scott, *James Madison's Notes of Debates in the Federal Convention of 1787 and Their Relation to a More Perfect Society of Nations* (Oxford University Press, 1918), seemingly used to shore up the cover of her notebook. No. 7, "Monks House, Rodmell, Sept. 7—Oct. 1, 1919," Berg.
51. Woolf wrote of the novel, "Hers, then, is the rarest of all powers. She could free life from its dependence on facts, with a few touches indicate the spirit of a face so that it needs no body; by speaking of the moor make the wind blow and

the thunder roar" (161). *The Common Reader*, first series, edited by Andrew McNeillie (Harcourt, 1984).
52. See Chapter 1 for an extended discussion of these passages in *Wuthering Heights* and also Charlotte Brontë's use of textbooks for diaries and other scribbling.
53. Bonnell 127, Brontë Parsonage Museum. See the Introduction for a picture of this (Fig. 1).
54. Some of Anne Brontë's poetry manuscripts utilize folding technology as well, such as "A dreadful darkness closes in," dated January 28, 1849, which is one sheet folded to make a small pamphlet, with the poem closed up on the inside. Bonnell 137, Brontë Parsonage Museum.
55. E6, Berg. See Roper, p. 213, for the full text of these two poems.
56. Other poems that have similar serious text on the verso: "It is not pride, it is not shame," E18, Berg, has "Ms. Brontë" written on the back in another hand and much larger than the verso poetry. "There was a time when my check burned," E7, Berg, has an illegible, scratched-out, partially visible word on the verso, in a similar large hand.
57. E11, Berg, May 19, 1840, 3½ by 1 inches.
58. British Library, vol. 2, the verso of page 28. Another scene of doodling: in *Jane Eyre*, her distracted penciling of her name on a scrap of paper while she is drawing leads to St. John discovering her true identity. Charlotte also wrote the 1847 poem "He saw my heart's woe, discerned my soul's anguish" on the back of a draft of a letter to W. S. Williams. Berg.
59. No date, E16 Berg.
60. Measures 3¼ by 4½ inches, E9, Berg. This famous poem is sometimes given the title "The Caged Bird" (although never by Emily). Derek Roper notes that the title was first added by A. C. Benson in the 1915 *Brontë Poems*. See Roper, *The Poems of Emily Brontë* (Clarendon, 1995), p. 251.
61. Emily Brontë, *Wuthering Heights*, p. 169.
62. Johanna Drucker, *Figuring the Word: Essays on Books, Writing, and Visual Poetics* (Granary, 1998), p. 227.
63. Charlotte also ripped and burned manuscript sheets in order to make them look like ancient, found artifacts, such as with "A Fragment," Bonnell 82 and 82b, Brontë Parsonage Museum.
64. Charlotte's strip of paper, Brontë Parsonage Museum, Bonnell 108.
65. Charlotte to Ellen Nussey, December 5 and 6, 1836. *Letters*, vol. 1, p. 156.
66. Charlotte Brontë, *Villette* (Harpers, 1900), p. 283.
67. Ibid., p. 352.
68. Ibid., p. 353.
69. Ibid., p. 123.
70. Charlotte mentions a character reading Radcliffe's *The Italian* in *Shirley*, and it's likely the family read *The Mysteries of Udolpho*, although I haven't been able to find definite proof of this.

71. Quoted in Alexander, *An Edition*, p. 341.
72. Branwell Brontë, "The History of the Young Men," Ashley MS 2468, British Library. See also Neufeldt, *The Works of Patrick Branwell Brontë*, vol. 1, p. 158.
73. James Hogg, *The Private Memoirs and Confessions of a Justified Sinner* (Grove Press, 1959), p. 227.
74. Charlotte might have read *Frankenstein* because she mentions its plot in an essay, although we don't know if Emily did, and it's not clear whether or not they read Maturin or Hogg's *Confessions*, although they did read Hogg's contributions to their beloved *Blackwood's Edinburgh Magazine*, some of which were gothic with supernatural elements, such as "The Mysterious Bride" about a ghost bride that leads to a man's murder. He published it under the pseudonym Ettrick Shepherd. *Blackwood's Edinburgh Magazine*, vol. 28, July–December 1830, pp. 943–50.
75. Kevin Jackson, *Invisible Forms: A Guide to Literary Curiosities* (Thomas Dunne, 2000), p. 159.
76. For instance, "It is not pride it is not shame," E18, Berg, no date, 2¾ by 2¾ inches.
77. Take, for example, E12, Berg, 1834–6, which has eight poems squeezed onto both sides of a 2½ by 3¼-inch sheet.
78. See E12; "How long will you remain? The midnight hour"; D14, Brontë Parsonage Museum, August 12, 1839; and "I'm standing in the forest now," undated, D3, Brontë Parsonage Museum.
79. See E12, for instance. W. D. Paden believes that some of these symbols refer to the initials of Gondal characters, which is possible in some cases, but they are never written as initials generally are—without "x's" between them and with periods to indicate that they are abbreviated. Paden, *An Investigation of Gondal* (Bookman, 1958).
80. Juliet Fleming, *Graffiti and the Writing Arts in Early Modern England* (Reaktion, 2001), p. 24.
81. Peter Bürger, *Theory of the Avant-Garde*, translated by Michael Shaw (University of Minnesota Press), 1984, p. 64. Considering the Brontës as precursors brings them into a history and set of theories that has been seen, until recently, as mostly male.
82. Virginia Jackson, p. 24. I am also inspired by the work done with Emily Dickinson's poems written on envelopes and parts of envelopes, especially the essays and photographs collected in the marvelous *Emily Dickinson: The Gorgeous Nothings*, edited by Marta Werner and Jen Bervin (New Directions, 2013).
83. Janet Gezari, *Last Things: Emily Brontë's Poems* (Oxford University Press, 2007), p. 1. See also Janet Gezari, editor, *Emily Jane Brontë: The Complete Poems* (Penguin, 1992). Maureen Peeck-O'Toole considers some of the poems under discussion here, but she has never seen the manuscripts. *Aspects of Lyric in the Poetry of Emily Brontë* (Rodopi, 1988).

84. Edward Chitham, *The Birth of Wuthering Heights: Emily Brontë at Work* (St. Martin's, 1998), pp. 9, 15, and chapter 3, and *A Life of Emily Brontë* (Blackwell, 1987), chapter 8. Chitham's general focus is on the later notebooks, although he does study the set of MSS designated D that are at the Brontë Parsonage Museum. He seems only to have seen these ones in person, however, which means he has studied less than half of Brontë's total poetry MSS.
85. Alexander and Sellars, pp. 381–2.
86. Virginia Jackson, p. 60.
87. For more on "extralinguistic messages," see Müller, p. 108.
88. Roper, p. 9.
89. Juliet Barker, *The Brontës* (St. Martin's, 1994), p. 153, and Chitham, *Birth of Wuthering Heights*, p. 15.
90. Paden calls this the "game of Gondal" (9) and Roper describes these activities as "inventive play, with parts spoken and perhaps performed" (8).
91. Clement Shorter, *Charlotte Brontë and Her Circle* (Greenwood, 1970), pp. 150–1.
92. Drucker, p. 66.
93. Peeck-O'Toole calls these MSS "workleaves," assuming that they are "trial runs" (3). I disagree with this assessment, which would mean that poems like "I'm happiest when most away" are only "trial runs."
94. Drucker, p. 115.
95. E13, Berg.
96. What appears to be the mysterious characters "HG" are written between the "Febuary [sic]" and the 1838. Roper believes that the HG refers to a Gondal character (30), which is possible, of course, with the "G" perhaps "Gleneden," a common last name in Gondal. Still, this doesn't explain why Brontë has incorporated the letters into the date. "G" could be the initial of a place, like Gondal or Gaaldine, with the "H" giving further specificity, like "Highlands" or a town. Or, it might indicate a time of day, noted in an unusual way, perhaps with the "H" meaning "hour" and the "g" something like "green" or "gold." The beginning of "To a Wreath of Snow" shares a leaf with a canceled poem, on the now first page of the 1839 notebook.
97. These facts about A.G.A. come from Paden's reconstruction of Gondal (pp. 30, 40). In both Gondal and Angria, colleges and other types of schools, such as the Palace of Instruction, contain prisons and dungeons where adults are locked up, generally for ethical rather than criminal failings. See Paden, pp. 60–1.
98. Paden believes "Weaned from life" is about a child imprisoned, but that is merely speculation based on "the morning of thy life," which could refer to a young adult (77). Many young characters in the Gondal tales end up in prisons, including Julius Brenzaida (who writes a poem on a dungeon wall in the Southern College) and Gerald S.

99. Paden calls these "record sheets" (12) and Roper considers them "storage" sheets (19). I disagree with this theory, following Peeck-O'Toole's lead in finding meaning in their adjacency on single sheets (4–5, 54).
100. See Roper, pp. 49–50, for the whole poem.
101. See Roper, p. 52.
102. McLaughlin, p. 11.
103. Gezari, p. 17.
104. Brontë, *Wuthering Heights*, p. 169.
105. I thank Susan Griffin for this idea about the torn edge and the sense of writing as partial.
106. Shorter, p. 146. He writes, "I have before me a little tin box about two inches long ... Within were four little pieces of paper neatly folded to the size of a sixpence" (146).
107. A photograph of this tiny snippet of paper is included in Barker, *Sixty Treasures*, p. 6.
108. Roper, p. 2.
109. Shorter, p. 146.
110. For more about storage boxes and the materiality of the Brontës' writing practice more generally, see Deborah Lutz, *The Brontë Cabinet: Three Lives in Nine Objects* (Norton, 2015).
111. From an interview with Martha Brown, first printed in *Yorkshireman*, and reprinted in Joanna Hutton, "Items from the Museum Cuttings Book," *Brontë Society Transactions*, vol. 14, no.3, 1963, pp. 28–9.
112. Diary paper written by both Anne and Emily Brontë, 1834, Brontë Parsonage Museum, Bonnell 131.
113. Walter Benjamin, *The Work of Art in the Age of Technical Reproducibility, and Other Writings on Media*, edited by Michael W. Jennings, Brigid Doherty, and Thomas Y. Levin (Belknap Press, 2008).

Notes to Chapter 5

1. George Eliot, *Middlemarch* (Penguin, 1994), p. 303.
2. Victoria Coulson, "Who Cares About Charlotte Wentworth? Fancy-Work in Henry James," *Henry James Review*, vol. 31, no. 1, 2010, p. 23.
3. Brontë's little books and rolled-paper crafts are discussed in Chapter 4, the fern album in Chapter 2. The only earlier draft of Brontë's novels that exists is the fragment of *Emma*, an unfinished novel, which has many edits on the page, but no cut and paste. The MS is in the Special Collections, Princeton University Library, RTCo1 (no. 196).
4. Elizabeth Gaskell, *The Life of Charlotte Brontë* (Penguin, 1997), p. 234.

5. Harriet Martineau, *Autobiography*, edited by Linda Peterson (Broadview, 2007), p. 325.
6. Both manuscripts are at the British Library. *Shirley*: Add MS 43477 and *Villette*: Add. 43, 480.
7. Christine Alexander and Jane Sellars discuss and picture the needle-case and these patterns. See *The Art of the Brontës* (Cambridge University Press, 1995), pp. 188–9 and 265–7. They also discuss other illustrations on cut-out paper for needle-cases made by Charlotte; see pp. 189, 199, 213, and 248.
8. Catherine J. Golden, *Posting It: The Victorian Revolution in Letter Writing* (Florida University Press, 2009), pp. 226–31.
9. The Jane Edwards album: British Library, Add 57724.
10. Lothar Müller explores late eighteenth- and nineteenth-century paper dolls, paper theaters, and other two- and three-dimensional artifacts made of paper, or "replicas of the external world." *White Magic: The Age of Paper*, translated by Jessica Spengler (Polity Press, 2014), pp. 221–4. See also Jane Toller, *The Regency and Victorian Crafts: Or, the Genteel Female—Her Arts and Pursuits* (Ward Lock, 1969), chapter 2; Talia Schaffer, *Novel Craft: Victorian Domestic Handicraft and Nineteenth-Century Fiction* (Oxford University Press, 2011), especially chapter 2; and Blair Whitton, *Paper Toys of the World* (Hobby House, 1986).
11. Toller, pp. 49–56.
12. For paper-mâché needlework boxes, see Mary C. Beaudry, *Findings: The Material Culture of Needlework and Sewing* (Yale University Press, 2006), p. 45.
13. George Eliot's desk was stolen in 2012 from a museum in Nuneaton, Warwickshire; Nightingale's desk is at the Florence Nightingale Museum, FNM:0371.
14. Raymond Lister, *Silhouettes: An Introduction to Their History and to the Art of Cutting and Painting Them* (Batsford, 1953).
15. Album of cut-paper designs, Victoria and Albert Museum, E3586-3643-1938.
16. Hans Christian Andersen, *A Fully Cut Fairytale,* Metropolitan Museum of Art, 2012.379. See also Hans Christian Andersen, HCA/XXIII-B-14-B and HCA/2005/226, Odense City Museum. Anderson made around 800 of these papercuts and some of them are miniature. See Beth Wagner Brust, *The Amazing Paper Cutting of Hand Christian Anderson* (Houghton Mifflin, 1994) and Jakob Stougaard-Nielsen, "The Fairy Tale and the Periodical: Hans Christian Andersen's Scrapbooks," *Book History*, vol. 16, 2013, pp. 132–54.
17. Silhouettes were common in the Austen family household, for instance. Detailed cut-paper outlines of the silhouettes of Austen's mother, her sister Cassandra, her father, and other family members were made by professionals. When her brother Edward Austen was adopted by the wealthy family of Thomas Knight in 1783, an intricate silhouette commemorated the formal presentation. Claire Tomalin, *Jane Austen: A Life* (Vintage, 1999), inset pictures between pages 76 and 77.

18. Elizabeth Gaskell, *Cranford* (Broadview Press, 2010), p. 188.
19. Elizabeth Gaskell, *Sylvia's Lovers* (Oxford, 1999), p. 387.
20. George Eliot, *Middlemarch*, British Library, Add MS 34034. One of the wafered-on pages comes at the very end, in the description of Dorothea's fate in her second marriage.
21. Emily Brontë, *Wuthering Heights* (Broadview, 2007), p. 155.
22. See Hannah Field, *Playing with the Book: Victorian Movable Picture Books and the Child Reader* (University of Minnesota Press, 2019).
23. Peter Haining, *Movable Books: An Illustrated History* (New English Library, 1979), pp. 20–1. In more elaborate types, the face on the last page is molded of materials like gutta-percha, so that it comes off of the last page, such as *The Hearty Old Boy, Who Looked Always the Same* (Dean and Son, 1865). See Blair Whitton, *Paper Toys of the World* (Hobby House, 1986), p. 18.
24. Haining, p. 10.
25. Such as the popular 1851 *Telescopic View of the Great Exhibition*, Victoria and Albert Museum, MISC. 49-1974, and the circa 1845 hand-colored view of the interior of the Thames Tunnel that opens concertina fashion. Not Book X, 375522, M-3-A, Huntington Library. See also Whitton, pp. 47–55, where he also explores panoramas and the historiscope.
26. Haining, pp. 30–53 and Whitton, pp. 56–79.
27. Haining details examples of these, including *The History of Little Fanny, Exemplified in A Series of Figures*, from 1811, and *The Paignion: With Sixty-five Figures, Which Can Be Placed in Any of Twelve Views to Form an Infinite Variety of Domestic Scenes*, from 1830. Whitton explores a wide array of paper dolls and soldiers, including many that were made to be cut out and dressed by children. See pp. 22–7, 92–120. Hannah Field reminds us that these are books that "overmaterialize," their formats exceeding the "merit of their content" (18).
28. Quoted in Teresa Ransom, *The Mysterious Miss Marie Corelli: Queen of Victorian Bestsellers* (Sutton, 1999), p. 63.
29. Charlotte wrote this essay when she was at school in Brussels, in June 1842. "Anne Askew: Imitation," with brown stitching on the upper-left corner, now coming apart, HM 2560, Huntington Library.
30. Part of the manuscript is at the Bodleian, MS. Eng. E,3764, and is digitized and discussed here: *Jane Austen's Fiction Manuscripts: A Digital Edition*, edited by Kathryn Sutherland (2010). Available at http://www.janeausten.ac.uk. Another part is at the Morgan Library, MA 1034. Sutherland says of the Bodleian one, "a handwritten note, held with the manuscript, states 'These three pins were removed by me for the purpose of / transcribing. I suggest that they be not put back in their / place, where they must sooner or later corrode the paper. / R. W. Chapman.'" The MS came with three paper patches, and there are straight pin marks in the MS pages where the patches were. Also, in the manuscript

fragment (two chapters only) of *Persuasion* at the British Library, a snipped-out piece of paper was attached as a revision using big sticky wafers. BL MS Egerton 3038.
31. Elizabeth Barrett Browning, Series I, box 1, folders 3 and 4, Ransom Center. See also https://sites.utexas.edu/ransomcentermagazine/2013/04/23/conservator-preserves-stitching. Sheets (letters, especially) sewn into albums and notebooks are easy to find, as well as repairs and neatening, such as George Eliot's stitched-together stubs in one of her notebooks. For example, at the Morgan Library, Kate Raven Haliday's "Scrapbook of text, drawings, and clippings, 1882 June 27–1891 Apr. 7," MA 4144, has sewn-in letters. Eliot's notebook, "Hebraic studies and miscellaneous notes," Pforzheimer Library, 707.
32. For example, see her "Irregular Verses," Commonplace Book, DCMS 120, Wordsworth Trust Library, Grasmere. See also Deborah Lynn Pfuntner, "Romantic Women Writers and Their Commonplace Books," Dissertation at Texas A&M University, 2016, pp. 40–1. A later French example is Marcel Proust, whose narrator in the last volume of *In Search of Lost Time* constructs his manuscript like a dress, pinning or gluing on extra pages and sticking on other pages with paste, like sewing patches over worn parts of dresses—all descriptions of how Proust himself put together his manuscript. *Time Regained* (Modern Library, 2002), pp. 509–10.
33. In 2013, Christopher Fletcher, Keeper of Special Collections at the Bodleian Library, wrote a blog post about pins in manuscripts: https://www.spectator.co.uk/article/jane-austen-s-pinny.
34. Gaskell Music Book, Manchester Central Library, Special Collections, MS F 823-894 C1, 2nd vol. Sala Commonplace Book, Morgan Library, 1859–94, MA 390.
35. Müller, p. 49.
36. Andrew Stauffer, "The Nineteenth-Century Archive in the Digital Age," *European Romantic Review*, vol. 23, no. 3, 2012, p. 336.
37. Dard Hunter, *Papermaking Through Eighteen Centuries* (Rudge, 1930), p. 215.
38. In Oscar Wilde's *The Importance of Being Earnest*, Algernon writes Jack's country address on his shirt-cuff at the end of Act 1, for instance, and in Arthur Conan Doyle's stories "The Hounds of the Baskervilles" and "The Naval Treaty" notes and appointments are scribbled onto shirt-cuffs.
39. Charles Dickens, *David Copperfield* (Penguin, 2004), p. 879. We also have Dora, who "carefully stitched up with a needle and thread all the leaves of the Cookery-Book which Jip had torn" (652).
40. These letters are now at the British Library, mounted between two pieces of glass so that the thread repairs can be easily seen. Add. MS 38, 732A-D. The account of the fate of the letters comes from Louise Heger, the daughter of the Hegers, who heard it from her mother. She then told it to M. H. Spielmann. See his "The Inner History of the Brontë-Heger Letters," *Fortnightly Review*, April 1919, pp. 345–50.

41. Before envelopes became common in the 1840s, letters were sealed using complicated folds, paper slits, wax, silk floss, and sewing. See Heather Wolfe, "'Neatly sealed, with silk, and Spanish wax or otherwise': The Practice of Letter-Locking with Silk Floss in Early Modern England," *In the Prayse of Writing: Early Manuscript Studies*, edited by S. P. Cerasano and Steven W. May (British Library, 2012), pp. 169–89, and James Daybell, *The Material Letter in Early Modern England: Manuscript Letters and the Culture and Practices of Letter Writing, 1512–1635* (Palgrave, 2012), pp. 106–7. He mentions a letter sealed with human hair.
42. Kislak Center, University of Pennsylvania Library, Ms. Coll. 1044, 1812.
43. Sara Sophia Hennell to George Eliot, 15 November 1854, Beinecke Library, GEN MSS 963. See also *The George Eliot Letters*, edited by Gordon S. Haight, vol. 2 (Yale University Press, 1954–78), pp. 186–7.
44. Eliot to Hennell, November 22, 1854. Haight, p. 188.
45. See William Sherman, *Used Books: Marking Readers in Renaissance England* (University of Pennsylvania Press, 2008), p. xvii, for examples.
46. Toller, p. 48. In the Harry S. Page Collection, Manchester Metropolitan University, Special Collections, there is a collection of handmade needle-cases from the nineteenth century, part of album number 4.
47. Brontë's needle booklet, Brontë Parsonage Museum, H175.
48. Beaudry, pp. 75–8 and Mary Andere, *Old Needlework Boxes and Tools: Their Story and How to Collect Them* (Drake Publishers, 1971), p. 76. There are many other instances of needlework made for friends as it was very common. For instance, Dorothy Wordsworth exchanged locks of hair, a thimble, and an embroidered handkerchief with her childhood friend Jane Pollard. See Pamela Woof, *Dorothy Wordsworth: Wonders of the Everyday* (Wordsworth Trust, 2013), p. 77. Charlotte Brontë also exchanged locks of hair and many handmade needlework gifts with her friend Ellen Nussey. See Deborah Lutz, *The Brontë Cabinet: Three Lives in Nine Objects* (Norton, 2015), chapter 2.
49. See Whitton, p. 133. The Huntington Library has a printed, commercially made paper doll that has been dressed with handmade clothing. Its skirt is formed of strips of hand-cut paper, ribbons, and other household scraps that one could find in a woman's sewing work box. Zelda Walker Gaudin collection of valentines and greeting cards, ephZWG [UNCATALOGED], Paper Dolls box 10.
50. Whitton, pp. 104–5, 109, 143–6.
51. The Page Collection, Manchester Metropolitan University, has a number of these nineteenth-century dressed prints collected from albums, with fur, velvet, seed pearls, and so on glued or sewn onto the paper figure. See especially #26.
52. Toller describes how these were made, including extra padding behind the feathers for a more rounded appearance. See pp. 58–9.

53. This picture, along with many other sand pictures, some of them valentines, is in the Page Collection, Manchester Metropolitan University, #4. Susan M. Stabile writes about women in eighteenth-century America handcrafting shellwork houses, which she calls "memory palaces in miniature" (14). *Memory's Daughters: The Material Culture of Remembrance in Eighteenth-Century America* (Cornell University Press, 2004).
54. Schaffer, p. 19.
55. See Heidi Brayman Hackel, *Reading Material in Early Modern England: Print, Gender, and Literacy* (Cambridge University Press, 2005), p. 206.
56. From Ellen Nussey's reminiscences, *The Letters of Charlotte Brontë: With a Selection of Letters by Family and Friends*, edited by Margaret Smith, vol. 1 (Oxford University Press, 1995), p. 609.
57. See Schaffer, pp. 21–2; Seth Lerer, "Devotion and Defacement: Reading Children's Marginalia," *Representations*, vol. 118, no. 1, 2012, p. 139; Wendy Wall, "Women in the Household," *The Cambridge Companion to Early Modern Women's Writing*, edited by Laura Lunger Knoppers (Cambridge University Press, 2009), p. 97; and Pfuntner, pp. 21, 74.
58. Christine Bayles Kortsch, *Dress Culture in Late Victorian Women's Fiction: Literacy, Textiles, and Activism* (Routledge, 2016), pp. 4–5. George Eliot took notes on Mary Linwood (1755–1845), who "imitated famous paintings in worsted embroidery. In 1798 she opened an exhibition of her work at Hanover square rooms, which contained one hundred copies of pictures by old and modern masters." Joseph Wiesenfarth, *A Writer's Notebook 1854–1879, and Uncollected Writings* (University of Virginia Press, 1981), p. 164n. See also Rozsika Parker, *The Subversive Stitch: Embroidery and the Making of the Feminine* (The Women's Press, 1984), pp. 144–6.
59. Schaffer, p. 63. Gaskell's sewing scissors and some of her sewing needles, in a bamboo case, are at the University of Manchester Library, JRL16111117 and JRL16111119.
60. Bayles Kortsch, p. 5.
61. David Nokes, *Jane Austen: A Life* (University of California Press, 1997), p. 128. There is also a needle-book Austen made for her niece Louisa Knight using felt, paper, yellow ribbon, and painted pictures, now at Jane Austen's House Museum.
62. Found in an 1823 album (a cross between a friendship and commonplace album) is one of these bookmarks, with "Lord Hear My Prayer," stitched into it, MS. Coll. 1129, Kislak Center, University of Pennsylvania Special Collections. See also Nerylla Taunton, *Antique Needlework Tools and Embroideries* (Antique Collectors Club, 1997), pp. 182–3.
63. A copy of the *Psalms* of David I. Watts that belonged to the Brontës' servant Tabitha Brown Ratcliffe has her inscription on the flyleaf and is preserved in

a linen bag, with a needlework inscription. Sotheby sale catalogue, December 13–15, 1916, #686. Embroidered bags for books, especially popular in the seventeenth century—usually with the embroidery matching the book in some way—are discussed in Doris V. Welsh, *The History of Miniature Books* (Fort Orange Press, 1987), p. 33, and Cyril Davenport, *English Embroidered Bookbindings* (Kegan Paul, 1899), pp. 16–18.

64. Virginia Woolf, *A Passionate Apprentice: The Early Journals 1897–1909*, edited by Mitchell A. Leaska (Pimlico, 2004), p. 222.
65. Davenport describes the Felbrigge Psalter, the cover of which he believes the nun Anne de Felbrigge worked, and numerous book covers embroidered by Princess Elizabeth. See pp. 29–37. Susan Frye describes many more seventeenth-century hand-embroidered book covers, especially in chapter 1. See *Pens and Needles: Women's Textualities in Early Modern England* (University of Pennsylvania Press, 2010).
66. Margaret D. Stetz, "*Keynotes*: A New Woman, Her Publisher, and Her Material," *Studies in the Literary Imagination*, vol. 30, no. 1, 1997, pp. 89–106.
67. Friendship album, Julia P. Wightman Collection, Morgan Library, 251019, 251019.
68. Michael Sadleir, *The Evolution of Publishers' Binding Styles, 1770–1900* (Constable and Co., 1930), pp. 39, 47.
69. Books from this collection are now held at the Houghton Library, Harvard University; Rare Books and Special Collections, University of Rochester; and the British Library. Two volumes of *The Works in Natural History by Gilbert White* at the British library are bound in Mary Wordsworth's dress. They were once part of Southey's library but they also have annotations made by Coleridge. Catalogue number: C.61.b.20.
70. For Dora's friendship album, see F. V. Morley, *Dora Wordsworth: Her Book* (Houghton Mifflin, 1925), p. 1.
71. Robert Southey, *The Life and Correspondence*, edited by Charles Cuthbert Southey, vol. 6. (Harper and Brothers, 1850), p. 17. Writing about early modern women, Susan Frye argues that "such work embodies ... the process of sewing within a network of household and community connections" (133).
72. Geoffrey Warren, *A Stitch in Time: Victorian and Edwardian Needlecraft* (David and Charles, 1976) describes pincushions with writing done in pins, like "may you be happy," p. 93.
73. Coulson discusses another of these pincushions, in Henry James's *The Spoils of Poynton,* given to Fleda Vetch by Owen Gereth with "F" marked out in pins. See Coulson, p. 24.
74. Suede boot, 1849, and handkerchief, Brontë Parsonage Museum, D124.1 and D87.
75. George Eliot, *The Mill on the Floss*, 1st ed. (Norton, 1994), pp. 167–8. A number of personal possessions that were handmade by George Eliot still exist,

such as her circa 1840–50 footstool, with its red-leaf design embroidered by her. Nuneaton Museum and Art Gallery, Donor ref: U/1/61/273 (51/11667). A brown leather case, or "housewife," holds her sewing tools, with mother-of-pearl handles, including scissors, thimble, bodkin, buttonhook, file, penknife, and crochet hook. Circa 1840–80, Nuneaton Museum and Art Gallery. A doll's cloak made of linen "is reported" to have been made by Eliot and her classmates at boarding school. Circa 1825/1835. The Herbert Art Gallery and Museum.

76. Charlotte Brontë, *Five Novelettes*, edited by Winifred Gérin (Folio, 1971), pp. 46 and 186.
77. Gaskell, *Cranford*, p. 160.
78. Sylvia Brown and John Considine discuss Francis, Lady Norton, who published a book called *A miscellany of poems, compos'd, and work'd with a needle, on the backs and seats and etc. of several chairs and stools* (1714). See *The Spacious Margin: Eighteenth-Century Printed Books and the Traces of Their Readers* (University of Alberta Press, 2012), p. 68.
79. Samuel Richardson, *Clarissa* (Penguin, 1986), p. 1412. In this will she bequeaths her finished pieces of needlework.
80. See Carol Humphrey, *Samplers* (Cambridge University Press, 1997); Taunton; and Frye, chapter 3.
81. The twentieth- and twenty-first-century (and still living) artist Elaine Reichek embroidered an exact replica of Emily Brontë's first sampler, but added "Elaine Reichek" after "Emily Brontë: Finished this Sampler/April the 22nd 1828." Part of the art here is in the doing—the choosing of the fabric and thread and then the activity of sewing it, very different from copying a manuscript.
82. Quoted in Toller, p. 69.
83. Johanna Drucker, *Figuring the Word: Essays on Books, Writing, and Visual Poetics* (Granary, 1998), p. 72.
84. Other types of samplers that have a special interest: map and solar system samplers that taught geography and the night skies to the maker. Mourning samplers commemorated the dead. Some girls depicted family trees, their homes, towns, and even celebrated the Great Exhibition of 1851. See Humphrey. One of these Great Exhibition samplers is pictured in Taunton, p. 187.
85. Elizabeth Parker's sampler, Victoria and Albert, T.6-1956. See also Bayles Kortsch, pp. 1–5.
86. See also Maureen Daly Goggin, "One English Woman's Story in Silken Ink: Filling in the Missing Strands in Elizabeth Parker's Circa 1830 Sampler," *Sampler and Antique Needlework Quarterly*, vol. 8, no. 4, 2002, pp. 39–49. She points out that red silk was often used for marking, so many girls used it to make marking samplers—rows of letters and numbers—as practice for marking household textiles or making monograms.
87. Wall text, "Bedlam: The Asylum and Beyond," Wellcome Collection, London, UK. The samplers are kept at the Mental Health Museum, Wakefield.

88. Drucker, p. 226.
89. *The Letters of Mrs. Gaskell*, edited by J. A. V. Chapple and Arthur Pollard (Manchester University Press, 1997), p. 59.
90. Anna Atkins, *Memoir of J.G. Children, including some unpublished poetry by his father and himself* (Printed [for private distribution only] by John Bowyer Nichols and Sons, 1853).
91. Ibid., p. 131.
92. Ibid., p. 287.
93. Anna Atkins, *Murder Will Out: A Story of Real Life* (Routledge, 1859), pp. 29–30.
94. Anna Atkins, *The Colonel: A Story of Fashionable Life*, vol. 1 (Hurst and Blackett, 1853), pp. 128–9.
95. Ibid., vol. 1, pp. 260–2.
96. William Henry Fox Talbot, *The Pencil of Nature* (Longman 1844), plate 9. See also Larry J. Schaaf, *Sun Gardens: Victorian Photograms by Anna Atkins* (Aperture, 1985).
97. Atkins was also an accomplished artist in watercolors. An album she created of her watercolors still exists in private hands.
98. Schaaf, 1985, pp. 27–8. Almost the same technology is still used for making blueprints today.
99. Wall text, "Blue Prints: The Pioneering Photographs of Anna Atkins," New York Public Library, New York City, New York.
100. Schaff, *Sun Gardens: Cyanotypes by Anna Atkins* (New York Public Library, 2019), p. 72.
101. Schaff, 1985, pp. 8–9.
102. Schaaf, 1985, p. 8. Parts or complete sets of this very rare book survive in approximately twenty archives and private collections, each one varying from the other. For more about this, see Schaaf, 2019.
103. Richard Menke remarks on "writing's conceptual preeminence in an age when every new inscription technology seemed to claim a status as a *something-graph* that made *something-grams*, as the newest *-graphy*" (5). *Literature, Print Culture, and Media Technologies, 1880–1900: Many Inventions* (Cambridge University Press, 2019).
104. Recently rediscovered and up for auction at Sothebys in 2021.
105. Cameron made her albumen photograms of ferns in the 1860s, such as this one: Victoria and Albert, PH.258-1982.
106. Bessie Rayner Belloc, Photogenic drawings of various objects, Yale Center for British Art, TR144.B4 1848. See also Carol Armstrong and Catherine de Zegher, editors, *Ocean Flowers: Impressions from Nature* (Princeton University Press, 2004), p. 190. They tell of a Mrs. C. C. Armstrong who created an album with albumen prints of ferns and real ferns decorating the pages of photographs, which she called *New Zealand Ferns* (ca. 1880), and of a Blanche Shelley, who did the same with ferns and daffodils, in 1854. See pp. 157, 245.

107. Quoted in *Sun Pictures: Catalogue 10, British Paper Negatives, 1839–1864* (Hans P. Kraus, 2001), p. 40, which also reproduces pages of Parkes's album.

Notes to Afterword

1. Elizabeth Gaskell, *Gothic Tales* (Penguin, 2000), p. 238.
2. *A Passionate Apprentice: The Early Journals 1897–1909*, edited by Mitchell A. Leaska (Pimlico, 2004), p. 159.
3. Ibid., pp. 159–60.
4. Jacques Derrida, *Archive Fever: A Freudian Impression*, translated by Eric Prenowitz (University of Chicago Press, 1995), p. 91.
5. Andrew Stauffer, *Book Traces: Nineteenth-Century Readers and the Future of the Library* (University of Pennsylvania Press, 2021).
6. Walter Benjamin, *The Work of Art in the Age of Technical Reproducibility, and Other Writings on Media*, edited by Michael W. Jennings, Brigid Doherty, and Thomas Y. Levin (Belknap Press, 2008).
7. See, for instance, the special journal issue edited by Mary Elizabeth Leighton and Lisa Surridge, "Object Lessons: The Victorians and the Material Text," *Cahiers victoriens et édouardiens*, vol. 84, 2016. Some of many books from the last twenty years that do this: Leah Price, *How to Do Things with Books* (Princeton University Press, 2012); Talia Schaffer, *Novel Craft: Victorian Domestic Handicraft and Nineteenth-Century Fiction* (Oxford University Press, 2011); Gerard Curtis, *Visual Words: Art and the Material Book in Victorian England* (Ashgate, 2002); and Kevin McLaughlin, *Paperwork: Fiction and Mass Mediacy in the Paper Age* (University of Pennsylvania Press, 2005). See also Paul Duguid, "Material Matters: The Past and Futurology of the Book," *The Future of the Book*, edited by Geoffrey Nunberg (University of California Press, 1996), pp. 63–101.
8. There have been some recent counter-movements, however, such as the rise in the popularity of artists' books. For instance, the Center for Book Arts in New York City is thriving.
9. Lisa Gitelman, *Paper Knowledge: Toward a Media History of Documents* (Duke University Press, 2014), p. 7.
10. Richard Menke, *Literature, Print Culture, and Media Technologies, 1880–1900: Many Inventions* (Cambridge University Press, 2019), p. 19.
11. Carolyn Steedman, *Dust: The Archive and Cultural History* (Rutgers University Press, 2002), p. 7.

Bibliography

1. Archival Sources

Citations of archival artifacts and manuscripts appear in the Notes. Some of the archives, libraries, and museums consulted that are not mentioned in the Notes can be found in the Acknowledgments.

2. Print Sources

Abbott, Ruth. "George Eliot, Meter, and the Matter of Ideas: The Yale Poetry Notebook." *ELH*, vol. 82, no. 4, 2005, pp. 1179–1211.
Ablow, Rachel, editor. *The Feeling of Reading: Affective Experience and Victorian Literature*. University of Michigan Press, 2010.
"Adventures of a Quire of Paper." *London Magazine*, vol. 48, 1779, August, pp. 355–8; September, pp. 395–8; October, pp. 448–52.
Alexander, Christine, editor. *An Edition of the Early Writings of Charlotte Brontë: The Glass Town Saga, 1826–1832*. 2 vols, Shakespeare Head Press, 1987.
Alexander, Christine. "Charlotte Brontë, Her School Friends, and the Roe Head Album." *Brontë Studies: The Journal of the Brontë Society*, vol. 29, no. 1, 2004, pp. 1–16.
Alexander, Christine and Juliet McMaster, editors. *The Child Writer from Austen to Woolf*. Cambridge University Press, 2005.
Alexander, Christine and Jane Sellars, editors. *The Art of the Brontës*. Cambridge University Press, 1995.
Allan, David. *Commonplace Books and Reading in Georgian England*. Cambridge University Press, 2010.
Allen, David Elliston. *The Victorian Fern Craze: A History of Pteridomania*. Hutchinson, 1969.
Alston, Robert. *Books with Manuscript: A Short Title Catalogue of Books with Manuscript Notes in the British Library*. British Library, 1994.
Altman, Janet Gurkin. *Epistolary Approaches to a Form*. Ohio State University Press, 1982.
Andere, Mary. *Old Needlework Boxes and Tools: Their Story and How to Collect Them*. Drake Publishers, 1971.
Armstrong, Carol and Catherine de Zegher, editors. *Ocean Flowers: Impressions from Nature*. Princeton University Press, 2004.
Armstrong, Nancy. *Victorian Glassworlds. Glass Culture and the Imagination. 1830–1880*. Oxford University Press, 2008.
Arnold, Matthew. *The Note-Books of Matthew Arnold*, edited by Howard Foster Lowry, Karl Young, and Waldo Hilary Dunn. Oxford University Press, 1952.
Atkins, Anna. *Perils of Fashion*. Colburn, 1852.
Atkins, Anna. *The Colonel: A Story of Fashionable Life*. Hurst and Blackett, 1853.
Atkins, Anna. *Memoir of J.G. Children*. Printed (for private distribution only) by John Bowyer Nichols and Sons, 1853.

Atkins, Anna. *Murder Will Out: A Story of Real Life*. Routledge, 1859.
Atkins, Anna. *A Page from the Peerage*. T. Cautley Newby, 1863.
Atkins, Anna and Larry J. Schaaf. *Sun Gardens: Victorian Photograms*. Aperture, 1985.
Attfield, Judy. *Wild Things: The Material Culture of Everyday Life*. Berg, 2000.
Austen, Jane. *Northanger Abbey*. Norton, 2002.
Austen, Jane. *Sense and Sensibility*. Norton Critical Edition, 2002.
Austen, Jane. *Pride and Prejudice*. Penguin Classics, 2003.
Austen, Jane. *Emma*. Longman, 2006.
Austen, Jane. *Juvenilia*, edited by Peter Sabor. Cambridge University Press, 2006.
Austen, Jane. *Jane Austen's Fiction Manuscripts: A Digital Edition*, edited by Kathryn Sutherland, 2010. http://www.janeausten.ac.uk.
Austen, Jane. *Jane Austen's Letters*, edited by Deirdre Le Faye. Oxford University Press, 2011.
Bachelard, Gaston. *The Poetics of Space*. Beacon Press, 1964.
Bacon, Francis. "Of Studies." *The Essays or Counsels, Civill or Morall*, edited by Michael Keirnan. Oxford, 1985.
Baker, William. "George Eliot's Readings in Nineteenth-Century Jewish Historians: A Note on the Background of 'Daniel Deronda.'" *Victorian Studies*, vol. 15, no. 4, 1972, pp. 463–73.
Baker, William. "George Eliot's Projected Napoleonic War Novel: An Unnoted Reading List." *Nineteenth-Century Fiction*, vol. 29, no. 4, 1975, pp. 453–60.
Baker, William. *The George Eliot—George Henry Lewes Library: An Annotated Catalogue of Their Books at Dr. Williams's Library, London*. Garland, 1977.
Baker, William. *The Libraries of George Eliot and George Henry Lewes*. University of Victoria Press, 1981.
Baker, William. "George Eliot: Notebooks—and Blotter." *The Library*, vol. S6-4, no. 1, 1982, pp. 80–4.
Baker, William. *Some George Eliot Notebooks: An Edition of the Carl H. Pforzheimer Library's George Eliot Holograph Notebooks, MSS 707, 708, 709, 710, 711*. 4 vols, Universität Salzburg, 1985.
Baker, William. "The Other George Eliot Notebooks at the Folger Shakespeare Library: A Survey." *The George Eliot, George Henry Lewes Newsletter*, no. 12/13, 1988, pp. 1–6.
Baker, William and Robert MacFarlane. "A Small Squealing Black Pig: George Eliot, Originality, and Plagiarism." *George Eliot—George Henry Lewes Studies*, no. 42/3, 2002, pp. 1–29.
Baldick, Chris. *In Frankenstein's Shadow: Myth, Monstrosity, and Nineteenth-Century Writing*. Clarendon, 1990.
Barker, Juliet. *Sixty Treasures: The Brontë Parsonage Museum*. Brontë Society, 1988.
Barker, Juliet. *The Brontës*. St. Martin's, 1994.
Barker, Juliet. *The Brontës: Wild Genius on the Moors—The Story of a Literary Family*. 2nd ed., Pegasus Books, 2012.
Barney, Stephen A., editor. *Annotation and Its Texts*. Oxford University Press, 1991.
Barthes, Roland. "Masson's Semiography." *The Responsibility of Forms*, translated by Richard Howard. University of California Press, 1991, pp. 153–6.
Batchen, Geoffrey. *Forget Me Not: Photography and Remembrance*. Princeton Architectural Press, 2004.
Bates, Amanda. *Samplers from the Museum Collection of North East England*. North East Regional Museums Hub, 2008.
Battles, Matthew. "In Praise of Doodling." *The American Scholar*, vol. 73, no. 4, 2004, pp. 105–8.
Bayles Kortsch, Christine. *Dress Culture in Late Victorian Women's Fiction: Literacy, Textiles, and Activism*. Routledge, 2016.
Beaty, Jerome. *Middlemarch from Notebook to Novel: A Study of George Eliot's Creative Method*. University of Illinois Press, 1960.

Beaudry, Mary C. *Findings: The Material Culture of Needlework and Sewing.* Yale University Press, 2006.
Benjamin, Walter. "Review of the Mendelssohns' Der Mensch in der Handschrift." *Walter Benjamin: Selected Writings,* vol. 2, translated by Rodney Livingstone and others, edited by Michael W. Jennings, Howard Eiland, and Gary Smith. Belknap, 1999, pp. 131–4.
Benjamin, Walter. "Unpacking My Library: A Talk about Collecting," *Walter Benjamin: Selected Writings,* vol. 2, translated by Rodney Livingstone and others, edited by Michael W. Jennings, Howard Eiland, and Gary Smith. Belknap, 1999, pp. 486–93.
Benjamin, Walter. *The Work of Art in the Age of Technical Reproducibility, and Other Writings on Media,* edited by Michael W. Jennings, Brigid Doherty, and Thomas Y. Levin. Belknap Press, 2008.
Benson, Arthur C., editor. *Brontë Poems: Selections from the Poetry of Charlotte, Emily, Anne and Branwell Brontë.* Smith, Elder, and Company, 1915.
Berg, Maggie. *Wuthering Heights: The Writing in the Margin.* Twayne, 1996.
Bermingham, Ann. *Learning to Draw: Studies in the Cultural History of a Polite and Useful Art.* Yale University Press, 2000.
Bernasconi, John R. *The English Desk and Bookcase.* College of Estate Management, 1981.
Bernstein, Susan David. *Roomscape: Women Writers in the British Museum from George Eliot to Virginia Woolf.* Edinburgh University Press, 2013.
Blair, Ann. *Too Much to Know: Managing Scholarly Information Before the Modern Age.* Yale University Press, 2010.
Blum, Andre. *On the Origin of Paper,* translated by Harry Miller Lyndenberg. R. R. Bowker, 1934.
Boden, Helen. *Dorothy Wordsworth, Her Write His Name: The Continental Journals, 1798–1820.* Thoemannes Continuum, 1995.
Bondy, Louis W. *Miniature Books: Their History from the Beginnings to the Present Day.* Sheppard Press, 1981.
Booth, Alison. *Homes and Haunts: Touring Writers' Shrines and Countries.* Oxford University Press, 2016.
Brake, Laurel, Bill Bell, and David Finkelstein. *Nineteenth-Century Media and the Construction of Identities.* Palgrave Macmillan, 2000.
Brewer, Luther A. *Marginalia.* Privately printed, 1926.
Bridge, Mark. *An Encyclopedia of Desks.* Apple Press, 1988.
Briggs, Asa. *Victorian Things.* University of Chicago Press, 1989.
Bristow, Joseph and Rebecca N. Mitchell. *Oscar Wilde's Chatterton: Literary History, Romanticism, and the Art of Forgery.* Yale University Press, 2015.
Broder, Janice. "Lady Bradshaigh Reads and Writes *Clarissa*: The Marginal Notes in Her First Edition." *Clarissa and Her Readers: New Essays for the Clarissa Project,* edited by Carol Houlihan Flynn and Edward Copeland. AMS Press, 1999, pp. 97–118.
Bromer, Anne C. and Julian Edison. *Miniature Books: 4,000 Year of Tiny Treasures.* Abrams, 2007.
Brontë, Anne. *Agnes Grey.* Penguin, 1989.
Brontë, Anne. *Tenant of Wildfell Hall.* Barnes and Noble, 2006.
Brontë, Charlotte. *Villette.* Harpers, 1900.
Brontë, Charlotte. *Five Novelettes,* edited by Winifred Gérin. Folio, 1971.
Brontë, Charlotte. *Shirley.* Oxford, 2008.
Brontë, Charlotte. *Jane Eyre.* Norton, 2016.
Brontë, Charlotte and Emily Brontë. *The Belgian Essays,* edited by Sue Lonoff. Yale University Press, 1996.
Brontë, Emily. *Wuthering Heights: The Complete Works of Emily Brontë,* edited by Clement K. Shorter, vol. 2. Hodder and Stoughton, 1911.

Brontë, Emily. *Gondal Poems*, edited by Helen Brown and Joan Mott. Shakespeare Head Press, 1938.

Brontë, Emily. *The Complete Poems of Emily Jane Brontë*, edited by C. W. Hatfield. Columbia University Press, 1995.

Brontë, Emily. *The Poems of Emily Brontë*, edited by Derek Roper and Edward Chitham. Clarendon, 1995.

Brontë, Emily. *Wuthering Heights*. Broadview, 2007.

Brontë Society. *Catalogue of the Bonnell Collection in the Brontë Parsonage Museum*. The Brontë Society, 1932. *Brontë Society Transactions*, vol. 21, no. 4, 1994, p. 4.

Brown, Kate E. "Beloved Objects: Mourning, Materiality, and Charlotte Brontë's 'Never-Ending Story.'" *English Literary History*, vol. 65, no. 2, 1998, pp. 395–421.

Brown, Sylvia and John Considine. *The Spacious Margin: Eighteenth-Century Printed Books and the Traces of Their Readers*. University of Alberta Press, 2012.

Browning, Elizabeth Barrett. *The Browning Collections: A Reconstruction with Other Memorabilia*, edited by Philip Kelley and Betty A. Coley. Mansell, 1984.

Brust, Beth Wagner. *The Amazing Paper Cutting of Hand Christian Anderson*. Houghton Mifflin, 1994.

Bürger, Peter. *Theory of the Avant-Garde*, translated by Michael Shaw. University of Minnesota Press, 1984.

Burns, Wayne. *Charles Reade: A Study in Victorian Authorship*. Bookman, 1961.

Bushell, Sally. *Text as Process: Creative Composition in Wordsworth, Tennyson, and Dickinson*. University of Virginia Press, 2009.

Byron, Lord. *Don Juan*. Penguin, 1996.

Capuano, Peter J. *Changing Hands: Industry, Evolution, and the Reconfiguration of the Victorian Body*. University of Michigan Press, 2015.

Carlyle, Thomas. *The French Revolution: A History*, vol. 1. Chapman and Hall, 1872.

Champness, Michael and David Trapnell. *Adhesive Wafer Seals: A Transient Victorian Phenomenon*. Chancery House, 1996.

Chartier, Roger. *Forms and Meanings: Texts, Performances, and Audiences from Codex to Computer*. University of Pennsylvania Press, 1995.

Chartier, Roger et al. *Correspondence: Models of Letter Writing from the Middle Ages to the Nineteenth Century*. Princeton University Press, 1997.

Chéroux, Clément et al., editors. *The Perfect Medium: Photography and the Occult*. Yale University Press, 2005.

Chitham, Edward. *A Life of Emily Brontë*. Blackwell, 1987.

Chitham, Edward. *The Birth of Wuthering Heights: Emily Brontë at Work*. St. Martin's, 1998.

Chorley, Henry. *Memorials of Mrs. Hemans*. Saunders and Otley, 1836.

Classen, Constance. "Touch in the Museum." *The Book of Touch*, edited by Constance Classen. Berg, 2005, pp. 275–88.

Cohen, Deborah. *Household Gods: The British and Their Possessions*. Yale University Press, 2006.

Colclough, Stephen, "Recovering the Reader: Commonplace Books and Diaries as Sources of Reading Experience." *Publishing History*, vol, 44, edited by Michael L. Turner. Cambridge University Press, 1998, pp. 5–37.

Coleman, D. C. *The British Paper Industry, 1495–1860: A Study in Industrial Growth*. Clarendon, 1958.

Coleridge, Samuel Taylor. *Collected Letters*, edited by E. L. Griggs. Oxford University Press, 1956–71.

Coleridge, Samuel Taylor. *The Notebooks of Samuel Taylor Coleridge*, edited by Kathleen Coburn and M. Christensen. 4 vols, Princeton University Press, 1980–90.

Coleridge, Samuel Taylor. *Coleridge's Notebooks: A Selection*, edited by Seamus Perry. Oxford University Press, 2002.
Collins, Wilkie. *The Dead Secret*. Bradbury and Evans, 1857.
Collins, Wilkie. *The Woman in White*. Penguin Classics, 2003.
Connell, Phillip. "Bibliomania: Book Collecting, Cultural Politics, and the Rise of Literary Heritage in Romantic Britain." *Representations*, vol. 71, 2000, pp. 24–47.
Cook, Davidson. "Emily Brontë's Poems: Some Textual Corrections and Unpublished Verses." *The Nineteenth Century and After*, vol. 100, no. 594, 1926, pp. 248–62.
Corelli, Marie. *The Sorrows of Satan*. Valancourt Books, 2008.
Coulson, Victoria. "Who Cares about Charlotte Wentworth? Fancy-Work in Henry James." *Henry James Review*, vol. 31, no. 1, 2010, pp. 21–6.
Croskery, Margaret Case. "Mothers Without Children, Unity Without Plot: Cranford's Radical Charm." *Nineteenth-Century Literature*, vol. 52, no. 2. 1997, pp. 198–220.
Crowther, Kathryn. "Charlotte Brontë's Textual Relics: Memorializing the Material in *Villette*." *Brontë Studies*, vol. 35, no. 2, 2010, pp. 128–36.
Curtis, Gerard. *Visual Words: Art and the Material Book in Victorian England*. Ashgate, 2002.
Dacome, Lucia. "Noting the Mind: Commonplace Books and the Pursuit of the Self in Eighteenth-Century Britain." *Journal of the History of Ideas*, vol. 65, 2004, pp. 603–25.
Daley, Jason. "X-Rays Reveal 'Hidden Library' on the Spines of Early Books." *Smithsonian Magazine*, June 6, 2016. https://www.smithsonianmag.com/smart-news/x-rays-reveal-hidden-library-spines-early-books-180959317.
Dames, Nicholas. *The Physiology of the Novel: Reading, Neural Science, and the Form of Victorian Fiction*. Oxford University Press, 2007.
Dane, Joseph. "Marks in Books: Provenance." *What Is a Book? The Study of Early Printed Books*. University of Notre Dame Press, 2012.
Darnton, Robert. "What Is the History of Books?" *The Book History Reader*, 2nd ed., edited by David Finkelstein and Alistair McCleery. Routledge, 2006, pp. 9–26.
Davenport, Cyril. *English Embroidered Bookbindings*. Kegan Paul, 1899.
Dávidházi, Péter. *The Romantic Cult of Shakespeare*. Palgrave, 1998.
Daybell, James. *The Material Letter in Early Modern England: Manuscript Letters and the Culture and Practices of Letter Writing, 1512–1635*. Palgrave, 2012.
De Certeau, Michel. *The Practice of Everyday Life*, 3rd ed., translated by Steven F. Rendall. University of California Press, 2011.
Derrida, Jacques. *Archive Fever: A Freudian Impression*, translated by Eric Prenowitz. University of Chicago Press, 1995.
Derrida, Jacques. *Paper Machine*, translated by Rachel Bowlby. Stanford University Press, 2005.
Di Bello, Patrizia. *Women's Albums and Photography in Victorian England: Ladies, Mothers, and Flirts*. Ashgate, 2007.
Dickens, Charles. "Our English Watering Place." *Household Words*, vol. 3, no. 71, 1851, pp. 433–6.
Dickens, Charles. *Great Expectations*. Penguin, 1996.
Dickens, Charles. *Bleak House*. Penguin Classics, 2003.
Dickens, Charles. *David Copperfield*. Penguin, 2004.
Dickenson, Emily. *The Gorgeous Nothings*, edited by Marta Werner and Jen Bervin. New Directions, 2013.
DiNoto, Andrea and David Winter. *The Pressed Plant: The Art of Botanical Specimen, Nature Prints, and Sun Pictures*. Stewart, Tabori and Chang, 1999.
Dinsdale, Ann, Sarah Laycock, and Julie Akhurst. *Brontë Relics: A Collection History*. Brontë Society, 2012.

Dixon, Ella Hepworth. *The Story of a Modern Woman*. Broadview, 2004.
Dodd, Valerie A. "A George Eliot Notebook." *Studies in Bibliography*, vol. 34, 1981, pp. 258–62.
Dolin, Tim. "Cranford and the Victorian Collection." *Victorian Studies*, vol. 36, no. 2, 1993, pp. 179–206.
Donoghue, Emma. *We Are Michael Field*. Absolute, 1998.
Doody, Margaret Anne. "Jane Austen's Reading." *The Jane Austen Handbook*, edited by J. David Grey. Athlone Press, 1986.
Dooley, Allen. *Author and Printer in Victorian England*. University of Virginia Press, 1992.
Drucker, Johanna. *Figuring the Word: Essays on Books, Writing, and Visual Poetics*. Granary, 1998.
Drucker, Johanna. *The Century of Artists' Books*, 2nd ed. Granary Books, 2004.
Dubansky, Mindell. *Blooks: The Art of Books That Aren't*. Dubansky, 2016.
Duguid, Paul. "Material Matters: The Past and Futurology of the Book." *The Future of the Book*, edited by Geoffrey Nunberg. University of California Press, 1996.
Duncan, Denis and Adam Smyth, editors. *Book Parts*. Oxford University Press, 2019.
Eagleton, Terry. *The Rape of Clarissa: Writing, Sexuality, and Class Struggle in Samuel Richardson*. Blackwell, 1982.
Earle, Rebecca. "Introduction: Letters, Writers, and the Historian." *Epistolary Selves: Models of Letter* Writing, edited by Rebecca Earlie. Ashgate, 1999, pp. 1–14.
Edwards, Elizabeth and Janice Hart, editors. *Photographs Objects Histories: On the Materiality of Images*. Routledge, 2004.
Elia, Anthony. "An Unknown Exegete: Uncovering the Biblical Scholarship of Elizabeth Barrett Browning." *Theological Librarianship*, vol. 7, no. 1, 2014, pp. 8–20.
Eliot, George. *Scenes of Clerical Life*. Houghton Mifflin, 1907.
Eliot, George. *The George Eliot Letters*, edited by Gordon S. Haight. 9 vols, Yale University Press, 1954–78.
Eliot, George. *George Eliot's Middlemarch Notebooks: A Transcription*, edited by John Clark Pratt and Victor A. Neufeldt. University of California Press, 1979.
Eliot, George. *George Eliot: Selected Essays, Poems, and Other Writings*, edited by A. S. Byatt and Nicholas Warren. Penguin, 1990.
Eliot, George. *Middlemarch*. Penguin, 1994.
Eliot, George. *The Mill on the Floss*. Norton, 1994.
Eliot, George. *Daniel Deronda*. Penguin, 1996.
Eliot, George. *Romola*. Penguin, 1996.
Eliot, George. *Adam Bede*. Wordsworth, 1997.
Eliot, George. *The Journals of George Eliot*, edited by Margaret Harris and Judith Johnston. Cambridge University Press, 1998.
Eliot, George. *Silas Marner*. Penguin, 2003.
Eliot, George. *Poems, Essays, Leaves from a Notebook*, vol. 5. *The Complete Works of George Eliot*. Dumont, n.d.
Eliot, George and Joseph Wiesenfarth. *A Writer's Notebook, 1854–1879, and Uncollected Writings*. Virginia University Press, 1981.
Elwin, Malcolm. *Charles Reade*. Russell and Russell, 1969.
Erickson, Lee. *The Economy of Literary Form: English Literature and the Industrialization of Publishing, 1800–1850*. Johns Hopkins University Press, 1996.
The Evangelical Magazine and Missionary Chronicle, vol. 6, 1829, p. 102.
Favret, Mary. "Mary Shelley's Sympathy and Irony: The Editor and Her Corpus." *The Other Mary Shelley: Beyond Frankenstein*. Oxford University Press, 1993, pp. 17–38.
Favret, Mary. *Romantic Correspondence: Women, Politics, and the Fiction of Letters*. Cambridge University Press, 1993.

Fay, Elizabeth. *Fashioning Faces: The Portraitive Mode in British Romanticism*. New Hampshire University Press, 2010.
Fennetaux, Ariane. "Female Crafts: Women and Bricoloage in Late Georgian Britain, 1750–1820." *Material Women, 1750–1950: Consuming Desires and Collecting Practices*, edited by Maureen Daly Goggin and Beth Fowkes Tobin. Ashgate, 2009, pp. 91–108.
Field, Hannah. *Playing with the Book: Victorian Movable Picture Books and the Child Reader*. University of Minnesota Press, 2019.
Field, Michael. *Works and Days: From the Journal of Michael Field*, edited by T. Sturge Moore and D. C. Sturge Moore. Murray, 1933.
Field, Michael. *Binary Star: Leaves from the Journal and Letters of Michael Field 1846–1914*, edited by Ivor C. Treby. St. Edmundsbury Press, 2006.
Field, Michael. *Michael Field, The Poet: Published and Manuscript Materials*, edited by Marion Thain and Ana Parejo Vadillo. Broadview Press, 2009.
Fleishman, Avrom. "George Eliot's Reading: A Chronological List." *George Eliot—George Henry Lewes Studies*, Supplement to No. 54/5, 2008, pp. 1–76.
Fleming, Juliet. *Graffiti and the Writing Arts in Early Modern England*. Reaktion, 2001.
Flint, Kate. *The Woman Reader, 1837–1914*. Clarendon, 1993.
Flint, Kate. "The Materiality of Middlemarch." *Middlemarch in the Twenty-First Century*, edited by Karen Chase. Oxford University Press, 2006.
Flint, Kate. "Travelling Readers." *The Feeling of Reading: Affective Experience and Victorian Literature*, edited by Rachel Ablow. University of Michigan Press, 2010.
Flint, Kate. "The Aesthetics of Book Destruction." *Book Destruction from the Medieval to the Contemporary*, edited by Gill Partington and Adam Smyth. Palgrave Macmillan, 2014, pp. 175–89.
Frawley, Maria. "Contextualizing Anne Brontë's Bible." *New Approaches to the Literary Art of Anne* Brontë, edited by Julie Nash and Barbara A. Suess. Ashgate, 2001, pp. 1–13.
Freedgood, Elaine. *The Ideas in Things*. Chicago University Press, 2006.
Freedgood, Elaine. "Ghostly Reference." *Representations*, vol. 125, no. 1, 2014, pp. 40–53.
Frye, Susan. *Pens and Needles: Women's Textualities in Early Modern England*. University of Pennsylvania Press, 2010.
Gallagher, Catherine. *The Body Economic: Life, Death and Sensation in Political Economy and the Victorian Novel*. Princeton University Press, 2006.
Gallagher, Catherine and Stephen Greenblatt. *Practicing New Historicism*. University of Chicago Press, 2000.
Garvey, Ellen Gruber. *Writing with Scissors: American Scrapbooks from the Civil War to the Harlem Renaissance*. Oxford University Press, 2012.
Gaskell, Elizabeth. *Wives and Daughters*. Penguin, 1996.
Gaskell, Elizabeth. *The Letters of Mrs. Gaskell*, edited by J. A. V. Chapple and Arthur Pollard. Manchester University Press, 1997.
Gaskell, Elizabeth. *The Life of Charlotte Brontë*. Penguin Classics, 1997.
Gaskell, Elizabeth. *Sylvia's Lovers*. Oxford, 1999.
Gaskell, Elizabeth. *Gothic Tales*. Penguin Classics, 2000.
Gaskell, Elizabeth. *North and South*. Norton Critical Edition, 2004.
Gaskell, Elizabeth. *Ruth*. Penguin, 2004.
Gaskell, Elizabeth. *Mary Barton*. Norton Critical Edition, 2008.
Gaskell, Elizabeth. *Cranford*. Broadview Press, 2010.
Gaskell, Elizabeth. *Further Letters of Mrs. Gaskell*, edited by John Chapple and Alan Shelston. Manchester University Press, 2019.
Gaze, Tim. *Asemic Movement*. January 1, 2008. http//isuu.com/eexxiitt.

Genette, Gerard. *Paratexts: Thresholds of Interpretation*, translated by Jane E. Lewin. Cambridge University Press, 1987.
Gérin, Winifred. *Emily Brontë: A Biography*. Clarendon Press, 1971.
Gernes, Todd S. "Recasting the Culture of Ephemera." *Popular Literacy: Studies in Cultural Practices and Poetics*, edited by John Trimbur, University of Pittsburgh Press, 2001, pp. 107–27.
Gezari, Janet, editor. *Emily Jane Brontë: The Complete Poems*. Penguin, 1992.
Gezari, Janet. *Last Things: Emily Brontë's Poems*. Oxford University Press, 2007.
Gillespie, Alexandra and Deidre Lynch, editors. *The Unfinished Book: Oxford Twenty-First Century Approaches to Literature*. Oxford University Press, 2020.
Gilson, David. "Jane Austen's Books." *The Book Collector*, vol. 23, 1974, pp. 27–39.
Gitelman, Lisa. *Scripts, Grooves, and Writing Machines: Representing Technology in the Edison Era*. Stanford University Press, 1999.
Gitelman, Lisa. "How Users Define New Media: A History of the Amusement Phonograph." *Rethinking Media Change: The Aesthetics of Transition*, edited by David Thorburn and Henry Jenkins. MIT Press, 2003.
Gitelman, Lisa. "Media, Materiality, and the Measure of the Digital, Or, the Case of Sheet Music and the Problem of Piano Rolls." *Memory Bytes: History, Technology, and Digital Culture*, edited by Lauren Rabinovitz and Abraham Geil. Duke University Press, 2004, pp. 199–217.
Gitelman, Lisa. "Unexpected Pleasures: Phonographs and Cultural Identities in America, 1895–1915." *Appropriating Technology: Vernacular Science and Social Power*, edited by Ron Eglash. University of Minnesota Press, 2004.
Gitelman, Lisa. *Always Already New: Media, History, and the Data of Culture*. MIT Press, 2006.
Gitelman, Lisa. "Mississippi MSS: Twain, Typing, and the Moving Panorama of Literary Production." *Residual Media*, edited by Charles Acland. University of Minnesota Press, 2007.
Gitelman, Lisa. "Ages, Epochs, Media." *On Periodization: Selected Papers from the English Institute*, edited by Virginia Jackson. English Institute, 2010.
Gitelman, Lisa. "Modes and Codes: Samuel F.B. Morse and the Question of Electronic Writing." *This Is Enlightenment*, edited by Clifford Siskin and William Warner. University of Chicago Press, 2010, pp. 120–38.
Gitelman, Lisa. "Print Culture (Other Than Codex): Job Printing and Its Importance." *Comparative Textual Media: Transforming the Humanities in the Postprint Era*, edited by N. Katherine Hayles and Jessica Pressman. University of Minnesota Press, 2013.
Gitelman, Lisa. *Paper Knowledge: Toward a Media History of Documents*. Duke University Press, 2014.
Gitelman, Lisa and Theresa Collins. "Medium Light: Revisiting Edisonian Modernity." *Critical Quarterly*, vol. 51, no. 2, 2009, pp. 1–14.
Glen, Heather. *Charlotte Brontë: The Imagination in History*. Oxford University Press, 2002.
Godburn, Mark R. *Nineteenth-Century Dust-Jackets*. Oak Knoll Press, 2016.
Goggin, Maureen Daly. "One English Woman's Story in Silken Ink: Filling in the Missing Strands in Elizabeth Parker's Circa 1830 Sampler." *Sampler and Antique Needlework Quarterly*, vol. 29, no. 4, 2002, pp. 39–49.
Goggin, Mareen Daly and Beth Fowkes Tobin, editors. *Women and the Material Culture of Needlework and Textiles*. Ashgate, 2009.
Golden, Amanda. "Virginia Woolf's Marginalia Manuscript." *Woolf Studies Annual*, vol. 18, 2012, pp. 109–17.
Golden, Catherine J., editor. *Book Illustrated: Text, Image, and Culture, 1770–1930*. Oak Knoll Press, 2000.
Golden, Catherine J. *Posting It: The Victorian Revolution in Letter Writing*. Florida University Press, 2009.

Golding, Alan. "'Drawing with Words': Susan Howe's Visual Poetics." *We Who Love to Be Astonished: Experimental Women's Writing and Performance Poetics*, edited by Laura Hinton and Cynthia Hogue. University of Alabama Press, 2001, pp. 152–65.
Gombrich, Ernst. "Pleasures of Boredom: Four Centuries of Doodles." *Uses of Images: Studies in the Social Function of Art and Visual Communication*. Phaidon, 1999.
Grafton, Anthony. *Commerce with the Classics: Ancient Books and Renaissance Readers*. University of Michigan Press, 1997.
Graver, Bruce. "Lucy Aiken's Marginalia to *Biographia Literaria*." *European Romantic Review*, vol. 14, no. 3, 2003, pp. 323–43.
Grossman, Jonathan H. *The Art of the Alibi: English Law Courts and the Novel*. Johns Hopkins University Press, 2002.
Grunwald, Martin. *Human Haptic Perception: Basics and Applications*. Birkhäuser, 2008.
Hack, Daniel. *The Material Interests of the Victorian Novel*. University of Virginia Press, 2005.
Hackel, Heidi Brayman. *Reading Material in Early Modern England: Print, Gender, and Literacy*. Cambridge University Press, 2005.
Haight, Gordon. "The George Eliot and George Henry Lewes Collection." *The Yale University Library Gazette*, vol. 46, no. 1, 1971, pp. 20–3.
Haight, Gordon. *George Eliot: A Biography*. Penguin, 1986.
Haining, Peter. *Movable Books*. New English Library, 1979.
Halsey, Kate. *Jane Austen and Her Readers*. Anthem Press, 2012.
Hardy, Thomas. *The Personal Notebooks of Thomas Hardy*, edited by Richard H. Taylor. Columbia University Press, 1979.
Hardy, Thomas. *The Literary Notebooks of Thomas Hardy*, edited by Lennart A. Björk. 3 vols, Macmillan, 1985.
Hardy, Thomas. *Thomas Hardy's "Studies, Specimens &c." Notebook*, edited by Pamela Dalziel and Michael Millgate. Oxford University Press, 1994.
Hardy, Thomas. *Thomas Hardy's "Facts" Notebook: A Critical Edition*, edited by William Greenslade. Routledge, 2004.
Hardy, Thomas. *Thomas Hardy's "Poetical Matter" Notebook*, edited by Pamela Dalziel and Michael Millgate. Oxford University Press, 2009.
Harman, Claire. *Myself and the Other Fellow: A Life of Robert Louis Stevenson*. Harper Collins, 2005.
Harris, David. *Portable Writing Desks*. Shire, 2000.
Hatfield, C. W., editor. *The Complete Poems of Emily Brontë*. Columbia University Press, 1941.
Havens, Earle. *Commonplace Books: A History of Manuscript Books from Antiquity to the Twentieth Century*. University Press of New England, 2001.
Havens, Hilary. "Adobe Photoshop and Eighteenth-Century Manuscripts: A New Approach to Digital Paleography." *Digital Humanities Quarterly*, vol. 8, no. 4, 2014, pp. 1-13.
Havens, Hilary. "Revisions and Revelations in Frances Burney's *Cecilia* Manuscript." *SEL: Studies in English Literature 1500–1900*, vol. 55, no. 3, 2015, pp. 537–58.
Havens, Hilary and Peter Sabor. "Editing *Evelina*." *XVII–XVIII: Revue de la Société d'Études Anglo-Américaines des XVIIe et XVIIIe Siècles*, vol. 71, 2014, pp. 285–305.
Hays, E. H. *The Pocket Magazine of Classic and Polite Literature*, vol. 6. Oxford University Press, 1820.
Haywood, J. F. *English Desks and Bureaux*. H.M.S.O., 1968.
Hemans, Felicia. *Felicia Hemans: Selected Poems, Letters. Reception Materials*, edited by Susan J. Wolfson. Princeton University Press, 2000.
Henry, Nancy. *George Eliot and the British Empire*. Cambridge University Press, 2002.
Henry, Nancy. *The Life of George Eliot: A Critical Biography*. Wiley Blackwell, 2012.

Hertenstein, Matthew and Sandra Weiss. *The Handbook of Touch: Neuroscience, Behavioral, and Health Perspectives.* Springer, 2011.
Hess, Jillian M. "Coleridge's Fly-Catchers: Adapting Commonplace-Book Form," *Journal of the History of Ideas*, vol. 73, no. 3, 2012, pp. 463–83.
Higden, David Leon. "George Eliot and the Art of the Epigraph." *Nineteenth-Century Fiction*, vol. 25, no. 2, 1970, pp. 127–51.
Hoffman, Jesse. "Dante Gabriel Rossetti's Bad Photographs." *Victorian Studies*, vol. 57, no. 1, 2014, pp. 57–87.
Hogg, James. *The Private Memoirs and Confessions of a Justified Sinner.* Grove Press, 1959.
Holgate, Ivy. "A Pilgrim at Haworth—1879." *Brontë Society Transactions*, vol. 14, no. 1, 1961, pp. 29–37.
Howe, Susan. *The Birth-Mark: Unsettling the Wilderness in American Literary History.* Wesleyan University Press, 1993.
Hughes, Linda. K. "George Eliot's 'Greek Vocabulary' Notebook (c. 1873) as Commodity and Rare Artefact." *Cahiers: Victoriens et Édouardiens*, vol. 84, 2016, pp. 1-20.
Hughs, Therle. *English Domestic Needlework.* Abbey Fine Arts, 1961.
"Human Skin as Binding." *Bookworm: An Illustrated Treasury of Old-Time Literature*, January 1, 1891, p. 148.
"Human Skin as a Binding." *Bookworm: An Illustrated Treasury of Old-Time Literature*, January 1, 1893, p. 103.
Humphrey, Carol. *Samplers.* Cambridge University Press, 1997.
Hunt, Leigh. *Autobiography.* Archibald Constable and Co., 1903.
Hunter, Dard. *Papermaking Through Eighteen Centuries.* Rudge, 1930.
Hutton, Joanna. "Items from the Museum Cuttings Book." *Brontë Society Transactions*, vol. 14, no. 3, 1963, pp. 26–30.
Hyman Aaron M. and Dana Leibsohn. "Washing the Archive." *Early American Literature*, vol. 55, no. 2, 2020, pp. 419–44.
Irwin, Jane, editor. *George Eliot's Daniel Deronda Notebooks.* Cambridge University Press, 1996.
Jackson, H. J. *Marginalia: Readers Writing Books.* Yale University Press, 2001.
Jackson, H. J. "'Marginal Frivolities': Readers' Notes as Evidence for the History of Reading." *Owners, Annotators, and the Signs of Reading*, edited by Robin Myers, Michael Harris, and Gilles Mandelbrote. British Library, 2005, pp. 137–53.
Jackson, H. J. *Romantic Readers: The Evidence of the Marginalia.* Yale University Press, 2005.
Jackson, H. J. "John Adams's Marginalia Then and Now." *The Libraries, Leadership, and Legacy of John Adams and Thomas Jefferson*, edited by Robert R. Baron and Conrad Edick Wright. Fulcrum, 2010, pp. 59–80.
Jackson, Kevin. *Invisible Forms: A Guide to Literary Curiosities.* Thomas Dunne, 2000.
Jackson, Virginia. *Dickinson's Misery: A Theory of Lyric Reading.* Princeton University Press, 2005.
Jacobs, Carol. "*Wuthering Heights*: At the Threshold of Interpretation." *Boundary 2: A Journal of Postmodern Literature and Culture*, vol. 7, no. 3, 1979, pp. 49–71.
Jalland, Pat. *Death in the Victorian Family.* Oxford University Press, 1996.
James, Henry. *The Complete Notebooks of Henry James*, edited by Leon Edel and Lyall H. Powers. Oxford University Press, 1987.
Janes, Dominic. "The Wordless Book: The Visual and Material Culture of Evangelism in Victorian Britain." *Material Religion*, vol. 12, no. 1, 2016, pp. 26–49.
Johns, Adrian. *The Nature of the Book: Print and Knowledge in the Making.* University of Chicago Press, 1998.
Johnson, Claudia. *Jane Austen's Cults and Cultures.* University of Chicago Press, 2012.
Kavanagh, James. *Emily Brontë.* Basil Blackwood, 1985.

Kimnach, Wilson H. and Kenneth P. Minkema, "The Material and Social Practices of Intellectual Work: Jonathan Edwards's Study." *The William and Mary* Quarterly, vol. 69, no. 4, 2012, pp. 683–730.

King, Amy M. *Bloom: The Botanical Vernacular in the English Novel.* Oxford University Press, 2003.

King, Kathryn R. "Of Needles and Pens and Women's Work." *Tulsa Studies in Women's Literature*, vol. 14, 1995, pp. 77–93.

Kitchel, Anna Theresa, editor. *Quarry for Middlemarch.* University of California Press, 1950.

Knoepflmacher, U. C. *Emily Brontë: Wuthering Heights.* Cambridge University Press, 1989.

Kooistra, Lorraine Janzen. *Poetry, Pictures, and Popular Publishing: The Illustrated Gift Book and Victorian Visual Culture, 1855–1875.* Ohio University Press, 2011.

Kucich, John. "George Eliot and Objects: Meaning as Matter in *The Mill on the Floss*." *Dickens Studies Annual: Essays in Victorian Fiction*, vol. 12, 1983, pp. 310–340. Rpt. in *The Mill on the Floss: An Authoritative Text, Backgrounds, and Contemporary Reactions, Criticism*, edited by Carol T. Christ. Norton, 1994.

Labarre, E. J. *Dictionary and Encyclopedia of Paper and Papermaking.* Oxford, 1955.

Lamb, Charles. "Detached Thoughts on Books and Reading." *London Magazine*, vol. 6, 1822, pp. 33–6.

Lamb, Charles. *Album Verses.* Moxon, 1830.

Lamb, Charles. *The Letters of Charles Lamb*, edited by Sir Thoma Noon Talfours. Moxon, 1841.

Landow, George P. and Ernest Chew. "Anthony Trollope's Marginalia in Macaulay's *Critical and Historical Essays*." *Notes and Queries*, vol. 48, no. 2, 2001, pp. 152–5.

Lang, Andrew. "Mrs. Radcliffe's Novels." *Cornhill Magazine*, vol. 82, 1900, pp. 24–34.

Langford, Martha. *Suspended Conversations: The Afterlife of Memory in Photographic Albums.* McGill-Queens University Press, 2001.

Latour, Bruno. *Reassembling the Social.* Oxford University Press, 2005.

Lau, Beth. "Editing Keats's Marginalia. *Text*, vol. 7, 1994, pp. 337–48.

The Laws of Piquet, edited by "Cavendish" (a pseudonym). Thomas De La Rue and Co., 1881.

Lee, Hermione. *Virginia Woolf.* Vintage, 1996.

Lee, Ruth Webb. *A History of Valentines.* Batsford, 1953.

Le Faye, Deirdre. "New Marginalia in Jane Austen's Books." *Book Collector*, vol. 49, no. 2, 2000, pp. 222–6.

Leighton, Mary Elizabeth and Lisa Surridge, editors. "Object Lessons: The Victorians and the Material Text." *Cahiers victoriens et édouardiens*, vol. 84, 2016. https://journals.openedition.org/cve/2864.

Lerer, Seth. *Error and the Academic Self.* Columbia University Press, 2002.

Lerer, Seth. "Devotion and Defacement: Reading Children's Marginalia." *Representations*, vol. 118, no. 1, 2012, pp. 126–53.

Leslie, Esther. "Dreams, Toys, and Tales." *Crafts*, vol. 146, 1997, pp. 26–31.

Levin, Susan M. *Dorothy Wordsworth and Romanticism.* Rutgers, 1987.

Lewis, Matthew. *The Monk.* Grove Press, 1952.

Liddington, Jill. *Female Fortune: Land, Gender, and Authority: The Anne Lister Diaries and Other Writings, 1833–36.* Rivers Oram Press, 1998.

Lilley, Charles A. *Selections for Autograph and Writing Albums.* Charles A. Lilley, 1879.

Liming, Sheila. *What a Library Means to a Woman: Edith Wharton and the Will to Collect Books.* University of Minnesota Press, 2020.

Lister, Anne. *I Know My Own Heart: The Diaries of Anne Lister, 1791–1840*, edited by Helena Whitbread. New York University Press, 1988.

Lister, Anne. *No Priest but Love: The Journals of Anne Lister from 1824–1826*, edited by Helena Whitbread. New York University Press, 1993.

Lister, Raymond. *Silhouettes: An Introduction to Their History and to the Art of Cutting and Painting Them*. Batsford, 1953.

Liu, Alan. "On the Autobiographical Present: Dorothy Wordsworth's *Grasmere Journals*." *Criticism*, vol. 26, no. 2, 1984, pp. 115–37.

Logan, Peter M. *Victorian Fetishism: Intellectuals and Primitives*. State University of New York Press, 2009.

Logan, Thad. *The Victorian Parlour: A Cultural Study*. Cambridge University Press, 2001.

Lowndes, Emma. *Turning Victorian Women into Ladies: The Life of Bessie Rayner Parkes, 1829–1925*. Academica, 2012.

Lumley, Edward, editor. *The Art of Judging the Character of Individuals from Their Handwriting and Style*. John Russel Smith, 1875.

Lupton, Christina. *Knowing Books: The Consciousness of Mediation in Eighteenth-Century Britain*. University of Pennsylvania Press, 2011.

Lutz, Deborah. *The Brontë Cabinet: Three Lives in Nine Objects*. Norton, 2015.

Lutz, Deborah. *Relics of Death in Nineteenth-Century Literature and Culture*. Cambridge University Press, 2015.

Lynch, Deidre Shauna. *Janeites: Austen's Disciples and Devotees*. Princeton University Press, 2000.

Lynch, Deidre Shauna. *Loving Literature: A Cultural History*. University of Chicago Press, 2015.

Lynch, Deidre Shauna. "Paper Slips: Album, Archiving, Accident." *Studies in Romanticism*, vol. 57, no. 1, 2018.

Machen, Arthur. *The Three Imposters*, 1895. Aegypan Press, 2005.

Macheski, Cecilia. "Penelope's Daughters: Images of Needlework in Eighteenth-Century Literature." *Fetter'd or Free? British Women Novelists, 1670–1815*, edited by Mary Anne Schofield and Cacelian Macheki. Ohio University Press, 1986, pp. 85–100.

Maclagan, David. *Line Let Loose: Scribbling, Doodling and Automatic Drawing*. Reaktion Books, 2014.

Maidment, Brian. *Reading Popular Prints, 1790–1870*, 2nd ed. Manchester University Press, 2001.

Maidment, Brian. *Comedy, Caricature, and the Social Order, 1820–50*. Manchester University Press, 2013.

Malafouris, Lambros. *How Things Shape the Mind: A Theory of Material Engagement*. MIT Press, 2013.

Mandell, Laura. "Felicia Hemans and the Gift-Book Aesthetic," *Cardiff Corvey: Reading the Romantic Text*, vol. 6, 2001, p. 1-12.

Mangin, Edward. *An Essay on Light Reading, as it may be supposed to influence moral conduct and literary taste*. James Carpenter, 1808.

Marcus, Sharon. *Between Women: Friendship, Desire, and Marriage in Victorian England*. Princeton University Press, 2007.

Marcus, Sharon. "The Theatrical Scrapbook." *Theatre Survey*, vol. 54, no. 2, 2013, pp. 283–307.

Marcus, Sharon. *The Drama of Celebrity*. Princeton University Press, 2019.

Marks, P. J. M. *The British Library Guide to Bookbinding: History and Techniques*. British Library, 1998.

Marsden, Jonathan, editor. *Victoria and Albert: Art and Love*. Royal Collection Trust, 2010.

Marsh, Jan. *Dante Gabriel Rossetti: Painter and Poet*. Phoenix, 2005.

Martin, Robert Bernard. *Tennyson: The Unquiet Heart*. Oxford University Press, 1980.

Martineau, Harriet. *Autobiography*, edited by Linda Peterson. Broadview, 2007.

Matthews, Samantha. "Psychological Crystal Palace? Late Victorian Confession Albums." *Book History*, vol. 3, 2000, pp. 125–54.

Matthews, Samantha. "Reading the 'Sign-Manual': Dickens and Signature." *Dickens Quarterly*, vol. 19, no. 4, 2002, pp. 232-42.
Matthews, Samantha. "Gems, Texts, and Confessions: Writing Readers in Late-Victorian Autographic Gift-Books." *Publishing History*, vol. 62, 2007, pp. 53-80.
Matthews, Samantha. "Album." *Victorian Review*, vol. 34, no. 1, 2008, pp. 13-17.
Matthews, Samantha. "Albums, Belongings, and Embodying the Feminine." *Bodies and Things in Nineteenth-Century Literature and Culture*, edited by Katharina Boehm. Palgrave Macmillan, 2012, pp. 107-29.
Maturin, Charles. *Melmoth the Wanderer*. Penguin, 2000.
Mavor, Elizabeth. *The Ladies of Llangollen: A Study in Romantic Friendship*. Michael Joseph, 1971.
Maxwell, Richard, editor. *The Victorian Illustrated Book*. University of Virginia Press, 2002.
McCaffery, Steve and Jed Rasula, editors. *Imagining Language: An Anthology*. MIT Press, 2001.
McDonald, Peter. "Ideas of the Book and Histories of Literature: After Theory?" *PMLA*, vol. 121, no. 1, 2006, pp. 214-28.
McGann, Jerome J. *The Textual Condition*. Princeton University Press, 1991.
McGann, Jerome J. *Radiant Textuality: Literature After the World Wide Web*. Palgrave, 2001.
McGill, Meredith L. "The Duplicity of the Pen." *Language Machines: Technologies of Literary and Cultural Production*, edited by Jeffrey Masten, Peter Stallybrass, and Nancy Vickers. Routledge, 1997, pp. 39-74.
McGill, Meredith L. "The Matter of the Text: Commerce, Print Culture, and the Authority of the State in American Copyright Law." *American Literary History*, vol. 9, no. 1, 1997, pp. 21-59.
McGill, Meredith L. *American Literature and the Culture of Reprinting, 1834-1853*. University of Pennsylvania Press, 2003.
McGill, Meredith L. "Common Places: Poetry, Illocality, and Temporal Dislocation in Thoreau's A Week on the Concord and Merrimack Rivers." *American Literary History*, vol. 19, 2007, pp. 357-74.
McGill, Meredith L. *The Traffic in Poems: Nineteenth-Century Poetry and Transatlantic Exchange*. Rutgers University Press, 2008.
McKelvy, William R. *The English Cult of Literature: Devoted Readers, 1774-1880*. University of Virginia Press, 2007.
McKitterick, David, editor. *The Cambridge History of the Book in Britain: Vol. 6, 1830-1914*. Cambridge University Press, 2009.
McLaughlin, Kevin. *Paperwork: Fiction and Mass Mediacy in the Paper Age*. University of Pennsylvania Press, 2005.
Menke, Richard. "*New Grub Street*'s Ecologies of Paper." *Victorian Studies*, vol. 61, no. 1, 2018, pp. 60-82.
Menke, Richard. *Literature, Print Culture, and Media Technologies, 1880-1900: Many Inventions*. Cambridge University Press, 2019.
Michie, Helena and Robyn Warhol. *Love Among the Archives: Writing the Lives of Sir George Scharf, Victorian Bachelor*. Edinburgh University Press, 2015.
Miller, Andrew. *Novels Behind Glass: Commodity Culture and Victorian Narrative*. Cambridge University Press, 1995.
Miller, Lucasta. *The Brontë Myth*. Jonathon Cape, 2001.
Moore, Virginia. *The Life and Eager Death of Emily Brontë: A Biography*. Rich and Cowan, 1936.
Moring, Meg M. "George Eliot's Scrupulous Research: The Facts behind Eliot's Use of the 'Keepsake in Middlemarch.'" *Victorian Periodicals Review*, vol. 26, no. 1, 1993, pp. 19-23.
Morley, F. V. *Dora Wordsworth: Her Book*. Houghton Mifflin, 1925.

Müller, Lothar. *White Magic: The Age of Paper*, translated by Jessica Spengler. Polity Press, 2014.
Myers, Robin, Michael Harris, and Giles Mandelbrote, editors. *Owners, Annotators, and the Signs of Reading*. Oak Knoll Press, 2005.
Myers, Robin, Michael Harris, and Giles Mandelbrote, editors. *Books on the Move: Tracking Copies Through Collections and the Book Trade*. British Library, 2007.
Neufeldt, Victor. *The Poems of Charlotte Brontë*. Garland, 1985.
Neufeldt, Victor. *The Works of Patrick Branwell Brontë*, vols 1–3. Routledge, 2015.
Nichols, Stephen. "On the Sociology of Medieval Manuscript Annotation." *Annotation and Its Texts*, edited by Stephen A. Barney. Oxford University Press, 1991, pp. 43–73.
Nokes, David. *Jane Austen: A Life*. University of California Press, 1997.
Norton, David. *A Textual History of the King James Bible*. Cambridge University Press, 2005.
Olmert, Michael. *The Smithsonian Book of Books*. Smithsonian Books, 1992.
Orgel, Stephen. *The Reader in the Book: A Study of Spaces and Traces*. Oxford University Press, 2015.
Ormond, Leonée. *Writing: The Arts and Living*. H.M.S.O., 1981.
Owings, Frank N. *The Keats Library*. Keats-Shelley Memorial Association, 1978.
Paden, William Doremus. *An Investigation of Gondal*. Bookman, 1958.
Page, Harry S. "Collecting Victoriana." *Manchester Review*, vol. 8, 1958, pp. 161–80.
Parker, Pamela Corpron. "Woman of Letters: Elizabeth Gaskell's Autograph Collection and Victorian Celebrity." *Material Women, 1750–1950: Consuming Desires and Collecting Practices*, edited by Maureen Daly Goggin and Beth Fowkes Tobin. Ashgate, 2009, pp. 265–78.
Parker, Rozsika. *The Subversive Stitch: Embroidery and the Making of the Feminine*. Women's Press, 1984.
Parsons, Eliza. *Castle of Wolfenbach*. Folio Press, 1968.
Pascoe, Judith. *The Hummingbird Cabinet: A Rare and Curious History of Romantic Collectors*. Cornell University Press, 2006.
Pearce, Susan. *On Collecting: An Investigation into Collecting in the European Tradition*. Routledge, 1995.
Peeck-O'Toole, Maureen. *Aspects of Lyric in the Poetry of Emily Brontë*. Rodopi, 1988.
Peltz, Lucy. "Facing the Text: The Amateur and Commercial Histories of Extra-Illustration, c. 1770–1840," *Owners, Annotators, and the Signs of Reading*, edited by Robin Myers, Michael Harris, and Giles Mandelbrote. Oak Knoll Press, 2005, pp. 91–135.
Perloff, Marjorie. *The Futurist Moment: Avant-Garde, Avant Guerre, and the Language of Rupture*. University of Chicago Press, 2003.
Persoon, James L. "Hardy's Pocket Milton: An Early Unpublished Poem." *English Language Notes*, vol. 25, no. 3, 1988, pp. 49–52.
Pettitt, Clare. "Peggotty's Work-Box: Victorian Souvenirs and Material Memory." *Romanticism and Victorianism on the Net*, vol. 53, 2009, pp. 1-27.
Pettitt, Clare. "Topos, Taxonomy and Travel in Nineteenth-Century Women's Scrapbooks." *Travel Writing, Visual Culture, and Form, 1760–1900*, edited by Mary Henes and Brian Murray. Palgrave, 2015, pp. 21–41.
Pfuntner, Deborah Lynn. "Romantic Women Writers and Their Commonplace Books." Dissertation at Texas A&M University, 2016.
Piper, Andrew. *Dreaming in Books: The Making of the Bibliographic Imagination in the Romantic Age*. University of Chicago Press, 2009.
Plotz, John. *Portable Property: Victorian Culture on the Move*. Princeton University Press, 2009.
Pratt, John Clark and Victor A. Neufeld, editors. *George Eliot's* Middlemarch *Notebooks: A Transcription*. University of California Press, 1979.

Price, Leah. *The Anthology and the Rise of the Novel: From Richardson to George Eliot.* Cambridge University Press, 2000.

Price, Leah. "Getting the Reading Out of It: Paper Recycling in Mayhew's London." *Bookish Histories: Books, Literature and Commercial Modernity, 1700–1900,* edited by Ina Ferris and Paul Keen. Palgrave Macmillan, 2009.

Price, Leah. *How to Do Things with Books in Victorian Britain.* Princeton University Press, 2012.

Proust, Marcel. *Time Regained,* translated by C. K. Scott Moncrieff and Terence Kilmartin. Modern Library, 2002.

Proust, Marcel. *Swann's Way,* translated by C. K. Scott Moncrieff and Terence Kilmartin. Modern Library, 2004.

Radcliffe, Anne. *Mysteries of Udolpho.* Penguin, 2001.

Ransom, Teresa. *The Mysterious Miss Marie Corelli: Queen of Victorian Bestsellers.* Sutton, 1999.

Rappoport, Jill. *Giving Women: Alliance and Exchange in Victorian Culture.* Oxford University Press, 2011.

Reade, Charles. *The Cloister and the Hearth.* Trübner and Co., 1862.

Reade, Charles. *Griffith Gaunt; Or, Jealousy.* Chapman and Hall, 1866.

Reade, Charles. *Put Yourself in His Place.* Fields, Osgood, and Co., 1870.

Reade, Charles. *Charles Reade, Dramatist, Novelist, Journalist, a Memoir,* vol. 1, written with Compton Reade. Chapman and Hall, 1887.

Reade, Charles. *The Double Marriage, or White Lies.* Chatto and Windus, 1891.

Reade, Charles. *A Terrible Temptation.* Collier, 1900.

Reader, Simon. "Oscar Wilde's Notebook on Philosophy." *Canadian Journal of Irish Studies,* vol. 36, no. 2, 2010, pp. 21–31.

Reader, Simon. "Social Notes: Oscar Wilde, Francis Bacon, and the Medium of Aphorism." *Journal of Victorian Culture,* vol. 18, no. 4, 2013, pp. 453–71.

"Recent Acquisitions." *Brontë Society Transactions,* vol. 21, no. 4, 1994, pp. 156–8.

Redford, Bruce. *The Converse of the Pen: Acts of Intimacy in the 18th-Century Familiar Letter.* University of Chicago Press, 1986.

Richardson, Samuel. *Clarissa.* Penguin, 1986.

Ritvo, Harriet. *The Animal Estate: The English and Other Creatures in Victorian England.* Harvard University Press, 1987.

Robinson, Oliver. "Bound for Glory: The Macabre Practice of Book Bindings Made of Human Skin." *Rare Book Review,* vol. 33, 2006, pp. 29–31.

Rose, Jonathan. *The Intellectual Life of the British Working Classes.* Yale University Press, 2001.

Rossetti, Christina. *The Complete Poems of Christina Rossetti: A Variorum Edition,* vol. 3, edited by R. W. Crump. Louisiana State University Press, 1990.

Rowlands, S. P. "An Old Fern Collection." *The British Fern Gazette,* vol. 6, no. 10, 1934, pp. 260–2.

Sadleir, Michael. *The Evolution of Publishers' Binding Styles, 1770–1900.* Constable and Co., 1930.

Saenger, Paul. *Space Between Words: The Origins of Silent Reading.* Stanford University Press, 1997.

Sánchez-Eppler, Karen. "Marks of Possession: Methods for an Impossible Subject." *PMLA,* vol. 126, no. 1, 2011, pp. 151–9.

Scarisbrick, Diana. *Ancestral Jewels.* Deutsch, 1989.

Schaaf, Larry J. *Sun Gardens: Victorian Photograms by Anna Atkins.* Aperture, 1985.

Schaaf, Larry J. *Sun Pictures. Catalogue 10. British Paper Negatives, 1839–1864*. Hans P. Kraus, Jr., 2001.
Schaaf, Larry J. *Sun Gardens: Cyanotypes by Anna Atkins*. New York Public Library, 2019.
Schaffer, Talia. *Novel Craft: Victorian Domestic Handicraft and Nineteenth-Century Fiction*. Oxford University Press, 2011.
Schaffer, Talia. *Romance's Rival: Familiar Marriage in Victorian Fiction*. Oxford University Press, 2016.
Schleuter, June. "Michael van Meer's *Album Amicorum*, with Illustrations of London, 1614–15." *Huntington Library Quarterly*, vol. 69. no. 2, 2006, pp. 301–14.
Schor, Naomi. *Reading in Detail: Aesthetics and the Feminine*. Methuen, 1987.
Schwenger, Peter. *Asemia: The Art of Writing*. University of Minnesota Press, 2019.
Scourse, Nicolette. *The Victorians and Their Flowers*. Croom Helm, 1983.
Secord, James. "Scrapbook Science." *Figuring It Out: Science, Gender, and Visual Culture*, edited by Ann B. Schteir and Bernard V. Lightman. University Press of New England, 2006, pp. 164–91.
Sedgwick, Eve Kosofsky. *Touching Feeling: Affect, Pedagogy, Performativity*. Duke University Press, 2003.
Seigert, Bernhard. *Relays: Literature as an Epoch of the Postal System*, translated by Kevin Repp. Stanford University Press, 1999.
Shelley, Mary. *Mary Shelley's Journals*, edited by Frederick Jones. University of Oklahoma Press, 1947.
Shelley, Mary. *Frankenstein*. Broadview Press, 2013.
Shelley, Mary. *The Frankenstein Notebooks*, edited Charles E. Robinson. 2 vols, Routledge, 2016.
Shelley, Percy Bysshe. *The Bodleian Shelley Manuscripts: A Facsimile Edition*, edited by Donald H. Reiman. 23 vols, Garland, 1986–2002.
Sheridan, Richard Brinsley. *The Rivals*. Crowell, 1884.
Sherman, William. "Toward a History of the Manicule." *Owners, Annotators, and the Signs of Reading*, edited by Robin Myers, Michael Harris, and Giles Mandelbrote. Oak Knoll Press, 2005, pp. 19–44.
Sherman, William. *Used Books: Marking Readers in Renaissance England*. University of Pennsylvania Press, 2008.
Shirai, Yoshiaki. "Ferndean: Charlotte Brontë in the Age of Pteridomania." *Brontë Studies*, vol. 28, no. 2, 2003, pp. 123–30.
Shorter, Clement King. "Relics of Emily Brontë." *The Woman at Home*, vol. 47, 1897. Rpt. in *The Bookman: An Illustrated Literary Journal*, no. 6, 1898, pp. 15–19.
Shorter, Clement King. *Charlotte Brontë and Her Circle*. Greenwood Press, 1970.
Shuttleworth, Sally. *George Eliot and Nineteenth-Century Science: The Make-Believe of a Beginning*. Cambridge University Press, 1984.
Siegel, Elizabeth et al. *Playing with Pictures: The Art of Victorian Photocollage*. Art Institute of Chicago, 2009.
Silver, Brenda. *Virginia Woolf's Reading Notebooks*. Princeton University Press, 1983.
Silverman, Gillian. *Bodies and Books*. University of Pennsylvania Press, 2012.
Siskin, Clifford. *The Work of Writing: Literature and Social Change in Britain, 1700–1830*. Johns Hopkins University Press, 1998.
Slights, William. *Managing Readers: Printed Marginalia in English Renaissance Books*. University of Michigan Press, 2001.
Smith, Gaye. "Sentimental Souvenirs: Victorian Scrap Albums from the Sir Harry Page Collection." *Catalogue of an Exhibition Held at the Holden Gallery*. Manchester Polytechnic Library, 1989.

Smith, Margaret, editor. *The Letters of Charlotte Brontë: With a Selection of Letters by Family and Friends*. 3 vols, Oxford University Press, 1995.

Southey, Robert. *The Life and Correspondence*, edited by Charles Cuthbert Southey, vol. 6. Harper and Brothers, 1850.

Spellerberg, Ian. *Reading and Writing Accessories: A Study of Paper-Knives, Paper Folders, Letter Openers and Mythical Page Turners*. Oak Knoll Press, 2016.

Spielmann, M. H. "The Inner History of the Brontë-Heger Letters." *Fortnightly Review*, April, 1919, pp. 345–50.

St. Clair, William. *The Reading Nation in the Romantic Period*. Cambridge University Press, 2004.

Stabile, Susan M. *Memory's Daughters: The Material Culture of Remembrance in Eighteenth-Century America*. Cornell University Press, 2004.

Stabile, Susan M. "Female Curiosities: The Transatlantic Female Commonplace Book." *Reading Women: Literacy, Authorship, and Culture in the Atlantic World, 1500–1800*, edited by Heidi Brayman Hackel and Catherine E. Kelly. University of Pennsylvania Press, 2008, pp. 217–44.

Stallybrass, Peter. "Books and Scrolls: Navigating the Bible." *Books and Readers in Early Modern England: Material Studies*, edited by Jennifer Anderson and Elizabeth Sauer. University of Pennsylvania Press, 2002, pp. 42–79.

Stauffer, Andrew. "Victorian Paperwork." *Victorian Poetry*, vol. 41, no. 4, 2003, pp. 526–31.

Stauffer, Andrew. "Byron, the Pyramids, and 'Uncertain Paper.'" *Wordsworth Circle*, vol. 36, no. 1, 2005, pp. 11–15.

Stauffer, Andrew. "Ruins of Paper: Dickens and the Necropolitan Library." *Romanticism and Victorianism on the Net*, vol. 47, 2007, pp. 1-28.

Stauffer, Andrew. "Legends of the Mummy Paper." *Printing History*, vol. 8, 2010, pp. 21–6.

Stauffer, Andrew. "Hemans by the Book." *European Romantic Review*, vol. 22, no. 3, 2011, pp. 373–80.

Stauffer, Andrew. "The Nineteenth-Century Archive in the Digital Age." *European Romantic Review*, vol. 23, no. 3, 2012, pp. 335–41.

Stauffer, Andrew. "Poetry, Romanticism, and the Practice of Nineteenth-Century Books." *Nineteenth-Century Contexts*, vol. 34, no. 5, 2012, pp. 411–26.

Stauffer, Andrew. *Book Traces: Nineteenth-Century Readers and the Future of the Library*. University of Pennsylvania Press, 2021.

Steedman, Carolyn. *Dust: The Archive and Cultural History*. Rutgers University Press, 2002.

Steinitz, Rebecca. "Diaries and Displacement in 'Wuthering Heights.'" *Studies in the Novel*, vol. 32, no. 4, 2000, pp. 406–19.

Stetz, Margaret D. "*Keynotes*: A New Woman, Her Publisher, and Her Material." *Studies in the Literary Imagination*, vol. 30, no. 1, 1997, pp. 89–106.

Stevenson, Robert Louis. *The Letters of Robert Louis Stevenson*, edited by Bradford A. Booth and Ernest Mehew, vol. 5. Yale University Press, 1995.

Stevenson, Robert Louis. *Strange Case of Dr. Jekyll and Mr. Hyde*. Norton, 2020.

Stewart, Garrett. "Reading Feeling and the 'Transferred Life': *The Mill on the Floss*." *The Feeling of Reading: Affective Experience and Victorian Literature*, edited by Rachel Ablow. University of Michigan Press, 2010, pp. 179–206.

Stewart, Susan. *On Longing: Narratives of the Miniature, the Gigantic, the Souvenir, the Collection*. Duke University Press, 1993.

Stewart, Susan. *The Ruins Lesson: Meaning and Material in Western Culture*. University of Chicago Press, 2020.

Stoddard, Roger. *Marks in Books, Illustrated and Explained.* Harvard University Press, 2005.
Stoker, Bram. *Dracula.* 1897. Norton Critical Edition, 1996.
Stougaard-Nielsen, Jakob. "The Fairy Tale and the Periodical: Hans Christian Andersen's Scrapbooks." *Book History,* vol. 16, 2013, pp. 132–54.
Suarez, Michael F. and Michael L. Turner, editors. *The Cambridge History of the Book in Britain: Vol. 5, 1695–1830.* Cambridge University Press, 2009.
Sutcliffe, E. G. "Charles Reade's Notebooks." *Studies in Philology,* vol. 27, 1930, pp. 64–109.
Sutherland, John. *The Stanford Companion to Victorian Fiction.* Stanford University Press, 1989.
Talbot, William Henry Fox. *The Pencil of Nature.* Longman, 1844.
Talley, Lee A. "The Case for Anne Brontë's Marginalia in the Author's Own Copy of *The Tenant of Wildfell Hall.*" *Brontë Studies,* vol. 32, no. 2, 2007, pp. 132–7.
Taunton, Nerylla. *Antique Needlework Tools and Embroideries.* Antique Collector's Club, 1997.
Tennyson, Alfred, Lord. *Tennyson's Poetry.* Norton, 1999.
Thackeray, William Makepeace. "Confessions of George Fitz-Boodle: Men's Wives, Mr. and Mrs. Frank Berry." *Fraser's Magazine,* vol. 27, 1843, pp. 707-721.
Thomas, Kate. *Postal Pleasures: Sex, Scandal, and Victorian Letters.* Oxford University Press, 2012.
Thompson, Andrew. "A George Eliot Holograph Notebook: An Edition." *George Eliot—George Henry Lewes Studies,* no. 50/1, 2006, pp. 1–109.
Thompson, Andrew. "George Eliot's Quarry for Romola: An Edition of the Notebook Held in the Morris L. Parrish Collection at Princeton University Library." *George Eliot—George Henry Lewes Studies,* vol. 66, no. 1/2, 2014, pp. 5–99.
Thompson, Andrew. "George Eliot's Florentine Notes: An Edition of the Notebook Held at the British Library, London." *George Eliot—George Henry Lewes Studies,* vol. 70, no. 1, 2018, pp. 1–86.
Thormahlen, Marianne. "Anne Brontë's Sacred Harmony: A Discovery." *Brontë Studies,* vol. 30, no. 2, 2005, pp. 93–102.
Thornton, Sara. *Advertising, Subjectivity and the Nineteenth-Century Novel: Dickens, Balzac, and the Language of the Walls.* Palgrave Macmillan, 2009.
Thorton, Tamara Platkins. *Handwriting in America: A Cultural History.* Yale University Press, 1996.
Toller, Jane. *The Regency and Victorian Crafts; or, the Genteel Female—Her Arts and Pursuits.* Ward Lock, 1969.
Tomalin, Claire. *Jane Austen: A Life.* Vintage, 1999.
Tucker, Susan, Katherine Ott, and Patricia P. Buckler, editors. *The Scrapbook in American Life.* Temple University Press, 2006.
Uglow, Jenny. *Elizabeth Gaskell: A Habit of Stories.* Faber and Faber, 1993.
Vine, Steven. *Emily Brontë.* New York: Twayne, 1998.
Waley, Daniel, editor. *George Eliot Blotter: A Commonplace Book.* The British Library, 1980.
Wall, Wendy. *The Imprint of Gender: Authorship and Publication in the English Renaissance.* Cornell University Press, 1993.
Wall, Wendy. "Women in the Household." *The Cambridge Companion to Early Modern Women's Writing,* edited by Laura Lunger Knoppers. Cambridge University Press, 2009.
Wark, Robert R. "The Gentle Pastime of Extra-Illustrating Books." *The Huntington Library Quarterly,* vol. 56, no. 2, 1993, pp. 151–65.
Warodell, Johan Adam. "Conrad the Doodler." *The Cambridge Quarterly,* vol. 43, no. 4, 2014, pp. 339–54.
Warren, Geoffrey. *A Stitch in Time: Victorian and Edwardian Needlecraft.* David and Charles, 1976.

Watson, Alex. *Romantic Marginality: Nation and Empire on the Borders of the Page*. Pickering and Chatto, 2012.
Watson, Nicola. *The Literary Tourist: Readers and Places in Romantic and Victorian Britain*. Palgrave, 2008.
Watson, Nicola. *The Author's Effects: On Writer's House Museums*. Oxford University Press, 2020.
Webb, Ruth. *A History of Valentines*. Studio Pubs, 1954.
Welsh, Doris V. *The History of Miniature Books*. Fort Orange Press, 1987.
Wheeler, M. D. "Mrs. Gaskell's Reading, and the Gaskell Sale Catalogue in Manchester Central Library." *Notes and Queries*, vol. 24, no. 1, 1977, p. 26.
Whitehouse, Tessa and N. H. Keeble, editors. *Textual Transformations: Purposing and Repurposing Books from Richard Baxter to Samuel Taylor Coleridge*. Oxford University Press, 2019.
Whittingham, Sarah . *Fern Fever: The History of Pteridomania*. Frances Lincoln, 2012.
Whitton, Blair. *Paper Toys of the World*. Hobby House, 1986.
Wiesenfarth, J. "George Eliot's Notes for *Adam Bede*." *Nineteenth-Century Fiction*, vol. 32, no. 2, 1977, pp. 127–65.
Wilson, Romer. *All Alone: The Life and Private History of Emily Jane Brontë*. Chatto and Windus, 1928.
Wise, Thomas J . *A Bibliography of the Writings in Prose and Verse of the Members of the Brontë Family*. Richard Clay and Sons, 1917.
Wise, Thomas J. *The Poems of Emily Jane Brontë and Anne Brontë*, vol. 12. The Shakespeare Head Press, 1932.
Wise, Thomas J. and John Alexander Symington, editors. *The Brontës: Their Lives, Friendship and Correspondence*. 4 vols, The Shakespeare Head Press, 1932.
Wolfe, Heather, "'Neatly sealed, with silk, and Spanish wax or otherwise': The Practice of Letter-Locking with Silk Floss in Early Modern England." *In the Prayse of Writing: Early Manuscript Studies*, edited by S. P. Cerasano and Steven W. May. British Library, 2012, pp. 169–89.
Wolosky, Shira. *Language Mysticism: The Negative Way of Language in Eliot, Beckett, and Celan*. Stanford University Press, 1995.
Wood, Claire. *Dickens and the Business of Death*. Cambridge University Press, 2015.
Woof, Pamela. "The Uses of Notebooks from Journal to Album, from Commonplace to Keepsake." *Coleridge Bulletin*, vol. 31, 2008, pp. 1–18.
Woof, Pamela. *Dorothy Wordsworth: Wonders of the Everyday*. Wordsworth Trust, 2013.
Woolf, Virginia. *The Diary of Virginia Woolf*, edited by Anne Oliver Bell, vol. 1. Harcourt, 1977.
Woolf, Virginia. *The Common Reader*, first series, edited by Andrew McNeillie. Harcourt, 1984.
Woolf, Virginia. *Three Guineas Reading Notebooks*, edited by Vara Neverow and Merry Pawlowski. eBook, Virginia Woolf website at Southern Connecticut State University, 2001.
Woolf, Virginia . *The Second Common Reader*. Mariner, 2003.
Woolf, Virginia. *A Passionate Apprentice: The Early Journals 1897–1909*, edited by Mitchell A. Leaska. Pimlico, 2004.
Wordsworth, Dorothy. *Her Write His Name: The Continental Journals, 1798–1820*, edited by Helen Boden. Thoemannes Continuum, 1995.
Wynne, Deborah. "Charlotte Brontë's Frocks and Shirley's Queer Textiles." *Literary Bric-à-brac and the Victorians: From Commodities to Oddities*, edited by Jonathon Shears and Jen Harrison. Ashgate, 2013, pp. 147–62.
Wynne, Deborah. "Reading Victorian Rags: Recycling, Redemption, and Dickens's Ragged Children." *Journal of Victorian Culture*, vol. 20, issue 1, 2015, pp. 34–49.
Yonge, Charlotte. *The Daisy Chain*. Macmillan, 1870.

Index

Note: Figures are indicated by an italic *f* following the page number. Notes are indicated by the suffix n.

"A Girl" (Michael Field) 91
Abbott, Ruth 74, 77, 178n56
abuse, revealed in sampler 134
Adam Bede (George Eliot) 20, 24
"Adventures of a Quire of Paper" 94
Agnes Grey (Anne Brontë) 24–25
Aikin, Lucy 12
albums
    art and purpose 34–35
    autograph 35, 48–51, 168n103, 168n106
    botanical 59–61, 60*f*, 171n137, 172n144
    commonplace books 35, 64–67, 81–82, 174n12
    friendship 36–47, 122*f*, 161n24
    memorial 161n23
    music books 35, 98, 160n7
    photography 61–62, 138–141
    souvenir 36, 56–62, 57*f*, 58*f*
    tourist 56–59
    see also poems, in friendship albums
Alexander, Christine 110
"And like myself lone wholey lone" (Emily Brontë) 107
Andersen, Hans Christian 121–122
Angria 18, 21, 88, 98, 109, 162n31, 190n97
archive fever 5–6, 144
Arnold, Matthew 66
Arrangement of British Plants (William Withering) 13
"A.S. Castlewood" (Emily Brontë) 102
asemic text 41–42, 164n48
Atkins, Anna 60–61, 136–142, 140*f*
Austen, Jane
    editing with pins 124–125, 127, 193n30
    embroidered bag 128
    Emma 81, 160n7, 161n18
    library 12
    marginalia 15, 18
    notebooks 181n98
    Pride and Prejudice 173n6
    silhouettes 192n17
Austin, Mary 158n105
autographs
    albums 35, 48–51, 168n103, 168n106
    collecting 167n92
    on fans 166n86
    graffiti 20–21, 154n62

Bacon, Francis 14
Baker, William 74–75
Bardi, Bardo de', in *Romola* 11, 78–79
Barthes, Roland 39, 43
Batchen, Geoffrey 14
Bayles Kortsch, Christine 127–128, 134
Beaty, Jerome 73
Bede, Seth, in *Adam Bede* 20
Benjamin, Walter 144–145
Berg, Maggie 30, 32
Berkeley, Georgina 62
bibles
    eating 14
    miniature 164n59
    recording dates in 26–27
    swearing on 23–24, 156n77
bibliomancy 23–24, 27, 107–108, 155n74
Biddell, Sydney 13, 14
bijous 81
bindings
    hand-embroidered 128, 129
    rebinding 55–56, 68, 128–130
    recursiveness in 170n121, 170n124
    using body parts 55, 170n120, 170n121, 170n124
    see also book covers
"blooks" (things that look like books) 44
blotters, George Eliot's 20, 65, 153n56
body, traces left on paper 5–6, 12–13, 147n13, 149n19, 150n25

body parts as parts of books 37, 54–55,
170n120, 170n121, 170n124,
171n131 *see also* hair
Boleyn, Anne 149n19
Boniface (saint) 25
book covers 97–98, 186n30 *see also* bindings
bookmarks 13, 83, 126, 128, 150n26
books
　associative properties 24–29
　making 105
　miniature 43–44, 88, 97–98, 97*f*, 164n59,
　　165n64, 182n103
　movable or action 124
　repurposed 32, 94–95, 103–105, 104*f*,
　　187n50
　skeuomorphism 43–44
　in *Wuthering Heights* 30
botanical albums 59–61, 60*f*, 171n137,
　172n144
Bradley, Katherine and Edith Cooper
　(Michael Field) 63–64, 67, 89–92
Bradshaigh, Lady 12, 149n16
Bree, Frances Elizabeth 62
Breton, André 101
British Algae: Cyanotype Impressions (Anne
　Atkins) 139, 140*f*
Brontë, Anne
　Agnes Grey 24–25
　bible 26–27, 157n99
　diaries 116, 117–118
　folded paper 188n54
　music books 98
Brontë, Branwell 88, 97–98, 109, 162n30
Brontë, Charlotte
　albums 37, 38, 40–41, 40*f*, 59, 162n30,
　　162n31, 171n137
　Angria 88, 109
　bibliomancy 107–108
　and books 12, 24–25, 156n78
　date-marking 87
　"I never can forget" 101
　Life of Charlotte Brontë, The (Elizabeth
　　Gaskell) 13, 14, 53–54
　manuscripts 96, 120–121
　marginalia 16–18, 17*f*, 19*f*
　miniature books 43–44, 97–98, 97*f*
　novels
　　Jane Eyre 32, 188n58
　　The Professor 96

　Shirley 38, 96, 152n46
　Villette 13, 108, 120–121, 131
　rolled-paper work 95
　sewing 124, 126, 131
　souvenirs of 53, 57–58, 58*f*
　writing method 120
Brontë, Emily
　asemic texts 42
　descriptions of 88–89, 117–118
　drafts 84–85, 111–112
　Gondal 21, 85–88, 105–106, 110–115,
　　190n96, 190n97, 190n98
　graffiti inscriptions 20–21
　manuscripts 5*f*, 84–85, 109–118, 112*f*,
　　113*f*, 139, 190n96
　marginalia 17–18
　miniaturization 110–111, 115–116
　notebooks 84–89, 86*f*
　poems
　　"And like myself lone wholey lone" 107
　　"A.S. Castlewood" 102
　　Gondal Poems 85–89, 86*f*
　　"I'm happiest when most
　　　away" 112–115, 112*f*
　　"She dried her tears and they did
　　　smile" 102
　　"To a Wreath of Snow / by A G
　　　Almeda" 112*f*, 113–115
　　"Weaned from Life and torn
　　　away" 112–115, 113*f*, 190n98
　reuse of paper 93, 105–107
　samplers 133
　temporality 87–89
　Wuthering Heights 9, 29–33, 123–124,
　　158n112 *see also* Earnshaw,
　　Catherine in *Wuthering Heights*
Brontë, Maria 25
Brontë, Patrick 12, 25, 162n30
Browning, Elizabeth Barrett 27, 83, 125,
　157n101, 162n30
Bürger, Peter 110
burials 94, 108–109, 117, 180n88, 184n8
Burns, Robert 154n62, 154n63, 170n122
Butler, Eleanor and Sarah Ponsonby (the
　"Ladies of Llangollen") 148n7,
　157n93
Byron, George Gordon, Lord 26, 96,
　154n63
Byron, Georgina Lucy 56–57,
　57*f*

calendars 99–101, 99f, 100f
Cameron, Julia Margaret 141
cards used to organise notes 71
Carlyle, Thomas 93, 107, 154n62
Carroll, Lewis 66, 181n98
carte-de-visite 61–62
Casaubon, in *Middlemarch* 78, 79–80
catalogues, library 148n7
Charles I, King 55
Children, J. G. 136–137
Chitham, Edward 110
cigar smoke 13
circulating libraries 13, 16, 129
Clarissa (Samuel Richardson) 10–11, 12, 132, 134, 149n16, 174n12
Clifford, Lady Anne 10, 65, 148n6
Cloister and the Hearth, The (Charles Reade) 72
cloth used in papermaking 93–94
Colclough, Stephen 64
Coleridge, Samuel Taylor 26, 64, 66
collaborative notebooks 89–91
collage
  editing the page 126–127
  photo 61–62
collecting 45–50, 56–62, 167n88, 167n92, 172n144
Collins, Wilkie, *The Law and the Lady* 54
Colonel: A Story of Fashionable Life, The (Anna Atkins) 137–138
commonplace books 35, 64–67, 81–82, 174n12
compositions in the margins of books 18, 152n50, 153n51
Conrad, Joseph 18
cookery books 152n49
Cooper, Edith and Katherine Bradley (Michael Field) 63–64, 67, 89–92
copying texts (transcription) 66–67, 74–75, 178n56
Corelli, Marie 65, 124
Coulson, Victoria 120
Crane, Walter 34
Cranford (Elizabeth Gaskell) 1, 45–47, 50–51, 95
curl-papers 96, 108
Curtis, Gerard 44, 50
cut and paste/pin 120, 124–125
cut-paper designs 42–43, 42f, 120–121
cyanotype 138–141, 140f

Cyanotypes of British and Foreign Flowering Plants and Ferns (Anna Atkins and Anne Dixon) 61, 141

Daisy Chain, The (Charlotte Yonge) 154n59
Dame Wonder's Transformations 124
date-marking 26–27, 38, 59–60, 87
David Copperfield (Charles Dickens) 54, 125
Dean and Sons 124
Derrida, Jacques 144
desks 117, 121
Dickens, Charles 16, 44, 54, 125, 146n6
Dixon, Anne 61, 141
Dixon, Ella Hepworth, *The Story of a Modern Woman* 65
Dolin, Tim 46
Don Juan (Lord Byron) 96
Donoghue, Emma 89
doodles 19f, 31, 106, 152n46, 188n58
Drucker, Joanna 41, 107, 111, 112, 134
dungeons in Angria and Gondal 21, 190n97, 190n98

E13 manuscript (Emily Brontë) 112–115, 112f, 113f, 190n96
Eagleton, Terry 6
Earnshaw, Catherine in *Wuthering Heights* 9, 29–33, 105, 107, 116
eating bibles 14
Edwards, Elizabeth 44
Edwards, Jane 121, 122f
Edwards, Jonathan 174n15
Egerton, George 129
Eliot, George
  asemic text 42
  autograph collecting 167n92
  bibliomancy 23–24, 155n74
  blotters 20, 65, 153n56
  calendar used for notes 99–101, 99f, 100f
  copying texts 67, 74–75, 178n56
  epigraphs 21, 77, 82–83
  found texts 21–22, 52–53, 65–66, 80–81
  graffiti 20, 148n8
  and Hennell, Sara Sophia 26, 76, 126
  "Journeys to Normandy in 1865 and Italy in 1864" 75–76, 75f
  library 11, 148n8, 148n12
  The Linnet's Life 28–29, 29f
  marginalia 14, 15
  memorializing 26–27

notebooks 7, 67, 68–69, 72–80, 173n8, 178n54, 178n56, 179n68
novels
  Adam Bede 20, 24
  Middlemarch 21–22, 52–53, 72–73, 72f, 77–83, 123
  The Mill on the Floss 13, 22–24, 29, 131
  Romola 11, 78–79
  Scenes of Clerical Life 95–96, 129, 184n8
  personal possessions 146n6, 197n75
  and The Prelude 27–28
  "Silly Novels by Lady Novelists" 15
  and Simcox, Edith 26
  standing ground 63, 82
Elizabeth, Princess (Queen Elizabeth I) 129
embroidery 126, 128, 129, 132 see also samplers
Emma (Jane Austen) 81, 160n7, 161n18
epigraphs (mottoes) 21, 77, 82–83, 155n67
Evelyn, John 171n131
extra-illustration (grangerization) 55–56

fabrics used to bind books 129–130, 130f
fans, autographs on 166n86
Fay, Elizabeth 49
fern albums 59, 171n137, 172n144
fetishes, books as 23–24
Field, Michael (Katharine Bradley and Edith Cooper) 63–64, 67, 89–92
finger marks 6, 150n25
fingernails 13, 54, 149n19
Fleming, Juliet 20, 24, 43, 55, 65, 109–110
Flint, Kate 15
folded paper 106, 188n54
Forman, Harry Buxton 96
found texts 21–22, 51–53, 65–66, 80–81, 108–109
Frankenstein (Mary Shelley) 108, 189n74
friendship albums 36–47, 122f, 161n24 see also autographs; poems, in friendship albums

Garth, Mary and Fred, in Middlemarch 82
Gaskell, Elizabeth
  albums 35, 36, 49–51
  The Life of Charlotte Brontë 13, 14, 53–54
  novels
    Cranford 1, 45–47, 50–51, 95
    Mary Barton 51–52, 169n108
    North and South 47
    Ruth 153n57
    Sylvia's Lovers 51, 123
    Wives and Daughters 47–48
  paper crafts 123
  "Squire's Story, The" 52
  writing process 44–46
Gaze, Tim 164n48
George Eliot Birthday Book, The 83
Gernes, Todd S. 38
Gezari, Janet 85, 110, 116
gifts 26, 47–48, 156n78, 157n91, 195n48 see also keepsakes
Gillespie, Alexandra 3
Gitelman, Lisa 67, 98, 103, 145
glass, writing on 20, 153n58, 154n59, 154n62, 154n63, 155n66
Golden, Catherine J. 121
Goldsmith, Oliver, The History of England 15
Gondal 18, 21, 84–88, 105–106, 110–115, 190n96, 190n97, 190n98
Gondal Poems notebook 85–89, 86f
gothic fiction 20, 96, 108–109, 155n66, 189n74
graffiti 20–21, 30–31, 153n58, 154n59, 154n62, 154n63, 155n66 see also inscriptions; marginalia; quotations written on walls and ceilings
Grammar of General Geography, A 17–18
grangerization (extra-illustration) 55–56
Griffith Gaunt; Or, Jealousy (Charles Reade) 71–72
Grossman, Jonathan 52

Hackel, Heidi Brayman 65, 66–67
hair
  in albums 37, 54–55, 171n131
  in book bindings 170n120, 170n121
  as bookmarks 13
  in lockets 137
  used in needlework 131, 133–134
handicrafts 124–136 see also paper crafts
handwriting 24, 42–43, 138, 139
haptic texts 14
Hard Cash (Charles Reade) 70–71
Hardy, Thomas 18, 66, 180n87
Hart, Janice 44
Haworth, souvenirs of 57–58, 58f
Hawtry, Eliza 157n91

Hays, E.H. 186n36
Heaton, Mary Frances 134–136, 135*f*
Hemans, Felicia 12, 37, 49, 65, 167n93, 174n12
Hennell, Sara Sophia 26, 76, 126, 167n92, 179n69
Herschel, Sir John 138, 139
Higden, David Leon 77
historical changes in paper culture 144–145
historical objects, collecting 49, 50, 56–57, 167n88
History of England, The (Oliver Goldsmith) 15
Hogarth Press 105
Hogg, James 108, 109, 189n74
Holder, William 25–26
Honresfeld manuscript (Emily Brontë) 84–85, 139
Hornby, Lady Emilia 57
Household Words 16
Howe, Susan 85
Howitt, Mary 44–45
Hughes, Linda K. 67
Hunt, Leigh 16
Hunter, Dard 125

"I never can forget" (Charlotte Brontë) 101
idea notebooks 180n87
"I'm happiest when most away" (Emily Brontë) 112–115, 112*f*
In Memoriam (Alfred Lord Tennyson) 96
indexes 15, 64, 70, 173n8, 177n44
inscriptions
 in books 15, 16, 25–26
 on doors and furniture 20, 148n8, 174n14
 see also glass, writing on; quotations written on walls and ceilings

Jackson, Heather 14, 16, 26, 64
Jackson, Kevin 109
Jackson, Virginia 97, 102, 110
Jacobs, Carol 30
Jane Eyre (Charlotte Brontë) 32, 188n58
Japan-work 121
John the Baptist 107
"Journeys to Normandy in 1865 and Italy in 1864" (George Eliot) 75–76, 75*f*

Kavanagh, James 30
Keats, John 18, 26, 156n89

Keepsake, The 81–82
keepsakes 46–47, 146n6 *see also* gifts; hair
Kitching, Agnes 39
Knoepflmacher, U.C. 158n112

"Ladies of Llangollen," the 148n7, 157n93
Lamb, Charles 13, 14, 163n36
Langford, Martha 37, 56, 59
Languish, Lydia in *The Rivals* 13
Last Things (Janet Gezari) 110
Law and the Lady, The (Wilkie Collins) 54
Lerer, Seth 78, 79
Leslie, Esther 98
letters
 Brontë, Charlotte 53, 125–126, 169n110
 Gaskell, Elizabeth 35, 45, 49–51
 in *Villette* 108
 see also grangerization (extra-illustration)
Lewes, Charles 11, 148n8
Lewes, George Henry 11, 16, 27, 74
Lewis, Matthew 96
libraries
 circulating 13, 16, 129
 personal 9, 10–12, 143
Life of Charlotte Brontë, The (Elizabeth Gaskell) 13, 14, 53–54
Linnet's Life, The 28–29, 29*f*
Linwood, Mary 197n58
Lister, Anne 6, 68, 173n5, 173n8, 176n31
literacy, women's 127–128, 132–133
Locke, John 64
Lockwood, in *Wuthering Heights* 30–31, 158n112
Logic (Isaac Watt) 103–105, 104*f*
Love Among the Archives (Michie and Warhol) 5
Lynch, Deidre 3, 20

Machen, Arthur, *The Three Imposters* 150n21
Magwitch, in *Great Expectations* 23
manicules 13, 151n28
manuscripts
 in autograph albums 51, 168n103, 168n106
 in Gothic fiction 108–109
 reuse of 96–97, 102–103, 105–107
 revisions to 120–121, 124–125
 storage of 44–45, 116–117
 see also Brontë, Emily, manuscripts

Marcus, Sharon 48
marginalia
  as aids to study 12, 14–15, 64, 157n91
  compositions in the margins 18, 152n50, 153n51
  criticism of 13, 15–16, 152n41
  doodles 19*f*, 31, 106, 152n46, 188n58
  graffiti 16–18, 17*f*
  intimate 26
  performative 15–16
marking possessions by sewing 131–132
Married Women's Property Acts 10
Martineau, Harriet 12, 49, 120, 146n2
Mary Barton (Elizabeth Gaskell) 51–52, 169n108
Matthews, Samantha 37, 39
Maturin, Charles, *Melmoth the Wanderer* 108
McLaughlin, Kevin 115
Melmoth the Wanderer (Charles Maturin) 108
Memoir of J.G. Children (Anna Atkins) 136–137
memorial albums 161n23
memorializing 26–27, 38, 59–60, 87
Menke, Richard 34
menstruation 6
mental illness 134–136
Metallic Book, Improved Patent 75, 75*f*
Michie, Helena 5
micrography 42–43
Middlemarch (George Eliot) 21–22, 52–53, 72–73, 72*f*, 77–83, 123
Mill on the Floss, The (George Eliot) 13, 22–24, 29, 131
Miller, Andrew 46
Milton, John, *Paradise Lost* 25–26
miniature books 43–44, 88, 97–98, 97*f*, 164n59, 165n64, 182n103
miniature friendship albums 43–44
mise en abîme 30–31, 40–41, 88–89, 139–140
Mitford, Mary Russell 28
Monk, The (Matthew Lewis) 96
Montaigne, Michel de 65
Moore, Thomas Sturge 91–92
Morris, Dinah, in *Adam Bede* 24
Mosses, album of British 59, 60*f*
mourning stationery, poem on 102
Müller, Lothar 49, 93, 125

Murder Will Out (Anna Atkins) 137
music books 35, 98, 160n7

needle-cards and -cases 126
needlework 127–136, 135*f*, 195n48, 198n84
  see also sewing
Nelson, Jane 37
Nicholls, Arthur 12, 116, 117
Nichols, Stephen 25
Nightingale, Florence 12, 60, 178n53
North and South (Elizabeth Gaskell) 47
notebooks
  books repurposed as 103–105, 104*f*
  Brontë, Emily 84–89, 86*f*
  buying and modifying 67–68
  drafts in 83–84
  Eliot, George 7, 67, 68–69, 72–80, 173n8, 178n54, 178n56, 179n68
  Field, Michael 89–90
  idea notebooks 180n87
  Reade, Charles 69–70
  see also commonplace books
nourishment, paper as 107–108

objet trouvé 105
odours in books 13, 31

packaging, domestic 98, 186n30
Paget, Violet (Vernon Lee) 177n44
paper
  making 93–94, 125
  menstruation pads 6
  as nourishment 107–108
  reuse of 93, 95–102, 105–107
  talismanic properties 107
paper crafts 42–43, 42*f*, 81–82, 95–96, 120–124
paper dolls 121, 122*f*, 126
paper pattern, poem pasted to 101
papers pinned to fabrics 65, 174n15
paper-ware (paper-mâché) 121
Paradise Lost (John Milton) 25–26
paratexts 32–33, 75–76, 147n3
Parker, Elizabeth 134
Parker, Pamela Corpron 49
Parkes, Bessie Rayner 141
Pascoe, Judith 49
peep-show books 124
Peltz, Lucy 95

226   INDEX

Pencil of Nature, The (William Henry Fox Talbot)   138
Pettitt, Clare   35, 41
Philomela   132, 134
photograms   138–141, 140*f*
photograph albums   61–62, 138–141
pincushions   130–131
pinpricks   13, 126
pins, editing with   124–125, 193n30
Piozzi, Hester   10, 26
place
   and date-marking   27–28, 38, 158n105
   souvenirs of   56–58, 57*f*, 58*f*
pockets in notebooks   75–76, 179n68
"poem objects"   101
poems
   composed as marginalia   18, 152n50, 153n51
   in friendship albums   38–39, 137, 161n24, 162n33, 163n36, 163n37, 167n93
Ponsonby, Sarah and Eleanor Butler (the "Ladies of Llangollen")   148n7, 157n93
potatoes, paper made from   94, 118
Prelude, The (William Wordsworth)   27
Price, Leah   18, 82, 83, 93
Pride and Prejudice (Jane Austen)   173n6
print artifacts, non-codex   98–99
prison poems of Emily Brontë   21, 112–115
Private Memoirs and Confessions of a Justified Sinner, The (James Hogg)   108, 109
Professor, The (Charlotte Brontë)   96
Proust, Marcel   28, 194n32
Put Yourself in His Place (Charles Reade)   72

"Quarry for *Middlemarch*" (George Eliot)   72–73, 72*f*
quotations written on walls and ceilings   65, 174n14

Raffles, John, in *Middlemarch*   80–81
rags used in papermaking   94
rape   132, 134
Reade, Charles   67, 69–72, 177n39
Reader, Simon   66
reading aloud   27, 127, 157n93
recursiveness
   in book bindings   170n122, 170n124
   in notebooks   76, 178n54, 178n56

Reichek, Elaine   198n81
relics, books as   25–26
religious texts   14, 23–24, 26–27, 107, 156n77, 159n119, 164n59
religious tracts   32, 105, 159n116, 159n118
reuse
   of books   32, 94–95, 103–105, 187n50
   of household items   98
   of manuscripts   96–97, 102–103, 105–107
   of paper   93, 95–102, 105–107
revisions to manuscripts   120, 124–125
rings   153n57, 153n58
Rivals, The (Richard Brinsley Sheridan)   13
Roe Head Album   40–41, 40*f*
rolled-paper work   95–96, 121
Romola (George Eliot)   11, 78–79
Roper, Derek   110, 116
Rossetti, Christina   181n98, 182n99
Rossetti, Dante Gabriel   180n88
"Rubaiyat of Omar Khayyam"   65
Russell's General Atlas of Modern Geography   16–18, 19*f*
Ruth (Elizabeth Gaskell)   153n57

Sadleir, Michael   129
St. Clair, William   96
saints   25
Sala, George Augustus   68
samplers   132–136, 135*f*, 198n84
Sampson, Ada   38
Sánchez-Eppler, Karen   10
sand pictures   126–127
Scenes of Clerical Life (George Eliot)   95–96, 129, 184n8
Schaffer, Talia   46, 95, 123, 127, 128
Schor, Naomi   2, 101
Schwenger, Peter   164n48
scrapbooks   35, 45, 103–105 *see also* albums
scribal publications   83–85, 97–98, 102
Sedgwick, Eve Kosofsky   78
Sellars, Jane   110
Seward, Anna   153n51
sewing
   bindings   68, 139
   needlework   127–136, 135*f*, 195n48, 198n84
   on paper   13, 124–126, 194n32
"She dried her tears and they did smile" (Emily Brontë)   102

INDEX

Shelley, Mary 55, 108, 189n74
Shelley, Percy Bysshe 55, 96
Sherman, William H. 10, 55, 65
Shirley (Charlotte Brontë) 38, 96, 152n46
shirt cuffs, writing on 125, 194n38
Shorter, Clement 116, 117
silhouette cutting 121, 123, 192n17
"Silly Novels by Lady Novelists" (George Eliot) 15
Silverman, Gillian 26
Simcox, Edith 26
skeuomorphism and books 43–44
skin, human, used for bookbinding 55, 170n124
Snow, Lucy in *Villette* 13, 108, 131
Sorrows of Satan, The (Marie Corelli) 65
Southey, Charles 129–130
Southey, Edith and Kate 129–130, 130*f*
Southey, Edith May 37
Southey, Robert 66, 129, 167n93
souvenir albums 36, 56–62, 57*f*, 58*f see also* autographs
"Squire's Story, The" (Elizabeth Gaskell) 52
Stallybrass, Peter 13
standing ground 63, 82
stationers 67, 176n29, 176n30
Stauffer, Andrew 14, 26, 125, 144
Steedman, Carolyn 4, 145
Stein, Gertrude 89
Sterne, Laurence, *Tristram Shandy* 71
Stetz, Margaret D 129
Stevenson, Bob 102–103
Stevenson, Robert Louis 102–103, 156n77, 159n116, 176n32
Stewart, Susan 43
Story of a Modern Woman, The (Ella Hepworth Dixon) 65
Stovin, Margaret 59–60
Strange Case of Dr. Jekyll and Mr. Hyde (Robert Louis Stevenson) 102, 159n116, 176n32
Strickland, Maggie 37, 38–39, 42–43, 42*f*
study, aids to 12, 14–15, 64, 157n91
Sylvia's Lovers (Elizabeth Gaskell) 51, 123
Symonds, John Addington 171n129
Symons, Arthur 171n129

tabs in notebooks 68
Talbot, William Henry Fox 138, 139
talismanic properties of paper 107
Temple Dictionary of the Bible, The 95
Tennyson, Alfred Lord 83, 96
Terrible Temptation, A (Charles Reade) 70, 71, 72
textile art, readable 130–136
Thackeray, William Makepeace 15, 51
Thomas, Sarah 38
Thos. De La Rue & Co. 99, 163n41
Three Imposters, The (Machen, Arthur) 150n21
Threipland, Eliza 41, 126
thrift, in *Cranford* 46–47, 95
Thyne, Amy 39
tin boxes 116–117
tipping in 56, 68
"To a Wreath of Snow / by A G Almeda—" (Emily Brontë) 112*f*, 113–115
toenails 54
Toller, Jane 134
touch 35, 37–38, 50, 160n12
tourist albums 56–59
toy-books 124
transcription (copying texts) 66–67, 74–75, 178n56
travel diaries 75–76, 75*f*
Tristram Shandy (Laurence Sterne) 71
tromp l'oeil 40–41, 40*f*
Tulliver, Maggie, in *Mill on the Floss, The* 22–24
typography 71–72

"useless" books 94–95

valentines 121
version books 176n32
Victoria, Queen 56, 61
Villette (Charlotte Brontë) 13, 108, 120–121, 131
Vincy, Rosamond, in *Middlemarch* 81–82

Wagner, Anne 37
wallpaper as book covers 97, 97*f*
Walton, George 55
Warhol, Robyn 5
Watsons, The (Jane Austen) 124–125, 127
Watt, Isaac, *Logic* 103–105, 104*f*
"Weaned from life and torn away" (Emily Brontë) 112–115, 113*f*, 190n98

Welch, Miss 18
"White Book" (Michael Field) 90
Wightman, Julia P. 43, 129
Wilde, Constance 48
Wilde, Oscar 66
will, Clarissa Harlowe's 10–11, 132, 134, 174n12
Wise, Thomas 55, 84–85, 170n120, 182n99
Wives and Daughters (Elizabeth Gaskell) 47–48
Woof, Pamela 66
wooing through books 26
Woolf, Virginia
  dirty books 150n25
  on marginalia 152n41
notebooks 83
and old books 33, 143–144
rebinding books 128
reusing books 104f, 187n50
scrapbooks 45, 103–105
Wordsworth, Dora 129, 167n93
Wordsworth, Dorothy 13, 66, 125
Wordsworth, William 13, 66, 83, 154n63
"Work and Days" (Michael Field) 89–90
wrappers, book 98
writers in George Eliot's novels 78–79
Wuthering Heights 9, 29–33, 123–124, 158n112 *see also* Earnshaw, Catherine in *Wuthering Heights*

Yonge, Charlotte, *The Daisy Chain* 154n59